Data Analysis for Database Design

Third edition

David Howe

Formerly Professor of Information Systems
De Montfort University

BUTTERWORTH
HEINEMANN

OXFORD   AMSTERDAM   BOSTON   LONDON   NEW YORK   PARIS
SAN DIEGO   SAN FRANCISCO   SINGAPORE   SYDNEY   TOKYO

Butterworth-Heinemann
An imprint of Elsevier Science
200 Wheeler Road, Burlington MA 01803

First published by Edward Arnold 1983
Second edition 1989
Third edition published by Butterworth-Heinemann
Reprinted 2002, 2003

British Library Cataloguing in Publication Data
A catalogue record for this book is available from the British Library

ISBN 0 7506 5086 0

For information on all Butterworth-Heinemann publications
please visit our website at www.bh.com

Typeset by Jayvee, Trivandrum, India
Printed and bound in Great Britain by MPG Books Ltd, Bodmin, Cornwall

Data Analysis for Database Design

Contents

Preface to the Third Edition

Readership

This book is intended to make the techniques of data analysis more readily available to students of systems analysis and database design. It examines the subject in some detail from a practical viewpoint. It is assumed that the reader has a background knowledge of computing and information systems, but no more than would be expected from an introductory course in computer studies.

Scope

In keeping the book within reasonable logical and physical bounds I have applied the following criteria.

Firstly, the book is about data analysis, not the wider field of systems analysis and design, or information systems management.

Secondly, although it is scarcely feasible to discuss data analysis without propounding some kind of methodology, my aim is to help the reader think about the problems and obtain a grasp of the basic tools, rather than to grind the axe of any particular methodology. For example, Chen's entity-relationship model is the basis for the discussion in Part 3, but no claim is made that this is an exposition of Chen's ideas; indeed I have freely selected and adapted his ideas to suit my own purpose. This book will have succeeded if it leaves readers better equipped to assimilate the ideas in any of the present or future 'brand-name' methodologies, or to devise methodologies of their own.

Thirdly, I have deliberately restricted the scale of the applications in the examples and exercises. It is important that the reader should tackle more substantial problems, but I believe that this is best done under some form of tutorial guidance, either on a course or on-the-job, as the ramifications of large-scale, or even medium-scale, applications are inevitably extensive. In this respect the role of the book is to free the tutor for more of this type of work.

Structure and content

The book is divided into five parts:

- A: Introduction
- 1: Databases and database management systems
- 2: Relational modelling
- 3: Entity-relationship modelling
- 4: Further topics

Part A establishes the need for data analysis; it differs from the rest of the book in its 'case history' style. The reader who is only too familiar with the problems introduced here may wish to skip quickly through this part.

Part 1 examines the concepts of *database* and *database management system* (DBMS). A DBMS is viewed not so much as a good thing in its own right, but more as a means of overcoming the problems of shared data. The architecture of a DBMS is discussed in terms of the ANSI/SPARC model.

Part 2 explains how a data model can be designed in a 'bottom-up' direction by applying normalisation techniques to the data items (attributes). The usual way of treating normalisation is to beat a trail down the first, second, third, fourth, and maybe fifth, normal form route, with Boyce/Codd normal form snapping hard at the heels of third normal form. I cannot see the merit of this approach, which seems to have become prevalent for historical reasons rather than for its intrinsic worth, and I have a sneaking feeling that it is sustained chiefly by its convenience as a source of examination questions. My approach has been to distinguish carefully between *duplicated* data and *redundant* data, and hence establish the Boyce/Codd rule directly. Tables (i.e. relations) that satisfy the Boyce/Codd rule are described as *well-normalised*. Even well-normalised tables may still contain redundant data; once this is eliminated the tables are said to be *fully-normalised*. Because the Boyce/Codd rule is stated in terms of the concept of a determinant, I often use the terms *determines* and *determinancy* where it might be more usual to find the opposite viewpoint being taken, coupled with the use of terms such as *is dependent on* and *dependency*. I have not dealt with fifth normal form explicitly as, although theoretically interesting, it is of little practical significance.

Part 3 builds on the results of Part 2, but takes an opposite 'top-down' approach which starts by identifying entity and relationship types, and then uses these to construct a framework into which the attributes may be slotted. Part 3 concludes with a discussion of how the design may be 'flexed' to improve its performance.

Part 4 covers several topics related to data analysis. The concepts of Part 3 are applied to distributed database systems. Data manipulation is discussed in terms of relational algebra, which is then applied to optimisation issues. The SQL language is introduced (based on SQL92). Object-orientation and object-relational developments (based on SQL99) are considered. The Codasyl (network) model is described in an appendix, as a contrast to the relational model.

Terminology

The terminology and diagrammatic conventions used deserve some comment. The term *table* has been preferred to *relation* for several reasons. Table is more meaningful at a first encounter with the subject, it avoids confusion between relation and relationship, and it avoids the barbarity of *relationship relation*. Having studied this material, the reader should have little difficulty in adapting to the use of relation instead of table, so I trust that those who know the difference between a table and a relation will forgive my lapse from grace. A further consideration is that SQL refers to tables rather than relations, possibly because some SQL tables are not relations.

In the discussion of entity-relationship modelling, I considered using a Unified Modeling Language (UML) style of notation, but found it easier to give tutorial explanations by using Chen's notation (1:1, 1:N, M:N) for representing the degree of a relationship, and my own 'blob' notation for representing obligatory and non-obligatory participation of an entity type in a relationship. In UML, an asterisk (*) on its own implies both a lower and upper bound (0..*) which is inconvenient when drawing a diagram in which only the upper bound is known or relevant for the discussion in hand. I have, however, introduced the UML multiplicity notation in Part 3, used it in the discussion of object-orientation in Part 4, and represented binary relationships by lines without Chen's diamond symbol for a relationship. Consequently, the transition to UML notation for class diagrams should be straightforward.

Questions and assignments

Merely reading about a subject does not, of itself, confer much practical skill or insight. Consequently, the text is interspersed with a large number of questions and several assignments; these frequently offer more than just routine practice, for they may amplify, anticipate or challenge the text, and together with the answer pointers at the end of each chapter they form an integral part of the book. The reader is assumed to have at least read the questions and answer pointers. For those with the resolve to tackle the questions (those who do not will surely reap their just reward!) estimated times are given for each question. These are 'thinking times' rather than 'writing out model answer times', and may be used in various ways. For example:

(i)   Ignore them. This is the best course of action if you are irritated at the thought of some kind of ectoplasmic author hovering over you with a stopwatch.
(ii)   If, on a first reading, you have not made any progress towards an answer within the allotted time, look up the answer pointer.
(iii)   On a second reading (assuming you have the stamina) try to sketch out the main features of the answer within the time stated.

The answer pointers should not be regarded as infallible model answers, but as aids to thinking about the questions. Some answer pointers do not cover all the points raised in a question, whereas others may offer additional commentary or even raise further questions. The assignments offer more substantial tasks which may be found useful for seminar or project work.

Comparison with the second edition

Minor changes have been made throughout the text, questions and answer pointers to bring the material up-to-date.
   There is little change to the coverage of database concepts and relational modelling in Part A, Part 1 and Part 2. Naming conventions are slightly different, for example part# is now written as partNo and Supplier-Part is written as SupplierPart.
   The treatment of entity-relationship modelling in Part 3 is essentially the same, but there are some changes to notation and terminology. The diamond symbol for a binary relationship has been dropped in favour of a simple relationship line. The term *participation condition* is preferred to *membership class*. The UML multiplicity

notation is introduced as an alternative to the degree and participation notation used in most of the book.

Part 4 is substantially new. The material on a proprietary DBMS has been replaced by chapters on distributed database systems, query optimisation and object-orientation. The chapter on the SQL language has been expanded and based on the SQL92 standard. Aspects of SQL99 are included in the object-orientation chapter.

Acknowledgements

It is a measure of the contribution of the pioneers in the database field that a tutorial book of this nature takes much of their work for granted. The brief annotated bibliography at the end of the book references some key primary sources. The bibliography also lists several texts, suitable for further reading, that include extensive (in some cases, annotated) references and bibliographies.

Finally, my personal acknowledgements. I would like to thank all those staff and students who contributed directly or indirectly to the first and second editions. For this third edition, special thanks are due to former colleagues at De Montfort University, in particular Adrian Larner, for comments on the second edition, to Ray Farmer for reviewing all the new chapters, to Stewart Thornton for reviewing Chapter 20, and to Brian Watts for advice on the Appendix. The final result is, of course, my responsibility.

I much appreciate the patience and skill of staff at Edward Arnold, and latterly Butterworth-Heinemann, who have been involved with this edition, including Nicki Dennis, Kirsty Stroud, Liz Gooster, Deborah Puleston and Matthew Flynn. My wife, Christine, has provided invaluable support and encouragement, without which I could not have completed the task.

David Howe
Ashby-de-la-Zouch
2001

Part A

Introduction

Part A sets the scene by using the experiences of an imaginary manufacturing company to explore the advantages and disadvantages associated with the sharing of data between applications.

A

Introduction

A.1 Database

A database is a collection of non-redundant data shareable between different application systems.

What does this definition mean? What is non-redundant data? Why share data? What problems arise in sharing data and how can they be overcome? We will begin to explore these questions by considering the problems encountered by a mythical manufacturing company, Torg Ltd, in the development of their computer systems.

A.2 Torg Ltd

The management of Torg Ltd, knowing that many pitfalls await the unwary in the development of computerised systems, had started cautiously by implementing a simple system for printing an up-to-date catalogue every month which listed the product reference number, the product description and the price of every product supplied by Torg. This Catalogue system maintained a master Catalogue file (Fig. A.1) comprising data items named productNo, productDescription, and price. At each month-end the Marketing department updated the file to reflect price changes, the addition of new products to the catalogue and the deletion of obsolete products. The update run printed a new catalogue listing which was then reprographed for circulation to customers.

Encouraged by the success of the Catalogue system, Torg decided to try something a little more ambitious, namely a Stock control system for the Stores department. The data items required for this system would be productNo, productDescription, quantity-InStock, and reOrderLevel. The quantityInStock of each product would be updated weekly with stock movement data, and an exception report would be printed showing those products for which the quantityInStock had fallen below the reOrderLevel.

Geoff Watson, the information systems manager, agreed with his chief (and only) systems analyst Tom Cross that since much of the data required by the Stock system was already held on the Catalogue system (viz. productNo, productDescription), it would be sensible to use the same master file for both systems. The Catalogue file was therefore extended to include quantityInStock and reOrderLevel data items and was renamed the Product file (Fig. A.2). Programs were written for the Stock system to handle stock movements and changes to reOrderLevel values. The update program in the Catalogue system had to be amended to cope with the additional data items in the Product file, but this was considered to be a trivial change. As illustrated in the diagram,

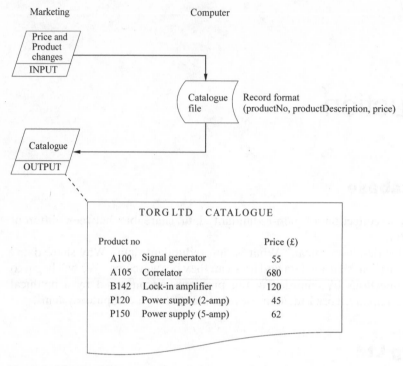

Fig. A.1 The Catalogue system

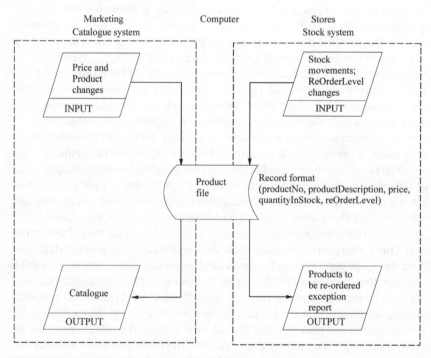

Fig. A.2 Joint Product file shared by Catalogue and Stock systems

the Stores department was responsible for the weekly updating of quantityInStock values and for the revision of reOrderLevel values when necessary. The Marketing department continued to be responsible for price changes and the addition and deletion of product records.

The Stock system was thoroughly tested and put into operation at the beginning of September. Early in October disaster struck. The latest product catalogue (Fig. A.3) had somehow acquired some additional columns of figures, namely the values of quantityInStock and reOrderLevel. Unfortunately, the error was not noticed until after the new catalogues had been distributed to customers. Several customers concluded that a company which could not print an intelligible catalogue was best avoided. A competitor discovered the meaning of the figures simply by telephoning one of the Torg secretaries. As a result the competitor identified several products for which Torg was having difficulty obtaining supplies and, by changing its marketing strategy, the competitor was able to win over some important Torg customers.

```
              TORG LTD CATALOGUE

Product no                        Price (£)

 A100   Signal generator          5501030040
 A105   Correlator                68000120025
 B142   Lock-in amplifier         12000000300
 P120   Power supply (2-amp)      4500840150
 P150   Power supply (5-amp)      6200030250
```

The erroneous
output: values of
quantityInStock
and reOrderLevel

Fig. A.3   The corrupted catalogue

An error in the Catalogue printing program was soon traced and corrected but the 'Catalogue Catastrophe', as it became popularly known within the company, prompted Watson to rethink the system's development policy. In future, he decided, each of the company's systems would be designed around its own master files. Not only would this application-centred approach eliminate the possibility of data being seen by an unauthorised program, but it would also make it possible to concentrate on the development of one application at a time.

To start the good work the Catalogue and Stock systems were split. The Catalogue system reverted to its original design and a new Stock system was designed around its own Stock file (Fig. A.4). The Product Design Department, who authorised the addition and deletion of products, was responsible for notifying both Marketing and Stores of such changes. This solution worked successfully at first, but after some while complaints were made by the Sales manager that the descriptions of products in the stock report were sometimes inconsistent with those in the catalogue. There were also instances of a product appearing in the catalogue but not in the stock report (and *vice versa*).

Investigation showed that there were several reasons for the discrepancies. One

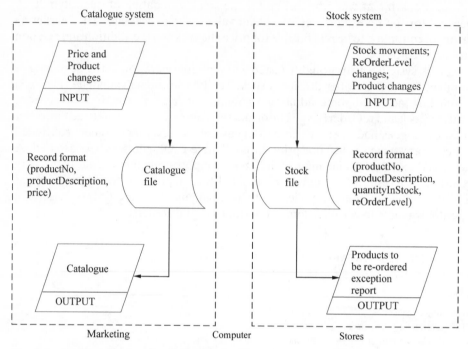

Fig. A.4   Application-centred solution. Separate Catalogue and Stock systems

problem was that Stores ran its update program weekly, whereas Marketing ran its update program monthly. Another problem was that mistakes by Product Design meant that Marketing and Stores did not always receive the same product change data. Sometimes data was accidentally omitted from an update run or entered incorrectly.

It became apparent that separate updating of the Catalogue and Stock files would almost inevitably lead to inconsistent data. After several rather acrimonious meetings, in which each of the parties blamed everyone else, it was agreed that the information systems department would write a 'consistency audit' program which would compare the two files and print a list of discrepancies. This program would be run every few months so that discrepancies could be identified and corrected. Furthermore, memos were sent to the clerical staff in Product Design, Marketing and Stores, emphasising the need for care in dealing with product changes.

During the next few years several other systems were implemented, including Production Scheduling, Purchasing, Payroll, and Customer Orders. The policy of developing each system in isolation had been continued, in the sense that each system had its own master files, but the growing need to communicate data between systems had led to the use of transfer files. For example, information about products ordered by customers was passed from the Customer Orders system to the Production Scheduling system via a transfer file. As the complexity of the systems grew, the number of transfer files proliferated (Fig. A.5).

The problem of consistency between systems was by now a real headache. Production Scheduling, Customer Orders, Purchasing, Catalogue and Stock Control systems all contained data on products, and much of the data was inconsistent. The

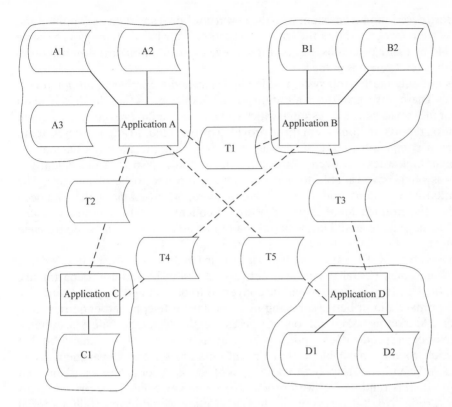

Fig. A.5   Proliferation of transfer files (T1–T5) to communicate between application systems

consistency audit program technique was still used, but it had become practically impossible to maintain consistency in the face of differing update cycles and data input errors. The proliferation of transfer files caused problems in scheduling work on the computer. The growth of Torg's business had necessitated upgrades to computer storage which could have been avoided if there were not so much duplicated data. Watson was also concerned about the time taken backing up the multiplicity of files and the risk that, in the event of a system crash, the files would not be restored correctly.

By this time *unproductive maintenance*, as Watson called it, was occupying a substantial amount of the programmers' time. The problem was well illustrated by the Payroll system for which some fifteen *ad hoc* report programs had been developed. These programs were not part of the main payroll suite but were run on request to provide management information. A new agreement between management and the Sports and Social Club that membership fees would be deducted automatically from members' pay meant that it was necessary to distinguish in the Payroll record between members and non-members. An extra data item was therefore added to the Payroll record so that club membership could be indicated. Certain Payroll programs which made use of the new data item naturally had to be amended, and this work Watson regarded as productive maintenance. The unproductive maintenance involved the amendment of the other Payroll programs, including all fifteen *ad hoc* report programs, which made no use of the new data item, but which had to be amended (in order to make their record descriptions consistent with the new record size) and then re-compiled and tested. Watson recognised that the root of the problem lay in the sharing of the same Payroll file by many programs, but that it was even less of a practical proposition to work with several versions of the file.

It was not only the Payroll system which had spawned a number of *ad hoc* report programs. There was a growing realisation among management that the data held on computer files was a valuable resource which could be tapped to provide management information reports to supplement those provided by the standard application systems. A common complaint voiced by management was that the information systems department took weeks, or even months, to write a report program. Consequently, a report was often not available to a manager until too late to be of any use. The information systems department replied that many report programs, which had been justified on the grounds that they would be used frequently, had been used once only, and that management should know better than to waste the time of an overstretched department.

Up to this point, all Torg's systems had been run in batch mode. Watson decided that the time had come to install a local area network accessible by end-user departments. Initially, the Catalogue system would be converted to on-line updating and retrieval, with the primary aim of better servicing by sales staff of telephoned enquiries from customers. Marketing asked for on-line access to the Catalogue file via either a productNo or a productDescription. Unfortunately, none of the standard file organisation routines available within the information systems department could provide a sufficiently fast response to both types of access. A serial file[1] was plainly out of the question. A random file[2] with productNo as the key would have provided fast access by productNo, but access by productDescription would have entailed a serial search. The same objection applied to an indexed sequential file.[3] The basic problem was that none of the file organisations permitted direct access via more than one key.[4] Eventually, a rather unsatisfactory solution was reached in which only productNo could be used for on-line access; retrieval by productDescription was dealt with by referring to a printed list produced in the monthly batch run.

With the implementation of the company's first networked application completed, Watson reviewed the state of computer systems development. The old policy of application-centred development had to all intents and purposes broken down. The spread of computer systems throughout the company had reached the point at which no major new system could be implemented without considering its interaction with existing computer systems. In spite of the experience gained over the years by the information systems department it seemed to be becoming harder rather than easier to cope with systems development. Perhaps a new manager would be able to sort things out. Watson handed in his resignation and set up as an independent consultant.

---

[1] i.e. where records are accessed in the order in which they are physically stored. On average, half the records in the file have to be read to locate a record with a given key.
[2] i.e. where a randomising algorithm is used to calculate a record's address from its key.
[3] i.e. where an index of record keys allows efficient access both in key sequence and directly to individual records.
[4] This is true of the conventional file organisation routines used at Torg Ltd, but not of the more sophisticated implementations discussed in Part 4.

A.3 Analysis

The problems experienced by Torg Ltd can be summarised as follows.

(1) The duplication of data between different master files is a potential source of inconsistent data.
(2) The sharing of data between systems poses a security problem.
(3) Unproductive maintenance can become a serious drain on the resources of an information systems department.
(4) Managers cannot exploit fully the data available to the computer because of delays in getting report programs written.
(5) The greater the number of existing computer systems, the longer it is likely to take to develop new systems, because there are more interactions to consider.
(6) File organisations supporting only single-key direct access may be inadequate, particularly for on-line systems.
(7) Systems were developed rather haphazardly. There was no coordinated view of the data as a whole, nor was there a proper systems development plan.

In the next chapter we contrast Torg's application-centred approach to systems design with a *database* approach and, in doing so, introduce the idea of a *database management system*.

Questions

1. Could the 'Catalogue Catastrophe' (section A.2) have been avoided by better program testing? What are the implications of your answer if a large number of application programs share the same file? (2 min)
2. The catalogue printing program worked correctly with a record format of (productNo, productDescription, price) as in Fig. A.1 but produced incorrect output (Fig. A.3) when its record description was altered to match the larger record size of the Product file in Fig. A.2. Suggest a cause for the incorrect output. Was there a bug in the original version of the program or not? Do you have any criticisms to make concerning the program or record design? (5 min)
3. Assuming that the Catalogue system and Stock system share a database as in Fig. A.2, discuss whether there is likely to be conflict over the ownership of data (i.e. the right to amend, add, delete, or restrict access to the data). (5 min)
4. The Product file in Fig. A.2 contains no redundant data. Does it follow that the file necessarily contains mutually consistent data? (2 min)
5. Which data items are common to both the Catalogue file and the Stock file in the application-centred solution of Fig. A.4? Are the data items common to both files the only source of inconsistency? (2 min)
6. Is better clerical procedures design the answer to inconsistent updating of duplicated data? (2 min)
7. Suppose duplication of data between application systems is allowed, but inconsistency is to be avoided by updating all copies of duplicated data 'simultaneously'. What are the implications of this procedure with regard to (a) batch systems, (b) on-line workstations, (c) recovery from computer malfunction? (10 min)
8. The use of transfer files (Fig. A.5) might be a security risk. Does the use of transfer

files have any advantages over allowing applications to access each other's master files directly?   (2 min)

9.   Why do you think 'The proliferation of transfer files caused problems in scheduling work on the computer'? (See section A.2.)   (3 min)

10.   Do you think the use of consistency audit programs is a good idea, or is it just papering over the cracks in a basically unsound approach?   (3 min)

Answer pointers

1.   Yes. But with a large number of programs to test the chance of faulty testing is increased. (Is the relationship linear?)

2.   One possible explanation is that the print-record-area was defined as being the same size as the printer page width and that the input record was moved to a print-record-area by a group move of the record as a whole. In each version of the program, the excess characters in the print-record-area would be padded automatically with spaces, but in each case the whole of the input record would be transferred to the print-record-area.

There was not a bug in the original version of the program unless the original specification included maintainability criteria which were not met. The problem would not have occurred if item-by-item moves had been used instead of a group move. The record design is unusual in that the productDescription values as stored on the Product file are already surrounded by the formatting blanks required to separate them from the productNo and price values on the printed output (otherwise a group move would not work). One might also wonder if it is wise to restrict prices to whole numbers of pounds.

3.   The Stores department might object to Marketing deleting the record for a product which has been withdrawn from the catalogue, but for which Stores still have supplies in stock which need to be scrapped.

4.   No. For example, an input error might mean that values of productDescription and productNo are inconsistent. The fact that there are two sources of updates to the Product file may also lead to inconsistency. Suppose that, because of an increase in the price of a product, it has been decided that its reOrderLevel should be reduced. If the updates performed by the Catalogue and Stock systems are not synchronised, the relevant product record will temporarily contain inconsistent values for price and reOrderLevel. A report derived from this file while it is in an inconsistent state would convey misleading information if it included the values of price and reOrderLevel. Similarly, the two reports shown in Fig. A.2 could be inconsistent.

5.   productNo, productDescription. No. See answer pointers for question 4.

6.   It may help, but cannot guarantee consistency.

7.   Some implications are: (a) all copies of the duplicated data must be available to the updating program when it is run, which may mean the mounting of a large number of files; (b) the response time to workstations may be unacceptably long because of the time taken to update all copies of the data; (c) the recovery procedure may be complicated by the larger number of files involved.

8.   Transfer files will usually have smaller records and give better security because only those data items to be transferred should be written to them; they may contain fewer records; they may have a more convenient file organisation; it is simpler to audit the contents of transfer files than to audit the operation of a program which accesses master files directly.

9. The need to mount several transfer files (both input and output files) simultaneously. The need to ensure that the input transfer files are at a consistent level of update.

10. As used by Torg, a case of papering over the cracks. We shall see later that even the best designed database is likely to contain some duplicated data, in which case the use of consistency audit programs is sensible, but as a check that all is well rather than as a firefighting exercise.

Part 1

Databases and database management systems

Part 1 examines the concepts of *database* and *database management system*.

Chapter 1 considers how the problems arising from the sharing of data can be overcome, at a price, by the use of a database management system.

Chapter 2 looks more closely at the architecture of a database management system, and distinguishes between *schema* and *data model* representations of the structure of the database itself.

1

Database systems

1.1 The database approach

The simplest way to reduce the incidence of inconsistent data is to eliminate unnecessary duplication of data; this in turn implies that data should be stored as a common pool shareable between application systems. This pool of data is the enterprise's database. The *application-centred* view of Figs A.4 and A.5 is replaced by the *database* view of Fig. 1.1.

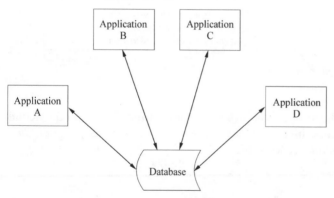

Fig. 1.1   Database view

Data which is unnecessarily duplicated is redundant in the sense that the duplication adds no new information; hence the use of the term *non-redundant* in our initial definition of a database (section A.1) as 'a collection of non-redundant data shareable between different application systems'.

Sharing data may ensure consistency but, as Torg found to their cost, other problems arise such as security and unproductive maintenance. To see how these problems can be overcome, consider first the security problem encountered by Torg with the sharing of a common Product file between the Catalogue and Stock control systems (Fig. A.2). It will help to emphasise the point being made if we assume that each of these systems is implemented as a number of separate programs (the conclusions remain the same whatever the program structure). Suppose then that the Catalogue system contains one program for price changes, another for printing the catalogue and a third for product changes (i.e. addition or deletion of products), while the Stock system contains two

programs, one for stock movements (i.e. changes of quantityInStock), and another
for printing the exception report showing products which need to be re-ordered.
The database in this example is a single file containing the data items productNo,
productDescription, price, quantityInStock, and reOrderLevel. To avoid compro-
mising security, each program should be restricted to seeing only those data items
to which it is entitled to have access. The Price-changes program needs only
productNo and price; the Stock-movements program needs only productNo and
quantityInStock, and so on (Fig. 1.2). In a database system, translation between the
global view of the data in the database and the local view expected by each application
program is performed by a generalised software interface known as a *database
management system* (Fig. 1.3).

System	Program	Data items required by program
Catalogue	Price-changes Print-catalogue Product-changes	productNo, price productNo, productDescription, price productNo, productDescription, price, quantityInStock, reOrderLevel
Stock	Stock-movements Re-order-report	productNo, quantityInStock productNo, productDescription quantityInStock, reOrderLevel

Fig. 1.2   Data items required by each program

This idea of separating the application program's view of the data from the actual
stored data is a key concept in database systems. It is known as *program/data
independence*, or *data independence* for short.

1.2   Program/data independence

The program/data independence which a database management system can provide
also offers a solution to the *unproductive maintenance* problem. Maintenance involving
the addition of a data item will be examined first, followed by a briefer look at some
other types of maintenance.

Addition of data item
With reference to Figs 1.2 and 1.3, suppose the Stock system is to be amended to
highlight for urgent action those products where quantityInStock has fallen, not just
below the reOrderLevel but below a minimumStockLevel. Suppose, that the additional
information needed is included in the database by adding a minimumStockLevel data
item to the existing Product file, and that the only application programs which need to
use this data item are the Re-order-report and the Product-changes program. If there
were no database management system to insulate the programs from changes in the
database, it would be necessary to amend all the programs in order to make them

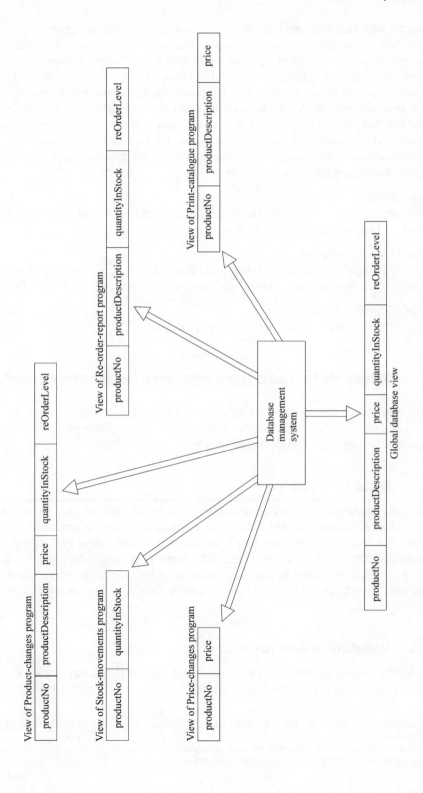

Fig. 1.3   The database management system as an interface between the global database view and the local views of application programs

consistent with the changed record size.[1] As it is, the only program amendments required are to the Re-order-report and the Product-changes programs (examples of *productive maintenance*). None of the other programs need to be amended, because the database management system will translate between the new stored database format and the unchanged views required by these programs. Of course it will be necessary to inform the database management system of (a) the change in the stored database format, (b) the new view required by the Re-order-report program, and (c) the new view required by the Product-changes program. Figure 1.4 shows the final situation.

Overall, a database management system can make the procedure for coping with a new data item simpler and more reliable.

Change of data item format
The format of a data item could be changed from, say, unpacked decimal to packed decimal[2] without affecting the application programs.

Change of file organisation
A serial sequential[3] file could be changed to allow random access to support a new on-line application. Existing programs would continue to see a serial sequential file.

Change of storage medium
Data could be transferred to a different storage device.

1.3   Other database management system facilities

Having established the utility of a database management system as a means of solving security and maintenance problems, we now review other facilities which are necessary or desirable in a database management system.

1.3.1   Data structuring

A database containing a mass of data items will be of little use unless the data is structured in a meaningful way. The database management system must therefore provide data structuring facilities which are capable of expressing the often complex relationships which may exist between data items (e.g. which products have been ordered by which customers in what quantities and which suppliers can supply them?). Moreover, it must be possible to access the data sufficiently quickly to satisfy the needs of a variety of users.

1.3.2   Validation and recovery

The sharing of data improves the consistency of the data, but makes the enterprise potentially more vulnerable to errors. Erroneous data inserted into the database by one

---

[1] Some operating systems allow data items to be added to the end of a record without existing programs requiring amendment.
[2] i.e. 8 bits per digit (unpacked) as against 4 bits per digit (packed).
[3] As typified by a sorted magnetic tape file or its equivalent on disk.

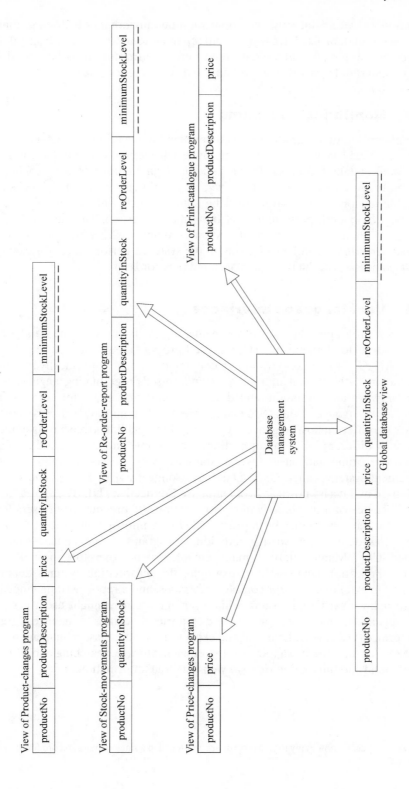

Fig. 1.4   Changes to the global and local views caused by the addition of the data item minimumStockLevel. Changes are underlined (– – – –). Note that the local views of the Stock-movements, Price-changes and Print-catalogue programs are unaffected

application will affect not only that application but any others which share that data. Similarly, loss of data may have widespread repercussions. Consequently, the database management system should validate data before permitting it to be stored in the database, and should provide comprehensive recovery procedures.

1.3.3   Monitoring and tuning

Different application programs may well have conflicting requirements. For example, application A may want fast access to employee data via employeeNumber; application B may want equally fast access to the same data via employeeName. Application C might be favoured by a large blocksize[1], application D by a small blocksize. An acceptable compromise solution must be sought which will satisfy all users while optimising the overall performance of the database system. This task will be made easier if the database management system contains facilities both for monitoring database performance and also for tuning the system's performance, for example by changing blocksizes or the physical placement of records.

1.3.4   User language interfaces

Application programs will need some means of interfacing with the database. One solution is to extend an existing standardised programming language (e.g. COBOL, FORTRAN, C, C++ or Java) by adding commands designed specifically for database manipulation. In this type of interface the standardised programming language is called a *host language* and the additional database commands are referred to as a *data manipulation language*. A database management system may allow access to the same database via different host languages, a feature which facilitates the sharing of the same database by different kinds of application, for example engineering and commercial applications. Some languages use a standard way of connecting to database management systems called Open Database Connectivity (ODBC). The version of ODBC used by Java is known as Java Database Connectivity (JDBC).

The existence of a database is likely to increase the pressure from users for easy access to the data, and it may be impracticable for an information systems department to meet this demand by writing individual programs in a language such as an extended C++. Many database management systems therefore provide several types of application language. For example, the information systems department might use an extended C++ for complex programs, and a report writing language for more straightforward applications, while user management might use a generalised query language to make their own *ad hoc* enquiries. Facilities to manage a graphical user interface (GUI) would normally be expected. The database management system may also offer multimedia support for the efficient storage, searching and retrieval of images, sound and full motion video as well as textual information.

---

[1]The blocksize specifies how many logical records are contained in a single physical record for data transfer and storage.

1.4 What constitutes a database management system?

Packages marketed as database management systems do not necessarily possess all the facilities described above, nor are the facilities they do possess necessarily implemented to the same level. For example, one system may have excellent program/data independence but be poor on recovery; another system may have extensive data structuring features but poor program/data independence. It is probably pointless to debate whether there is a minimum set of facilities which are essential to a database management system; what matters is whether the user's needs are met or not, and different users can have widely different priorities.

1.5 Disadvantages

The database approach solves some problems but raises others. To be successful a database system needs skilled design and management. Staff with the necessary expertise are in short supply and expensive. A database management system is itself likely to be expensive, it may be incompatible with any other available database management system, and may even restrict the user's choice of hardware. Finally, the speed of processing data will be adversely affected by the presence of the additional interface between the programs and the data, and also by the need to compromise between the demands of different applications.

1.6 Database vs database management system

It is important to distinguish between the use of a database and the use of a database management system. The benefits of shared data (e.g. consistency) can be obtained by using a database. The function of a database management system is to overcome problems attendant on the use of a database (e.g. security, unproductive maintenance). If these problems are not considered significant for an enterprise, or if more cost-effective solutions can be found for their particular circumstances, then there is no need to use a database management system.

1.7 Scope of a database

In practice it is not usually feasible to construct a single database covering the whole of an enterprise's activities, as there is so much detail to consider that it may be impossible to complete the system within an acceptable timescale. It is often better to construct a number of separate databases, each one covering a single well-defined application area (e.g. Personnel/Payroll/Manufacturing), but with each database being designed to fit into an overall outline business plan. The scope of an application area should be small enough to be manageable, but large enough to provide adequate benefits from sharing data between the individual applications.

Questions

1.   Does the problem of unproductive maintenance arise only in an application-centred approach, only in a database approach, or in both?   (2 min)

2.   Were Watson's problems caused by the lack of a database, or a lack of planning? Would a database approach have helped him in planning the development of Torg's systems?   (10 min)

3.   A college database contains the following data items:

Student data items
studentNo, name, address, balanceOf FeesDue
Course data items
courseNo, courseTitle, totalEnrolments, syllabus, hours
Lecturer data items
lecturerName, title, roomNo, telephoneNo, salary

Which of the above data items would you expect to find in the local view of each of the following application programs:

(a)   New-student-enrolments
(b)   Print-prospectus
(c)   Print-staff-telephone-directory
(d)   Print-enrolment-statistics
(e)   Print-student-address-labels?   (5 min)

4.   In section 1.2 it was assumed that the new data item, minimumStockLevel, would be incorporated into the database by extending the existing Product file. Instead, minimumStockLevel could have been included in a separate file with the format:

productNo, minimumStockLevel

If this idea is taken to its logical conclusion, there would be a separate file for each data item other than productNo. For example, the Product file data would be stored as five separate files:

productNo, productDescription
productNo, price
productNo, quantityInStock
productNo, reOrderLevel
productNo, minimumStockLevel

This is known as a transposed file structure. Discuss the merits of this approach with respect to program/data independence (especially the addition of a data item). Would a database management system be of any use as an interface to a transposed file structure and, if so, what kind of translation might it perform between the global database view and the local views of the application programs?   (10 min)

5.   Can the problem of fast provision of *ad hoc* reports for managers be solved without using a database management system?   (1 min)

6.   Section 1.7 refers to the idea of an application area. By considering the functions involved, suggest three possible application areas for each of the following: (a) a manufacturing industry; (b) a utility (e.g. gas, water, electricity).   (3 min)

Assignment

1. Write a scenario along the lines of that in section A.2, but this time highlighting the problems of using a database management system.

Answer pointers

1. Usually in both. Of course, a database management system may be used to overcome the problem. If an application is such that every program accesses the whole of the database, and if this situation always remains true (perhaps because there is no need for the system to change) then there is no call for unproductive maintenance.
2. If by 'database approach' one implies a planned approach, then the question is tautologous. A vague idea that a database would be a good thing would probably only make matters worse.
3. For example:

> New-student-enrolments: studentNo, name, address, balanceOf FeesDue;
> Print-staff-telephone-directory: lecturerName, title, telephoneNo;
> Print-student-address-labels: studentNo, name, address.

Your answer may differ depending on your assumptions. For instance, the staff telephone directory might include roomNo. Incidentally, this would be a very uninteresting database (in fact it would scarcely deserve the name) if there were no connection between the student, course and lecturer data. It would become a more interesting, realistic and useful database if the different kinds of data were linked by relationships showing which students were enrolled on which courses, which lecturers taught which courses, and so on. The analysis and representation of such relationships will be important topics in later chapters.
4. The addition of a new data item requires only the addition of a new file to the database. Existing programs which do not need the new data item will not be affected. A database management system could translate between the transposed file structure and conventional record structures like those in Fig. 1.4. This arrangement would provide a more convenient local view for each program, and would reduce the number of files a program would need to handle.
5. Generalised file interrogation packages are available for use with conventional file structures. Packages of this kind may be able to process only one file at a time, which may restrict their usefulness compared with a database enquiry language.
6. (a)   Personnel/Payroll; Production scheduling and control; Sales and Marketing.
   (b)   Personnel/Payroll; Spares and repairs; Customer billing.

2

Database management system architecture

2.1 Introduction

The previous chapter conveyed the idea of a database management system (DBMS) as providing an interface between a global view of the data and the local views of the application programs. This was essentially a two-level DBMS architecture. In the present chapter a more careful analysis of the functions of a DBMS will show that three levels of data view can usefully be distinguished.

2.2 A three-level architecture

First a definition. A data view which is specified in a language which the DBMS software is designed to understand will be called a *schema*. The discussion in Chapter 1 implied that a DBMS should cater for two types of schema, namely *global schema* and *local schema*. In fact, in this two-level architecture, the global schema would need to contain two essentially different types of information. There is information about what data is available in the database, and information about the way that data is stored and accessed. Taken together with the local schema there are then three schemas. For consistency with general usage, the three schemas will be referred to from now on as the *conceptual*, *internal* and *external* schemas. These three terms are defined below.

2.3 The conceptual schema

The *conceptual schema* is a description of all the data of interest to the enterprise which is to be stored in the database. It specifies the logical data content of the database and the constraints which apply to the data. For example:

(1)   The data held on customers is customerNo, name, address, ...
(2)   The data held on products is productNo, description, price, ...
(3)   Customers place orders for products.
(4)   An employee may not work simultaneously for more than one department.
(5)   The age of an employee on the payroll may not exceed 99 years.
(6)   Age must be a numeric data item.
(7)   Personnel data (namely . . .) may be accessed only by the following users . . . .
(8)   A product may be a final assembly, sub-assembly or component.
(9)   The distinction between a full-time and a part-time employee is that . . . .

This list hints at the comprehensiveness which a conceptual schema might possess. As might be expected, database management systems differ in the degree of comprehensiveness, and ease of use, of their conceptual schema facilities.

As the enterprise evolves, so the conceptual schema will have to be changed. If the conceptual schema is an accurate model of the enterprise, then any change seen by the enterprise as being a straightforward development in its way of doing business should imply a straightforward change in the conceptual schema. On the other hand, no one should be surprised if a radical change to the enterprise necessitates a radical change to the conceptual schema. The conceptual schema is therefore to be thought of as a relatively stable, long-term view of the data, which is capable of evolving with the enterprise.

2.4 The external schema

An *external schema* describes the local view of the database required by an application program. If several programs require identical local views they may share the same external schema.

Properties of the data such as the format of data items or the sequence in which data is seen (e.g. customerName sequence) may be specified by an external schema, but it cannot override any of the constraints imposed by the conceptual schema.

2.5 The internal schema

The *internal schema* describes how the stored data is implemented at the level of stored records, stored record formats, indexes, hashing algorithms, pointers, blocksizes, storage media, and the like.

2.6 Mapping

The DBMS software is responsible for mapping between the three types of schema. It must be capable of checking the schemas for consistency (e.g. that each external schema is capable of being derived from the conceptual schema), and must use the information in the schemas to map between each external schema and the internal schema via the conceptual schema.

The relationships between the three types of schema are shown in Fig. 2.1. The conceptual schema is the hub of the architecture. Each external schema provides one, or more, programs with a local view which can be derived from the conceptual schema; the internal schema describes how the conceptual schema is physically implemented.

2.7 DBMS components

Few, if any, available DBMS systems adhere strictly to the three-level architecture illustrated in Fig. 2.1, but the diagram does indicate the components which one would

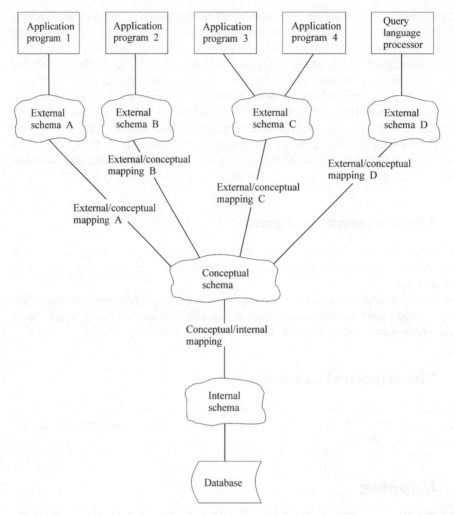

Fig. 2.1 The relationship between application programs and database in a three-level DBMS architecture. (Note that programs 3 and 4 share the same external schema, and that one program is a generalised query language processor)

expect to find in some shape or form in a typical DBMS. These include:

(1) User language interfaces, normally including a data manipulation language (DML), as described in section 1.3.4.
(2) An external schema data description language.
(3) A conceptual schema data description language.
(4) An internal schema data description language.
(5) A database control system (DBCS) which will access the database in response to DML commands.

The operation of the database control system is illustrated in Fig. 2.2. Suppose application program 1 issues a DML command to store a new record in the database. The DBCS consults the application program's external schema, the external/

conceptual mapping, the conceptual schema, the conceptual/internal mapping, and the internal schema, in order to find out how the record should be stored. The DBCS can then command the operating system to store the record in the database. Finally, a message is returned to the application program to say whether or not the store operation has been successful.

The process as represented in Fig. 2.2 is interpretive in that the DBCS consults each schema and mapping every time it receives a DML command. A system implemented in this way would provide very good program/data independence (for example, the internal schema could be changed between successive DML commands without the application program being aware of the change) but the performance of the system would be unacceptably slow for many applications. In practice, a DBMS is likely to compile mappings in advance, so that a more direct path is provided between application program and database.

A more detailed example of the sequence of events in a store operation is shown in Fig. 2.3. Both Figs 2.2 and 2.3 are intended to be suggestive, rather than prescriptive, of the structure and operation of a DBMS. In Fig. 2.3, the external schema contains just one record type, costRecord (in general, an external schema would contain several record types and relationships between records); this external schema maps on to part of one conceptual schema record type, Inventory (in general, an external schema could

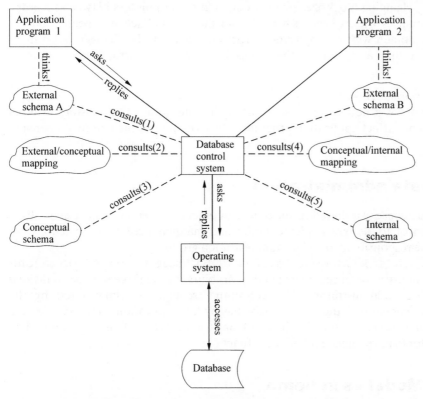

Fig. 2.2   The way in which an application program accesses the database via the database control system. The sequence in which the schemas and mappings are consulted following a DML command from program 1 is shown by the numbers in parentheses

be derived from several conceptual record types and relationships); the conceptual schema in turn maps on to the internal schema (once again, the mapping could be more complex than the direct correspondence between Inventory and Stored Inventory).

2.8   Advantages of three-level architecture

The three-level architecture simplifies the design and management of a database system by providing a higher level of program/data independence than is possible with a one- or two-level architecture. The clear separation of external, conceptual and internal schemas offers a standard against which a DBMS may be assessed. Some of the implications of the three-level architecture with respect to program/data independence are listed below.

Change in conceptual schema
A change to the conceptual schema (the addition of a data item, say) will not affect any existing application program, unless its external schema is incompatible with the new conceptual schema.

Change in internal schema
Changing patterns of data usage may necessitate tuning of the database system (for example, by changing blocksizes or providing additional pointers between records). The separation of the external schemas from the internal schema means that the latter can be tuned without application programs having to be changed. Also there is no danger that a change to the internal schema will corrupt the conceptual schema.

Change in external schema
The definition of a new external schema, or the alteration of an existing external schema will not affect application programs which do not use the external schema in question.

2.9   Data administration

Because a database is a shared resource it is, in practice, essential to have centralised coordination of its design, implementation and maintenance. These functions are normally the responsibility of a data administration group.

The three-level architecture proposed for the DBMS suggests a possible structure for the data administration group, in which responsibility for the three schemas is divided between three administrators. The conceptual schema is administered by the enterprise administrator, the external schemas by the application administrator, and the internal schema by the database administrator. We will use the term data administrator to cover any, or all, of these functions.

2.10   Model vs schema

As defined above, a schema is a specification of a data view expressed in the language used by a particular database management system. Schemas written for one DBMS

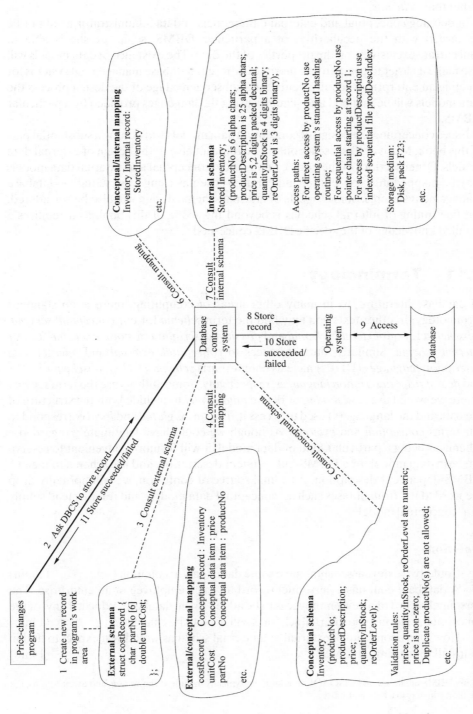

Fig. 2.3 The sequence of events for a store operation

would not normally be intelligible to a different DBMS[1]. There are therefore advantages in adopting higher-level descriptions of the data, descriptions which are independent of any DBMS software. We will refer to such descriptions as *data models* rather than *schemas*.

In defining conceptual and external data models, a data administrator need not be concerned with the peculiarities of a particular DBMS, so he or she is able to concentrate exclusively on the properties of the data. The existence of data models will also make it easier to compare the merits of different database management systems for meeting an enterprise's requirements. At a subsequent stage of the design process the data models will be mapped into schemas using the languages provided by a particular DBMS.

Issues concerning the design of conceptual data models will occupy a substantial part of this book. Much of this discussion will be relevant also to the design of external data models. Other sections of the book examine how conceptual and external data models may be mapped into conceptual and external schemas using representative database management systems. Some aspects of internal schema design will also be considered, but fine tuning of internal schemas is beyond the scope of this book as it requires a detailed knowledge of the specific DBMS concerned.

2.11   Terminology

In database literature, as in many other areas of computing, there is no standard terminology. In other texts you may find the term *schema* for our *conceptual schema*, *subschema* for our *external schema*, and *physical description* or *storage schema* for our *internal schema*. Similarly, our references to *conceptual, external* and *internal data description languages* (DDLs) have as counterparts *schema DDLs, subschema DDLs* and *data storage description languages*, respectively. Some authors use the term *schema* where we would use *data model*, or define *data model* to include both the structure of the data and the language(s) used to access it. The terms *global* and *local* correspond to our terms *conceptual* and *external*. Although we could have legitimately regarded a schema as being a particular kind of data model, it will be more convenient to reserve the term data model for a DBMS-independent description, and use schema to mean a DBMS-dependent description. As a final source of confusion, we will normally drop the word 'data' from phrases such as 'conceptual data model', and refer instead simply to a 'conceptual model'.

Questions

1.   Could two external schemas have some data items in common?   (1 min)
2.   A database contains a personnel record for each employee of an enterprise. The personnel record of a new employee is to be added to the database. Which, if any, of the conceptual, external and internal schemas will need to be changed?   (1 min)
3.   How many conceptual, external and internal schemas would you expect to find in an installation using a DBMS?   (1 min)

---

[1] Many DBMS are based on an ISO SQL standard, but typically include variations on, and extensions to, the standard which restrict compatibility.

4. Suggest four, or more, reasons why the store operation illustrated in Fig. 2.3 might be unsuccessful. (2 min)

5. Why might there be a security risk if the DBMS and operating system software are designed independently? (1 min)

6. Compare the merits of:
(a) sharing an external schema between several application programs; and
(b) defining a separate external schema for each application program. (2 min)

7. Separation of the external schemas from the internal schema allows the latter to be tuned without changes having to be made to application programs. In what way might an application program become aware of a change in the internal schema? (1 min)

8. Suppose a particular DBMS allows only complete conceptual record types to be included in an external schema, so that an application program using the external schema always sees all the data items in a record. Compare this external schema structure with one in which it is possible to specify which data items are required. Which structure offers (a) the best program/data independence, and (b) the best security. (2 min)

9. In principle, the size of a data item could be defined differently in the external and internal schemas (3 characters versus 5 characters, or 1 decimal point versus 2 decimal points, say). If this were permitted by a DBMS, what problems would need to be resolved in connection with retrieval and amendment operations? (5 min)

10. Is there such a thing as an internal data model? (3 min)

11. Is the three-level DBMS architecture the best thing since sliced bread, or is it altogether too clever? (10 min)

Assignments

1. In section 1.6 (Chapter 1) it was stated that the function of a DBMS is to overcome problems attendant on the use of a database. In this an unduly harsh assessment? Argue the case for a more charitable view, namely that a DBMS offers a consistent set of facilities which would otherwise be provided in a piecemeal fashion.

2. Summarise the claims made in advertisements for database management systems. Comment on the validity of these claims.

3. If you are familiar with a particular DBMS, classify its facilities into conceptual, external and internal schema facilities. Assess how well the DBMS conforms to the three-level architecture, and outline the advantages and disadvantages of any deviations which you have identified.

Answer pointers

1. Yes. If you are in doubt return to Chapter 1.

2. None of them if, as is normally the case, the same type of information is to be held for both new and existing employees. If the information about the new employee is to include a new type of data item, then the conceptual schema, the internal schema, and the external schemas for those application programs which will use the new data item will have to be changed.

3. One conceptual schema, one internal schema, and several external schemas, for each database. Some installations may have several databases, one for each application area (see section 1.7). Occasionally, more than one DBMS is used in the same installation. An alternative answer is that, if the installation's security is adequate, you won't find any schemas unless you have the necessary authority.

4.   (a) The database already contains an Inventory record with the same productNo as the record to be stored. Note that the conceptual schema forbids duplicate values of productNo. (b) The value of price is zero or non-numeric; see conceptual schema rules. (c) Disk pack F23 is not on-line. (d) Disk write error. (e) Failure of the central processing unit. (f) Power failure. (g) Database has been opened for inquiry only, not update.

5.   By accessing the operating system directly, for example to dump the database, an intruder may be able to by-pass security checks in the DBMS. In practice, most database management systems have been tacked on to existing operating systems.

6.   Under option (a) one can be sure that each application program has exactly the same view of the data. If the programs do not need the same view, or if their views may differ in the future, then option (a) could cause maintenance and security problems. Sharing external schemas reduces the number of external schemas and external/conceptual mappings which have to be created. If a DBMS allows an application program to use a dummy external schema name, which can be separately equated to an actual external schema name, then option (a) could easily be converted into option (b).

7.   Change in response time.

8.   Specification of individual data items gives best program/data independence and security.

9.   How will the different data item descriptions be aligned? From the left, right, implied decimal point? Will truncation from left or right of numeric data be allowed? If an external three character value ABC amends an internal five character value VWXYZ, should the result be ABCYZ or ABC followed by two spaces, or what? If an internal three character data item is retrieved into an external five character data item what values should be inserted in the extra two characters?

10.   On our definitions a data model is DBMS-independent, but an internal schema is highly DBMS-dependent. An internal data model would have to be a DBMS-independent description of the storage structure of a database. Such a language could form the basis of a system for automatic conversion between different database management systems.

11.   Depends what you want. Consider the extremes of a completely static environment and a highly dynamic environment. A good answer should also assess the merits of sliced bread.

Part 2

Relational modelling

Part 2 explains how a conceptual data model, free of redundancy, can be designed using a 'bottom-up' approach which focuses on the interdependence of data attributes.

Chapter 3 describes the basic building block of this approach, namely the *table*.

Chapter 4 makes an important distinction between *redundant* and *duplicated* data, and emphasises the crucial role of *enterprise rules* in distinguishing redundancy from mere duplication.

Chapter 5 examines the problems posed by *repeating groups* and shows how they may be eliminated.

Chapter 6 is central to the theme of Part 2. The ideas discussed in the previous chapters are developed via the concepts of *determinant* and *identifier* into a statement of the *Boyce/Codd rule*, which a table must obey to be free of redundancy.

Chapter 7 shows that the Boyce/Codd rule, although a necessary condition, is not always sufficient to guarantee freedom from redundancy.

3

Tables

3.1 Introduction

The description of a conceptual model should not only be independent of any DBMS, it should not even presuppose the use of a computer system at all. This being so, it would be best to avoid the use of terms such as *record* and *file* in the description of a conceptual model, since these terms have strong internal schema connotations.

A conceptual model should provide a view of the data which is as logically simple as possible. The question of exactly what constitutes logical simplicity is ultimately a matter of individual judgement. Many people would accept that one criterion for a logically simple structure is that it should be composed of as few elementary building blocks as possible; however, the choice of elementary building blocks is likely to be more contentious. The building block which we will concentrate on initially, and one which is widely used in describing conceptual models, is the *table*, or *relation*. For the reasons given in the preface, we will use the term table rather than relation. However, it is important to note that table is used in the specialised sense described below.

3.2 Tables

In the *relational model*, data is structured into simple tables. Figure 3.1a shows an example of a table. The table name is Stock; the table contains three *columns* each headed by the name of an *attribute type*, and four *rows*.[1] The intersection of each row and column in the table contains an *attribute occurrence*, otherwise known as an *attribute value*. For instance, bolt is an attribute value of the attribute type partDescription.

In the interests of logical simplicity a number of restrictions will be applied to tables:

(1) The ordering of rows is not significant; that is, the rows can be interchanged without affecting the information content of the table.
(2) The ordering of columns is not significant. (We can ensure that this is so by insisting that each column within a table has a distinct attribute type name.)
(3) Each row/column intersection contains a single attribute value. Multiple values are not allowed.
(4) Each row in a table must be distinct; no two rows can have the same attribute values throughout. (The significance of this rule is that a row can always be uniquely identified by quoting an appropriate combination of attribute values.)

---

[1] A *row* is commonly referred to as a *tuple*, but we will not use this term.

Figure 3.1a is an example of a *table occurrence*, that is it contains attribute values. Figure 3.1b is an example of a *table type*; it contains the table name and the attribute types, but not the attribute values.

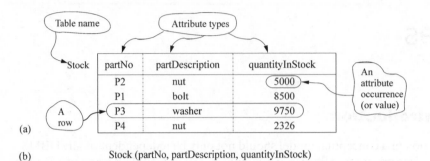

(a)

(b)   Stock (partNo, partDescription, quantityInStock)

Fig. 3.1   Examples of a table occurrence and a table type
(a)   Table occurrence
(b)   Table type

In order to make the ensuing discussion less cumbersome, the term *table* used on its own may mean either *table occurrence*, or *table type*, or both, depending on context. The terms *attribute type* and *attribute value* may be abbreviated to *attribute* and *value*, respectively. Phrases such as 'the partNo attribute value is Z80' will be abbreviated to 'the partNo value is Z80', or simply 'the partNo is Z80'. The suffix '(s)' will be appended to an attribute name when referring to several values of the attribute, as in 'The partNo(s) shown in Figure 3.1a are P2, P1, P3 and P4'.

Table names are usually written in the singular (e.g. Employee rather than Employees). They will be written with an initial capital for each word and with no spaces in the name (e.g. StaffContract). Attribute names will be written in the same way except that the first word will not have an initial capital (e.g. quantityInStock).

3.3   Nulls

An attribute occurrence may be *null*, that is not yet known or not applicable. For example, the number of eggs an ostrich will lay may be applicable but not yet known, whereas the number of eggs an elephant will lay is not applicable. As we will not usually need to distinguish between different kinds of null, any null occurrence in a table will usually be represented by a blank, but this should not be taken to mean that null and blank are synonymous.

3.4   Normalisation

A table which satisfies restriction 3 of section 3.2 will be called a *normalised* table. A table which violates restriction 3 is said to be *unnormalised*. The aim of the next few chapters is to develop some simple tests which will reveal whether a table possesses certain undesirable properties, notably redundant attribute values. A set of tables which passes these tests will be called *fully-normalised*, and will form a useful basis for the description of a conceptual model.

Questions

1. What is wrong with the following table?

Book

bookNo	title	author
246	Biology	Chan
172	Physics	Green, Newton
246	Biology	Chan

(1 min)

2. For the table shown in question 1, identify the table name and the attribute types. Is 'Physics' an attribute value or an attribute type? (1 min)
3. A table is to contain a list of the make and colour of every car recorded in a survey. The table will be used to count the number of cars of each colour within each make. A table type Car (make, colour) is unsuitable because there could be only one row for each distinct combination of make and colour. There would be no way of recording how many cars had been observed with each make/colour combination. Suggest a suitable table type. (2 min)
4. The following table is intended to show that orderNo 123 is for partNo(s) P4 and P7, and orderNo 138 is for partNo(s) P2, P4 and P8. The value of orderNo is blank in rows 2, 4 and 5. What is wrong with the table? How could the problem be overcome?

Order

orderNo	partNo	quantityOrdered
123	P4	5
	P7	12
138	P2	10
	P4	20
	P8	16

(1 min)

5. The table:

  Register (studentNo, surname, firstForename, secondForename)

is used to record names of students on a course.
(a) Why might it be advisable to forbid null occurrences for studentNo? (1 min)
(b) Use the example of the Register table to illustrate why one might want to represent 'not yet known' and 'not applicable' by different types of null. (1 min)

Answer pointers

1. Attribute type author has multiple values in the second row. Also, rows 1 and 3 are identical, so the table does not conform to the relational model. The multiple values can be eliminated by replacing row 2 by two rows:

  172 Physics Green
  172 Physics Newton

Deletion of one of the duplicate rows would then make the table consistent with the relational model.

2.   Table name is Book. Attribute types are bookNo, title, author. 'Physics' is an attribute value.

3.   Car (make, colour, count) where each value of the count attribute gives the number of vehicles recorded of a given make and colour. An alternative solution is Car (registrationNo, make, colour).

4.   The ordering of rows is significant. For example, if row 2 is swapped with row 5 it would appear that orderNo 123 is for partNo(s) P4 and P8, and orderNo 138 is for partNo(s) P2, P4 and P7. Notice also that, if the same partNo were ordered in the same quantity on different orderNo(s), there could be identical rows in the table. To overcome the problem repeat the orderNo value 123 in row 2, and repeat the orderNo value 138 in rows 4 and 5. The layout shown in question 4 might be suitable for an internal schema in which each row in the table is represented as a record occurrence, but it is an unnecessarily complex layout for a conceptual schema.

5.   (a)   It would be impossible to distinguish between rows where the full names (surname, firstForename and secondForename) were the same. Notice that two such rows would be identical in the sense that the corresponding surname, firstForename and secondForename values would be equal and both studentNo occurrences would be null. However, we cannot say that the two studentNo occurrences are equal. Where null means 'value not known', there is no way of determining whether or not one null is equal to another. Where null means 'not applicable', it makes no sense to ask if one 'not applicable' occurrence is equal to another. Null is a state rather than an actual value, though for simplicity we will sometimes refer to null values. The slippery nature of nulls leads some authorities to argue that they should not be permitted in the relational model, and that actual values should always be used. For example, 'value not known' could be represented by '?' and 'not applicable' by '!' (assuming that these characters can be reserved for these purposes).

(b)   A student's forenames might not be known when he or she is initially enrolled on the register, so they could be entered as 'not yet known'. If a student does not have a second forename, it could be entered as 'not applicable'.

4

Redundant vs duplicated data

4.1　Introduction

As we have seen, a major advantage of the database approach is that inconsistency can be reduced by eliminating redundant data. Also, it seems likely that the elimination of redundancy will lead to a simpler conceptual model which more accurately reflects the real world. This chapter gives a fairly informal introduction to the identification and elimination of redundant data.

4.2　Redundant vs duplicated data

Care must be taken to distinguish between *duplicated* data and *redundant* data. Duplicated data is present when an attribute has two (or more) identical values. A data value is redundant if you can delete it without information being lost. Redundancy is *unnecessary* duplication.

Table Part in Fig. 4.1a contains duplicated data, because the value nut occurs twice for the attribute partDescription. The table does *not*, however, contain redundant data. If, as in Fig. 4.1b, the value nut is deleted from the row P2 nut, you will no longer be able to tell from the table what the description of part P2 should be.

Part	partNo	partDescription
	P2	nut
	P1	bolt
	P3	washer
(a)	P4	nut

Part	partNo	partDescription
	P2	—
	P1	bolt
	P3	washer
(b)	P4	nut

Fig. 4.1　Non-redundant duplication
(a)　Duplication but no redundancy
(b)　Deletion of duplicated but non-redundant data value causes loss of information

In contrast, table SupplierPart in Fig. 4.2a contains duplicated data which *is* redundant. This table shows which suppliers supply which parts, and also the descriptions of the parts. Notice that the fact that partNo P1 is a bolt is duplicated, and that the duplication is redundant because, even if the value bolt were deleted from one of the occurrences of P1 bolt, you could still tell from the table that P1 is a bolt. In

Fig. 4.2b, the value bolt has been deleted from the fourth row, but the description of partNo P1 can still be deduced from the first row. (There is a hidden assumption here — can you tell what it is? See question 6 below.)

SupplierPart	supplierNo	partNo	partDescription
	S2	P1	bolt
	S7	P6	bolt
	S2	P4	nut
	S5	P1	bolt

(a)

SupplierPart	supplierNo	partNo	partDescription
	S2	P1	bolt
	S7	P6	bolt
	S2	P4	nut
	S5	P1	—

(b)

Fig. 4.2   Redundant duplication
(a)   Redundantly duplicated data
(b)   Deletion of redundantly duplicated data value causes no loss of information

Is there any other redundancy in Fig. 4.2a? The supplierNo S2 is duplicated, and so is partNo P1, but in neither case is the duplication redundant. For example, deletion of S2 from the third row would mean that you cannot tell who supplies partNo P4.

Questions

1.   Which of the following statements is true?
(a)   Duplicated data is always redundant.
(b)   Some duplicated data is redundant.   (1 min)
2.   What information would be lost if the value nut were deleted from the fourth row of the table in Fig. 4.1a?   (1 min)
3.   Suppose another row P7 nut were added to the table in Fig. 4.1a. Would this new value of nut be redundant? How can you tell?   (1 min)
4.   In Fig. 4.2a, which of the following are examples of redundant duplication of data values?
(a)   The two occurrences of the partNo value P1.
(b)   The two occurrences of the partDescription value bolt in rows 1 and 4.
(c)   The two occurrences of the partDescription value bolt in rows 2 and 4.   (1 min)
5.   The CustomerPart table below shows the quantities in which customers have ordered parts.

CustomerPart	customerNo	customerName	partNo	partDescription	quantity
	C4	Carter	P7	Pin	5
	C4	Carter	P2	nut	100
	C2	Carter	P2	nut	200
	C8	Brown	P4	nut	5

In the CustomerPart table, which of the following are examples of redundant duplication of data values? Explain briefly your reasoning.
(a)   The two occurrences of the customerNo value C4.
(b)   The two occurrences of Carter in rows 1 and 2.
(c)   The two occurrences of Carter in rows 1 and 3.
(d)   The two occurrences of nut in rows 3 and 4.
(e)   The two occurrences of 5 in rows 1 and 4.   (2 min)
6.   Under what circumstances would it not be true that the missing partDescription in Fig. 4.2b could be deduced from the other data in this table?   (2 min)

4.3   Elimination of redundancy

Although the redundancy in Fig. 4.2a has apparently been eliminated in the Fig. 4.2b version, the latter is still an unsatisfactory way of structuring the data. The dash in the fourth row means 'I'm not going to tell you what the partDescription is, but you can find out from somewhere else in the table'. A structure which requires such a cumbersome interpretation is not consistent with our aim of designing simple conceptual models.

A much more satisfactory solution is to split the table into two as in Fig. 4.3. One table, SupplierPart1, shows which supplier supplies which part, and the other table, Part1, contains the description of each part. Two points should be noted. Firstly, the connection between the two tables is made by including partNo in each table. Secondly, the row P1 bolt, which appears twice in Fig. 4.2a, can appear only once in table Part1 because of the rule that identical rows are not allowed. Convince yourself that no information has been lost by discarding the duplicate row.

SupplierPart1	supplierNo	partNo
	S2	P1
	S7	P6
	S2	P4
	S5	P1

(a)

Part1	partNo	partDescription
	P1	bolt
	P6	bolt
	P4	nut

(b)

Fig. 4.3   Elimination of redundancy by table splitting

For the present, try to see intuitively how a table which can contain redundant data should be split into tables which do not contain redundant data. Later on we will present rules that will help you in this process.

Questions

1.   The table below shows the names and qualifications of employees. Each employee has precisely one employee number, and any given employee number is assigned to precisely one employee (i.e. employees cannot share the same employee number).

Employee	employeeNo	employeeName	qualification
	E1	Smith	BSc
	E1	Smith	MSc
	E1	Smith	PhD
	E2	Jones	BA
	E3	Jones	BA
	E3	Jones	PhD

(a) How many employees called Smith are there in this table?
(b) How many employees called Jones are there in this table?
(c) Which attribute values are redundant in this table?
(d) Show how the redundancy can be eliminated by splitting the table into two.
(e) Satisfy yourself that the original Employee table can be derived from the new tables.   (3 min)
2. Show how the redundancy can be eliminated from the CustomerPart table in question 5 of section 4.2 by splitting the table into three.   (3 min)

4.4   Deceptive appearances

The discussion in the previous sections of this chapter is not entirely accurate, because it is implied that table structures that permit redundancy can be recognised simply by inspection of sample table occurrences. One reason why this is not so is that the attribute values in a table are normally subject to amendment, insertion and deletion.

Suppose the fourth row were deleted from the SupplierPart table in Fig. 4.2a, to give the SupplierPart2 table of Fig. 4.4. Inspection of SupplierPart2, as opposed to SupplierPart, does not reveal any redundant data. In fact, SupplierPart2 could be consistent with a rule that no two suppliers may supply the same partNo. If this rule does apply, the table structure would be satisfactory as it stands; if not, it would need to be split, as in Fig. 4.3, in order to eliminate the possibility of its holding redundant data.

SupplierPart2	supplierNo	partNo	partDescription
	S2	P1	bolt
	S7	P6	bolt
	S2	P4	nut

Fig. 4.4   Could this table contain redundant data?

The opposite situation is illustrated by the SupplierPart3 table in Fig. 4.5. In this example a further row S3 P4 collar has been added to the original SupplierPart data of Fig. 4.2a. In the discussion of SupplierPart it was implicitly assumed that a given partNo value had exactly one (possibly null) associated partDescription value, but it might have been true that a given partNo value could have several associated partDescription values, as exemplified by SupplierPart3 where P4 is described variously as a nut and a collar. The data P1 bolt is duplicated in SupplierPart3, but there is no redundancy. If bolt were deleted from the first row, the missing value could not be deduced from the remaining data, because supplier S2 does not have to use the same description as supplier S5 for partNo P1.

SupplierPart3	supplierNo	partNo	partDescription
	S2	P1	bolt
	S7	P6	bolt
	S2	P4	nut
	S5	P1	bolt
	S3	P4	collar

Fig. 4.5   A given partNo value may have more than one partDescription value

4.5   Enterprise rules

The above discussion shows that a 'snapshot' of a table is not a reliable guide as to whether the table could contain redundant data. What one really needs to know are the underlying rules which govern the data. We will call any rule which is applicable to the conceptual model of an enterprise's data, an enterprise rule. Examples of the kind of enterprise rule in which we will be particularly interested are:

(1)   A given partNo value has exactly one associated partDescription value.
(2)   A given partDescription value may be associated with many partNo values.
(3)   A given supplierNo value may be associated with many partNo values.
(4)   A given partNo value may be associated with many supplierNo values.

Unless otherwise stated, it will be assumed that an enterprise rule such as (1), above, must be obeyed by any single snapshot of the data, but need not necessarily be obeyed by a series of snapshots viewed together. That is, at any given time a partNo value has exactly one associated partDescription value, but the partDescription value could be changed between snapshots.

An important task for the data administrator is to discover the enterprise rules which apply to the conceptual model. Once the rules are known it becomes possible to design a conceptual model that is free of redundancy.

Questions

1.   The following enterprise rules apply to information held in a library's catalogue:
(a)   bookNo uniquely identifies a book;
(b)   a book may be written by several authors;
(c)   a book has only one title.
Write an occurrence of the table:

Book (bookNo, title, authorName)

using the following data:

BookNo 811203 has the title Introduction to Biology and is written by Brown.
BookNo 811204 has the title Microprocessor Systems and is written by Jones and Smith.   (1 min)

2. With reference to question 1, and assuming that none of the enterprise rules are known to you:

(a)   can you deduce any of the enterprise rules merely by inspecting the table occurrence that you have written?

(b)   if you are told that a bookNo uniquely identifies a book, which of the other enterprise rules can you deduce from an inspection of the table?   (3 min)

3.   As part of a fact finding investigation you are told that each employee has a unique employeeNo. Does this mean that:

(a)   an employee has only one employeeNo;

(b)   no two employees share the same employeeNo;

(c)   all employees have the same employeeNo;

(d)   some combination of the above?   (5 min)

4.   An enterprise rule states that an employee has only one salary. Would this normally mean, as far as the conceptual model is concerned:

(a)   an employee's salary is never changed;

(b)   an historical record of employees' salaries is not required;

(c)   every employee has the same salary?   (1 min)

5.   The examples of enterprise rules given in section 4.5 are expressed in the form:

'A given supplierNo value may be associated with many partNo values.'

Would the following statement have the same meaning as the one above?

'A supplier may supply many parts.'   (2 min)

Answer pointers

Section 4.2

1.   (a) False.   (b) True.

2.   The fact that partNo P4 is a nut.

3.   The new value would be a duplicate value, but not a redundant value. Deletion of the value would cause loss of information.

4.   (a)   Non-redundant. If P1 is deleted from the first row, you still know that S2 supplies a bolt, but you don't know what type of bolt. For example, it could be a P1 or a P6. A partDescription value does not uniquely identify a part.

(b)   Redundant.

(c)   Non-redundant. If one of the bolt values is deleted from either row 2 or 4, the remaining row will not provide the missing information. (Row 1 would come to the rescue if the deletion were from row 4.)

5.   (a) Non-redundant. Attribute customerName does not uniquely identify a customer, so deletion of (say) the first C4 means you don't know who ordered the P7 — it was ordered by a Carter, but which one? (b) Redundant. (c) Non-redundant. (d) Non-redundant. (e) Non-redundant.

6.   partNo P1 might have more than one description, possibly because the description is that used by the supplier. Supplier S2 might call a P1 a bolt, but supplier S5 might call it a rivet. Points like this will turn out to be very important in the analysis of data.

Section 4.3

1. (a) One. Employee E1. (b) Two. Employees E2 and E3. (c) Two of the Smiths in rows 1–3. One of the Jones in rows 5 and 6.

(d)

Employee1

employeeNo	employeeName
E1	Smith
E2	Jones
E3	Jones

EmployeeQual1

employeeNo	qualification
E1	BSc
E1	MSc
E1	PhD
E2	BA
E3	BA
E3	PhD

2.

Customer1

customerNo	customerName
C4	Carter
C2	Carter
C8	Brown

Part1

partNo	partDescription
P7	pin
P2	nut
P4	nut

CustomerPart1

customerNo	partNo	quantity
C4	P7	5
C4	P2	100
C2	P2	200
C8	P4	5

Section 4.5

1. Book

bookNo	title	authorName
811203	Introduction to Biology	Brown
811204	Microprocessor Systems	Jones
811204	Microprocessor Systems	Smith

2. (a) You can tell that a given bookNo may be associated with several authorName(s) but you cannot be sure that a bookNo uniquely identifies a book. Perhaps bookNo 811204 is a classification number applicable to all books about microprocessors. If so, the two Microprocessor Systems titles might be completely different books, and there might be an enterprise rule that only one authorName is recorded for each book. Alternatively, bookNo might refer to the date on which the book was catalogued. You cannot tell that a book has only one title. Notice also that the meaning of the word 'book' is ambiguous. Does it mean a 'work' or a 'copy'? A library may stock several copies of the same work. Assumptions about the meaning an enterprise attaches to an attribute should always be checked. A suspicious mind is a valuable asset (as long as it doesn't become neurotic).

(b)   You can tell that a book may be associated with several authorName(s). You cannot tell that a book has only one title; it may just be that there is currently no instance of a book with several titles, but that it would be perfectly valid to add rows such as:

811205	Twelfth Night	Shakespeare
811205	What You Will	Shakespeare

Notice that, on its own, inspection of a table occurrence may reveal permissive enterprise rules (a given bookNo may have several associated authorName(s)); it cannot reveal a restrictive rule (a given bookNo has only one title) as it is conceivable that further rows that would contravene the restriction could be added. Inspection of table occurrences may provide clues, but the determination of a valid set of enterprise rules requires a more extensive fact finding investigation.

3.   I would expect the statement to mean that both (a) and (b) apply, but if you want to analyse the statement thoroughly, I suggest you convene a discussion group equipped with a pile of dictionaries and some comfortable chairs. The real point of this question is that statements of this kind may be interpreted differently by different people, for example users, systems analysts and data administrators. Different interpretations will lead to different enterprise rules and different conceptual models. Although you may, quite rightly, decry its sloppy use, it must be recognised that natural language often is ambiguous, and that it is a waste of time for an enterprise to issue an edict that ambiguous statements are henceforth forbidden.

4.   The statement would normally mean that (b) is true but (a) and (c) are false. Stated more precisely, the rule would probably mean that the database defined by the conceptual model can store only one salary attribute value for each employee at any one time.

5.   The second statement has the advantage that it declares that the nature of the association is to do with 'Supply' rather than, say, 'Manufacture', though there is still room for further clarification ('Could supply'?, 'Does supply'?; either of these?). The first statement does not make it clear whether a supplierNo value identifies a supplier uniquely (similarly for partNo and part), whereas the second statement does not say how suppliers and parts are identified. The second statement might be interpreted as meaning that a supplier may supply many copies of the same part (partNo X25 in a quantity of 100, say) rather than that the supplier may supply many kinds of part (X25, X32, R48, say).

   In this text it is not practicable to state enterprise rules with absolute precision, without indulging in verbal gymnastics which may confuse rather than clarify the subject. If assumptions are not explicitly stated, then reasonable assumptions should be made by the reader. Remember, however, that in the 'real world' a reasonable assumption that turns out to be false can have catastrophic consequences.

5

Repeating groups

5.1 Introduction

One of the properties of a normalised table, as defined in Chapter 3, is that an attribute must have only one value in each row. The present chapter looks more closely at the reasons for this rule, and then discusses ways in which tables may be structured so that the rule is obeyed.

What constitutes a single value for an attribute? Suppose partNo values are defined as two-character codes, the first character being alphabetic (not necessarily a P, as used in the examples) and the second character numeric. Each two-character code represents a part that may be supplied by a supplier. In Fig. 5.1a, row 1 contains a single value (P1) of partNo, as does row 3 (P6). Conversely, row 2 contains multiple values (P1, P4) of partNo, as does row 4 (P8, P2, P6).

The relational model does allow the values of an attribute to have an internal structure, but it is not aware of that structure and cannot access it directly (though it could do so via a suitably written function or procedure). A simple example is that the supplierName value Wells (Fig. 5.1) has an internal structure consisting of the individual letters W, e, l, l, s. However, it is Wells as a whole that constitutes a single value of supplierName known to the relational model, not the individual letters making up the name.

In fact, the relational model allows any degree of complexity in the internal structure of an attribute value. For example, a single attribute value could be the complete score of Beethoven's ninth symphony, or a circuit diagram, or a picture of an oak tree. Whatever the complexity of the internal structure, only a single value of the attribute type is allowed at each row/column intersection.

5.2 Repeating groups

Suppose that a supplier can supply several parts, and that the attributes of interest are supplierNo, supplierName, and partNo. If each row of a table were allowed to contain several partNo values, the table structure of Fig. 5.1a could be used. Here, partNo is an example of a *repeating group*. (In this case the group consists of just one attribute.) This table structure is unnecessarily complex because a repeating group is itself a table. For example, the last row of SupplierPart contains a single supplierNo value (S9), a single supplierName value (Edwards), but a table of partNo values (P8, P2, P6). SupplierPart therefore consists of one table type embedded within another.

SupplierPart	supplierNo	supplierName	partNo
	S5	Wells	P1
	S2	Heath	P1, P4
	S7	Barron	P6
(a)	S9	Edwards	P8, P2, P6

SupplierPart	supplierNo	supplierName	partNo
	S5	Wells	P1
	S2	Heath	P1
			P4
	S7	Barron	P6
	S9	Edwards	P8
			P2
(b)			P6

Fig. 5.1   Repeating group layouts
(a)   Horizontal layout
(b)   Vertical layout

Several other drawbacks flow from the use in Fig. 5.1a of an embedded table structure for SupplierPart.

(1)   The table is an asymmetrical representation of symmetrical data. The data is symmetrical in the sense that a supplier may supply many parts, and a part may be supplied by many suppliers. The representation is asymmetrical because in any one row of the table, a given supplierNo may be associated with a list of partNo(s), but a given partNo may not be associated with a list of supplierNo(s).
(2)   The rows can be sorted into supplierNo order, or supplierName order, but not into partNo order.
(3)   The rows are of different length because of variation in the number of partNo values per row.
(4)   If rows are forced to be a fixed length, they will need to be padded with nulls.
(5)   There might not be a definite upper limit to the number of partNo values in a row. It is simpler to allow an unlimited number of rows than an unlimited row length.

Another way of representing repeating group values is shown in Fig. 5.1b. The vertical layout of the repeating group avoids problems (3), (4) and (5) in the above list, but violates the rule that the order of rows in a table is not significant; for example, moving row 3 to the end of the table would mean that partNo P4 is supplied by supplier S9, not supplier S2.

Questions

1.   Rewrite the table occurrence of Fig. 5.1b in such a way that the supplier attributes become the repeating group.   (3 min)
2.   A table type is written as a table name followed by a list of its attribute types enclosed in brackets. Suggest a way of writing down a table type when it contains a repeating group (i.e. an embedded table type). Use the tables in Fig. 5.1 and in the answer to question 1 as examples.   (2 min)

3. By royal decree, any supplier to the Ruritanian royal household must supply exactly three products (e.g. supplier Harridges supplies caviare, pumpkins, and jellied eels). The royal warrant to supply any given product is awarded to only one supplier. Assuming that the product names are represented in a table as a repeating group with a horizontal layout, which of the objections in section 5.2 apply? (3 min)

4. Which of the drawbacks listed in section 5.2 could be applied in some sense to an attribute whose individual values may be of variable length, for example supplierName? (2 min)

5.3 Elimination of repeating groups (normalisation)

The easiest way of eliminating a repeating group is to write out the table occurrence using a vertical layout for the repeating group and then fill in the blanks by duplicating the non-repeating data as necessary. Applying this process to Fig. 5.1b yields Fig. 5.2. In terms of table types, the normalisation is achieved by deleting the name of the embedded table type together with the brackets around its attributes. Thus, the table type corresponding to Fig. 5.1b is:

SupplierPart (supplierNo, supplierName, Part (partNo))

whereas the table type corresponding to Fig. 5.2 is:

SupplierPart (supplierNo, supplierName, partNo)

SupplierPart	supplierNo	supplierName	partNo
	S5	Wells	P1
	S2	Heath	P1
	S2	Heath	P4
	S7	Barron	P6
	S9	Edwards	P8
	S9	Edwards	P2
	S9	Edwards	P6

Fig. 5.2 Elimination of repeating group. Duplicated data has been inserted in rows 3, 6 and 7

Another way of eliminating a repeating group, and one which may shortcut part of the further normalisation procedures to be discussed later, is to split the table into two, so that the repeating group appears in one table and the rest of the attributes in another. However, it is not sufficient to put the repeating group into a table on its own; a link between the two new tables must be set up. In the example of Fig. 5.1b, splitting off the partNo repeating group on its own gives the result shown in Fig. 5.3a, in which information has been lost about who supplies what. Figure 5.3b shows how to link the tables by including supplierNo in both new tables. Techniques for deriving links between tables are considered more fully in later chapters.

Supplier	supplierNo	supplierName
	S5	Wells
	S2	Heath
	S7	Barron
	S9	Edwards

Part	partNo
	P1
	P4
	P6
	P8
	P2

(a)

Supplier	supplierNo	supplierName
	S5	Wells
	S2	Heath
	S7	Barron
	S9	Edwards

SuppPart	supplierNo	partNo
	S5	P1
	S2	P1
	S2	P4
	S7	P6
	S9	P8
	S9	P2
	S9	P6

Table types:
Supplier(supplierNo, supplierName)
(b)   SuppPart(supplierNo, partNo)

Fig. 5.3   Wrong and right ways of splitting off a repeating group into a new table
(a)   Splitting off the partNo repeating group on its own causes loss of information. Who supplies what?
(b)   supplierNo provides the link between the two tables. Compare with part (a)

Questions

1.   The following table is used to show the skills of each employee and the dates on which employees qualified in their skills.

Personnel (employeeNo, employeeName, salary,
          Skill (skillName, dateAcquired))

Write down normalised table types, using each of the methods described above.

(2 min)

2.   The answer pointer for question 2 in the previous section gave the following two equivalent table types:

SupplierPart (supplierNo, supplierName, Part (partNo))
PartSupplier (partNo, Supplier (supplierNo, supplierName))

Normalise each table type by deleting the name of the embedded table and the brackets around its attributes. Is the same result obtained in each case? Is the result symmetrical between supplierNo and partNo?   (1 min)

3.   Normalise the table:

PartSupplier (partNo, Supplier (supplierNo, supplierName))

by splitting off the repeating group into a new table. Compare your solution with Fig. 5.3b.   (2 min)

4.   Does the table structure of Fig. 5.2 contain (a) duplicated data, (b) redundant data?
(1 min)

5.   Does the table structure of Fig. 5.3b contain (a) duplicated data, (b) redundant data, (c) a consistency problem?   (2 min)

Assignments

Leave these assignments until a second reading unless you are confident that you have mastered repeating groups.

1. The following table contains two repeating groups.

Dept (deptNo, deptName, Employee (employeeNo, employeeName),
Machine (machineType, quantity))

The table contains details of the employees and machines which belong to each department; it is not intended to show any other connection between employees and machines, such as which employees operate which machines. The quantity attribute refers to the number of machines of a given machineType within a given department (e.g. 6 lathes, 4 drills). Write down a table occurrence for Dept. Invent your own data. Discuss whether this table structure is a satisfactory way of representing the data.

2. Discuss whether there are any significant differences between the table type Dept in assignment 1, and the table type:

Dept (deptNo, deptName, Employee (employeeNo, employeeName,
Machine (machineType, quantity)))

5.4 Separate attribute types

The table structure shown in Fig. 5.4 tries to avoid a repeating group by using the separate attribute names firstPartNo, secondPartNo, and thirdPartNo. Suppose there is no significant distinction between the partNo values in a row; they represent merely different parts supplied by a supplier. If so, this structure is unnecessarily complicated, apart from being open to most of the objections raised previously against repeating groups.

SupplierPart (supplierNo, supplierName, firstPartNo, secondPartNo, thirdPartNo)

SupplierPart	supplierNo	supplierName	firstPartNo	secondPartNo	thirdPartNo
	S5	Wells	P1		
	S2	Heath	P1	P4	
	S7	Barron	P6		
	S9	Edwards	P8	P2	P6

Fig. 5.4 Separate attribute names for each partNo. Compare with the SupplierPart (supplierNo, supplierName, partNo) structure of Figs 5.1 and 5.2

In other circumstances, however, the table structure could be perfectly acceptable. Suppose the meaning of firstPartNo, secondPartNo, and thirdPartNo is that a supplier who is out of stock for the firstPartNo may substitute the secondPartNo, and if the latter is also out of stock then the thirdPartNo may be supplied. In this case there is a real distinction between the partNo attributes, as interchanging the values within a row would invalidate the data.

Finally, an example which is less clear-cut. A table is to contain values of personNo (social security, or national insurance number, for instance), surname, and up to two forenames. Two ways of structuring the table are shown in Fig. 5.5.

Person1 appears to be the simpler structure. It suffers from the minor disadvantage that some secondForename(s) may be null, and from a further disadvantage (which may, or may not, matter) that it is restricted to a fixed number of forenames. It would be a good structure for handling queries such as 'what is the full name of personNo XJ51P?' or 'list the personNo(s) of all those whose firstForename is Peter'. It would be less suitable for queries such as 'list personNo(s) of all those who have Mary as a forename', because the latter query would involve a search on two attributes, not one.

Person2, in contrast, looks rather more complicated. It does, however, avoid the use of nulls, and does permit an unlimited number of forenames to be stored should this become necessary. Person2 would be good for handling queries such as 'list the personNo(s) of all those who have Mary as a forename.' It would be less suitable for queries such as 'what is the full name of personNo XJ51P', as two rows must be retrieved. Another criticism of the table is that it contains redundant surnames. Although this redundancy could be eliminated by splitting the table into two, the resulting structure would not gain much in terms of simplicity.

In general, the choice between the table structures exemplified by Person1 and Person2 depends very much on the way the data will be used. It is a choice which frequently offers plenty of scope for argument, and one where each case must be considered on its merits.

Person1 (personNo, surname, firstForename, secondForename)

Person1	personNo	surname	firstForename	secondForename
	YE24D	Harris	Christine	Mary
	YG82J	Brown	Peter	
	XJ37T	Cotson	David	John
	XJ51P	Nixon	Mary	Susan
	PR14F	Jones	Sarah	
(a)	RT59A	Cotson	Peter	Paul

Person2 (personNo, surname, forename, forenameSequence)

Person2	personNo	surname	forename	forenameSequence
	YE24D	Harris	Christine	1
	YE24D	Harris	Mary	2
	YE82J	Brown	Peter	1
	XJ37T	Cotson	John	2
	XJ37T	Cotson	David	1
	XJ51P	Nixon	Mary	1
	XJ51P	Nixon	Susan	2
	PR14F	Jones	Sarah	1
	RT59A	Cotson	Peter	1
(b)	RT59A	Cotson	Paul	2

Fig. 5.5　Two ways of structuring the same data

Questions

1. A table is to contain information about employees, including their qualifications and the dates on which the qualifications were acquired. Comment on the relative merits of the following table structures:

> Employee1 (employeeNo, qualification, dateAcquired)
> Employee2 (employeeNo, qual1, date1, qual2, date2, qual3, date3)

> (2 min)

2. A table is to hold the dates of birth, death, and accession to the throne of the kings and queens of England. Define two table types for this data, one using a single date attribute type, the other using three date attribute types. Compare the merits of the two table structures. (5 min)

3. A fixture table contains details of each fixture for a football league. The details comprise fixtureDate, homeTeam, awayTeam, venue. Compare the merits of using separate attribute types for homeTeam and awayTeam, with the use of a single attribute type team. (5 min)

4. A bakery supplies standing orders to customers. A customer may order several items for delivery on each day of the working week (Monday to Saturday inclusive). The quantity in which an item is ordered by a customer may vary according to the day of the week. Two ways of structuring the data are shown below. Compare their relative merits.

> StandingOrder1 (customerNo, itemName, qty1, qty2, qty3, qty4, qty5, qty6)
> StandingOrder2 (customerNo, itemName, dayName, qty)   (5 min)

5. Can the substitute parts problem of section 5.4 be solved using only one partNo column, rather than three? (3 min)

6. Split Person2 (Fig. 5.5b) into two tables in such a way that the redundant surname values are eliminated. (3 min)

Answer pointers

Section 5.2

1. PartSupplier

| partNo | Supplier | |
	supplierNo	supplierName
P1	S5	Wells
	S2	Heath
P4	S2	Heath
P6	S7	Barron
	S9	Edwards
P8	S9	Edwards
P2	S9	Edwards

You may have omitted the table name Supplier, which has been included here to stress the presence of an embedded table. Some of the supplier names are redundant, and could therefore have been omitted.

2. For Fig. 5.1:

SupplierPart (supplierNo, supplierName, Part (partNo))

For the solution to question 1:

PartSupplier (partNo, Supplier (supplierNo, supplierName))

3. The objections which apply are:
(a)   the embedded Product table introduces unnecessary complexity;
(b)   the rows can be sorted into supplierName order, but not productName order.
Lack of symmetry is not a valid objection because the data is itself asymmetrical (a supplier may supply many products, but a product is supplied by only one supplier). The constraints stated in the question mean that rows are of fixed length and do not contain nulls.

4. In general, items (3), (4) and (5) apply if 'number of characters' is substituted for 'number of partNo values'. Item (5) would not normally apply to supplierName, but it might well apply to an attribute such as documentText and suggest its ultimate replacement by a fixed length attribute, documentLine. In the earlier stages of design all the individual values taken by an attribute will be assumed to be of the same fixed length, but at a later stage of physical design it will be worth considering whether fixed or variable length formats should be used, as these decisions will affect storage requirements and processing complexity.

Items (3), (4) and (5) are physical rather than logical drawbacks to repeating groups, and are therefore the least cogent objections in the present context.

Section 5.3

1. Deletion of the embedded table name and brackets gives:

Personnel (employeeNo, employeeName, salary, skillName, dateAcquired)

Splitting off the repeating group gives:

Employee (employeeNo, employeeName, salary)
EmpSkill (employeeNo, skillName, dateAcquired)

where employeeNo provides the link between the two tables.

2. Bearing in mind that a table name can be chosen arbitrarily, and that the ordering of columns in a table is not significant, the result in each case is:

SupplierPart (supplierNo, supplierName, partNo)

which is symmetrical between supplierNo and partNo.

3. There are two routes to the solution, the difference being in the way the link between the two new tables is set up initially. The simplest route is to create a Supplier (supplierNo, supplierName) table and a Part (partNo) table, and then link the two by 'posting' supplierNo into the Part table, to give the same solution as in Fig. 5.3b, namely:

Supplier (supplierNo, supplierName)
SuppPart (supplierNo, partNo)

An alternative route would be to post partNo into Supplier, giving:

Supplier (supplierNo, supplierName, partNo)
Part (partNo)

Now, the Part table doesn't contain any information that is not already available in Supplier, so Part can be deleted, giving an end result which is essentially the same as Fig. 5.2. The fact that the two routes give different solutions is, on the face of it, rather worrying. At present our concern is simply to eliminate repeating groups; the further normalisation steps introduced later on will remove the problem.

4. (a) Yes. (b) Yes. If any given supplierNo value is associated with only one supplierName value, then one Heath value and two Edwards values are redundant. Different suppliers could have the same name (although there is no instance of this in Fig. 5.2) so supplierNo values S2 and S9 are not redundant.

5. (a) Yes. (b) No. (Try deleting an S2 or P6 value, say.) (c) A consistency problem occurs if there is an enterprise rule that for any supplierNo value appearing in SuppPart there must be a corresponding supplierNo value in Supplier (or *vice versa*). Of course, Supplier might contain approved suppliers, while SuppPart might contain only actual suppliers, in which case a given supplierNo value might appear in Supplier but not in SuppPart.

Section 5.4

1. Employee2 might have the edge on Employee1 if there is an upper limit of three qualifications and if there is a distinction between the three qualification attributes (e.g. sub-degree, graduate, postgraduate). Employee1 is a more general solution. In doubtful cases, it is better to err on the side of generality in the design of a conceptual model, as this will mean fewer maintenance problems. If the conceptual and internal schemas are sufficiently independent, the choice of an Employee1 type of structure for the conceptual schema does not preclude the use of an Employee2 type of structure for the internal schema. The latter could always be changed if the upper limit on qualifications exceeds three. However, the use of the Employee2 type of structure for the conceptual schema might lead to the writing of application programs which are dependent on the upper limit being three.

Another possibility is to use the Employee1 structure, but allow each qualification value to be a string of qualifications. Each employee would have just one 'qualification' such as 'BA, MSc, PhD'. Note that this is a single value, not a repeating group. What are the merits and demerits of this solution?

2. Compare:

Royalty1 (monarch, dateOfBirth, dateOfDeath, dateOfAccession)
Royalty2 (monarch, date, typeOfDate)

Are the date values for a monarch interchangeable? Compare queries such as 'at what age did Charles II die?', 'which monarchs were born, died, or acceded to the throne, between 1066 and 1660?' Incidentally, would there be any advantage in replacing the attribute monarch by separate attributes king and queen?

3. As each fixture involves precisely two teams, the use of separate homeTeam and awayTeam attributes looks quite attractive. There is a snag in that occasionally teams may play at a neutral ground, in which case it might be safer to have just one team attribute plus a homeOrAway attribute.

4. StandingOrder1 has the advantage of being more compact. There is a significant difference (day of the week) between the quantity attributes, and a fixed upper limit to their number. StandingOrder1 would service quite happily queries such as 'what is customerNo C2's standing order for french rolls on a Thursday (i.e. the qty4 value)?', or 'list all customerNo C1's standing orders'. StandingOrder2 would be better for a query such as 'which of our customers have ordered french rolls in quantities of 200?' You may find it helpful to study the sample table occurrences in Fig. 5.6 in reaching your own conclusions.

5. Yes. For example, you could denote each group of associated parts by a substitutionGroupNo, and the position of each part within a group by a substitutionLevelNo, giving the table type:

> SupplierPart (supplierNo, supplierName, partNo, substitutionGroupNo,
> substitutionLevelNo)

6. PersonSurname (personNo, surname)
PersonForename (personNo, forename, forenameSequence)

If you are not sure why this eliminates the redundant surname values, try writing down the table occurrences for these two tables, using the data in Fig. 5.5b and remembering that duplicate rows are not allowed.

StandingOrder1

customerNo	itemName	qty1	qty2	qty3	qty4	qty5	qty6
C1	french roll	50	200	150	0	200	100
C1	strudel	25	75	100	0	80	100
C2	french roll	80	250	300	200	150	0

StandingOrder2	customerNo	itemName	dayName	qty
	C1	french roll	Mon	50
	C1	french roll	Tues	200
	C1	french roll	Wed	150
	C1	french roll	Fri	200
	C1	french roll	Sat	100
	C1	strudel	Mon	25
	C1	strudel	Tues	75
	C1	strudel	Wed	100
	C1	strudel	Fri	80
	C1	strudel	Sat	100
	C2	french roll	Mon	80
	C2	french roll	Tues	250
	C2	french roll	Wed	300
	C2	french roll	Thurs	200
	C2	french roll	Fri	150

Fig. 5.6   See answer pointer to question 4, section 5.4

6

Determinants and identifiers

6.1 Introduction

This chapter introduces a simple formal rule which a table must obey if it is to be free of redundancy. To apply the rule it is first necessary to understand what is meant by the terms *determinant* and *identifier*.

6.2 Determinants

Consider the attributes within a table type. If the enterprise rules are such that duplicate values of attribute A are always associated with the same value of attribute B (within any given occurrence of the table), then attribute A is a *determinant* of attribute B. In the special case where duplicate values of A are not allowed within a table occurrence, A is necessarily a determinant of B.

If A is a determinant of B, we will say that A *determines* B and B *is determined by* (or *is dependent on*) A. The value of attribute B may be duplicated elsewhere in the table, it may be a null, and it may be updated (if so, a new table occurrence is created in which duplicate values of A must still be associated with a single, though now updated, value of B). If a_1 and a_2 are non-duplicate values of A, they may be associated with the same, or different values of B.

Less rigorously, we may say that A is a determinant of B if each value of A has precisely one (possibly null) associated value of B. Although ambiguous (why?), statements in this form will be used for the sake of conciseness in what follows.

Figure 6.1 shows some sample data for the table type:

> Stock (partNo, partDescription, quantityInStock)

If we are told that each possible partNo value has precisely one associated partDescription value (e.g. partNo P2 has just one description, nut), then we can say that partNo is a determinant of partDescription. Similarly, if each possible partNo

Stock	partNo	partDescription	quantityInStock
	P2	nut	5000
	P1	bolt	8300
	P3	washer	9750
	P4	nut	2326

Fig. 6.1   Stock table occurrence

value has only one associated quantityInStock value then we know that partNo is a determinant of quantityInStock.

Are there any other determinants in the table? It is easy to see from the data in Fig. 6.1 that partDescription cannot be a determinant of partNo, because the value nut is associated with more than one partNo—namely P2 and P4. Similarly, partDescription cannot be a determinant of quantityInStock.

Could quantityInStock be a determinant of, say, partNo? Possibly; after all each quantityInStock value shown in the table *is* associated with a single partNo value. However, if quantityInStock really is a determinant of partNo it would mean that no two partNo(s) could be stocked in the same quantities, and this does seem a rather unlikely enterprise rule. This example emphasises that a table occurrence cannot be relied upon for identifying determinants; it is the underlying enterprise rules which count.

Questions

1. Suppose the quantityInStock of part P1 in Fig. 6.1 were changed to 5000. Could you then be certain, merely by inspecting the table, as to whether quantityInStock is a determinant or not?   (1 min)
2. Repeat question 1, but this time change the quantityInStock of partNo P4 to 5000 (leave P1 at 8300).   (1 min)
3. A table type is defined as:

>   Employee (employeeNo, employeeName, salary)

Each employee has a unique employeeNo which distinguishes him or her from any other employee. Known enterprise rules are that an employee has only one name and salary, but different employees may have the same name and/or the same salary. Which attribute, or attributes, are definitely determinants?   (3 min)
4. (a)   State a further enterprise rule for the Employee table of question 3 which would make employeeName a determinant of salary.   (1 min)
(b)   Would your enterprise rule mean that employeeName would also be a determinant of employeeNo?   (1 min)

6.3   Superfluous attributes

If partNo determines quantityInStock, it follows that the composite attribute {partNo, partDescription} also determines quantityInStock. (Curly brackets { } will be used to denote a composite attribute, or composite value.) For example (with reference to Fig. 6.1), if you are given the composite value {P2, nut} you can find the single associated quantityInStock value (5000). However, if partNo alone is a determinant of quantityInStock, you really only need to know the partNo value; knowledge of the partDescription value is superfluous. We will assume that a determinant does not contain any superfluous attributes. This does not mean that a determinant cannot be composite, as will be seen from the example in section 6.5.

6.4   Determinancy diagrams

A simple way of showing determinants, and the attributes they determine, is to draw a *determinancy diagram*. The fact that attribute A is a determinant of attribute B is shown by an arrow as in Fig. 6.2a. If, in addition, B is a determinant of A, there will be arrowheads pointing in both directions (Fig. 6.2b).

(a)
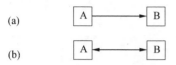

(b)

Fig. 6.2   Determinancy diagrams
(a)   Attribute A is a determinant of attribute B
(b)   Attribute A is a determinant of attribute B, and attribute B is a determinant of attribute A

If, in the Stock table example of section 6.2, partNo is a determinant of both partDescription and quantityInStock, and there are no other determinants, the determinancy diagram would be as shown in Fig. 6.3.

Determinancy diagrams provide a powerful means of expressing enterprise rules in a way which is not bedevilled by the ambiguities of English narrative. Being more precise and concise, a determinancy diagram is easier to check and interpret than even the best narrative description. Looking at Fig. 6.3, it is immediately apparent that each partNo value is associated with only one partDescription value and one quantityInStock value; that a given quantityInStock value may be associated with many partNo values and many partDescription values (otherwise there would be arrows from quantityInStock to partNo and partDescription); and finally that a given partDescription value may be associated with many partNo and quantityInStock values.

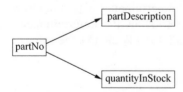

Fig. 6.3   Determinancy diagram for Stock table

Questions

1.   (a)   Draw a determinancy diagram for question 3 of section 6.2, showing the determinancies which definitely exist.   (2 min)
(b)   Amend your diagram to include the enterprise rule that all employees with the same name get the same salary.   (1 min)
2.   Each customer is identified by a customerNo and each salesperson by a salespersonNo. A determinancy diagram including customerNo, salespersonNo and salespersonName is shown below. The association represented between customers and salespersons is that a salesperson services a customer.

Which of the following enterprise rules are consistent with the diagram?
(a)   A customer may be serviced by several salespersons.
(b)   A salesperson may service many customers.
(c)   Several salespersons may have the same name.
(d)   A salesperson may have several names.   (2 min)

6.5   Composite determinants

Table SupplierPart (Fig. 6.4) shows which suppliers supply which parts. The enterprise rules are:

(1)   A supplier is identified by a single supplierNo, and a part is identified by a single partNo.
(2)   Each supplier has only one supplierName, but different suppliers may have the same supplierName.
(3)   A supplier may supply many different parts in many different packsizes.
(4)   A part may be supplied by many different suppliers in many different packsizes.
(5)   A given supplier supplies a given part in just one packsize.

SupplierPart	supplierNo	supplierName	partNo	packsize
	S2	Jones	P1	10
	S7	Smith	P6	25
	S2	Jones	P4	40
	S5	Jones	P1	20

Fig. 6.4   SupplierPart table

The determinants can be recognised easily by drawing a determinancy diagram. Draw a box for each attribute (Fig. 6.5a), then draw arrows to show the determinancies between attributes (Fig. 6.5b). Notice that, because of rules (3), (4) and (5), the value of

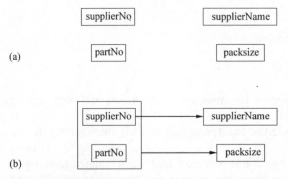

Fig. 6.5   Construction of determinancy diagram for SupplierPart
(a)   Attributes
(b)   Determinancies inserted. {supplierNo, partNo} is a composite determinant for packsize

packsize is determined by the composite attribute {supplierNo, partNo}. The value of supplierNo on its own is insufficient to determine the packsize (e.g. S2 supplies in packsizes of 10 and 40). Likewise the value of partNo alone is insufficient to determine packsize (e.g. P1 is supplied in packsizes of 10 and 20). However, the value of the composite attribute {supplierNo, partNo} does determine packsize (e.g. S2 supplies P1 in just one packsize, namely 10). The existence of this composite determinant is shown on the determinancy diagram by enclosing its constituent attributes within the larger box.

Questions

1. Explain, in your own words, why in Fig. 6.5b the arrow to supplierName comes from supplierNo, but the arrow to packsize comes from the box surrounding {supplierNo, partNo}.   (1 min)

2. There are no arrows between supplierName and packsize in Fig. 6.5b. Why not?
                                                                          (1 min)

3. Shoes are sold in a variety of styles and sizes. A style is identified by a styleNo. Each style has a single description (e.g. men's slippers) and the same description may apply to several styles. The attribute weeklySales represents the number of shoes of a particular size and style sold in the previous week (e.g. 25 pairs, styleNo 17, size 8). The attribute monthlyStyleValue represents the total sales value in the previous month for each style. Draw a determinancy diagram for the attributes styleNo, styleDescription, size, weeklySales, monthlyStyleValue.   (3 min)

6.6 Transitive determinants

If attribute A is a determinant of attribute B, and attribute B is a determinant of attribute C, then attribute A must be a determinant of attribute C. Attribute A is said to *transitively determine* attribute C; conversely, attribute C is said to be *transitively dependent* on attribute A.[1] The corresponding determinancy diagram could be drawn as in Fig. 6.6a, or else as in Fig. 6.6b. In general, Fig. 6.6a will be preferred as it is less cluttered and is less likely to cause errors in later stages of the normalisation process. Attribute A is said to *directly determine* attribute B; conversely, attribute B is *directly dependent* on attribute A.

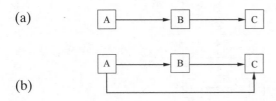

(a)

(b)

Fig. 6.6   Transitive dependency of C on A

[1] To be precise, the transitive determinancy/dependency is not considered to exist if, in addition to the determinancies stated, A is itself determined by B or C.

Questions

1. For each of the following determinancy diagrams, identify each determinant and the attribute(s) it directly determines. Omit any transitive dependencies.   (4 min)

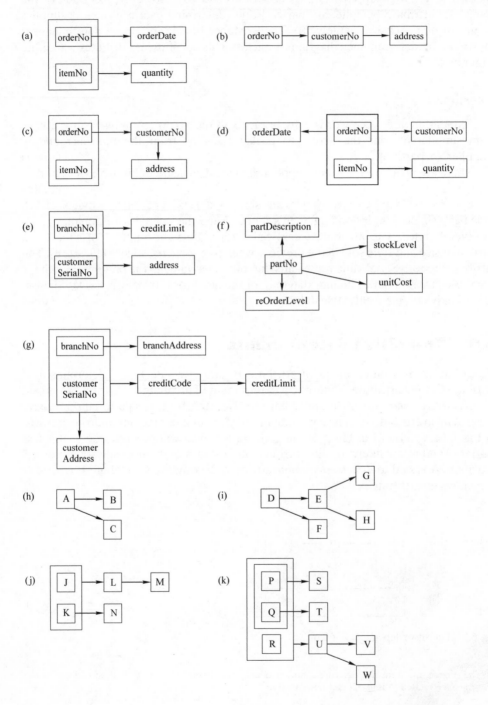

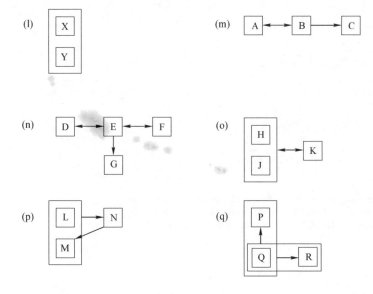

2. For each diagram in question 1 identify any transitive dependencies which exist. Express your answers in the form: 'Attribute X is transitively dependent on attribute Y via attribute Z.' (3 min)

3. Write down typical table occurrences which are consistent with each of the determinancy diagrams in question 1. Include examples of redundant attribute values wherever possible. For diagrams (h)–(q), use subscripted lower case letters to represent attribute values: for example $a_1, a_2, a_3, \ldots$ as values of attribute A; $b_1, b_2, b_3, \ldots$ as values of attribute B. (5 min each)

6.7   Terminology

Strictly speaking, phrases such as 'A determines B' and 'B is dependent on A' should have been expressed as 'A functionally determines B' and 'B is functionally dependent on A'. In Fig. 6.7a there is no functional dependency between orderNo and itemNo, but there is certainly an association between them (a non-functional dependency) as evidenced by the larger box. Figure 6.7b is quite different to Fig. 6.7a, in that the former represents two independent tables whereas the latter represents a single table which shows the items on each order. In general, the words *functional* and *functionally* will be omitted for the sake of brevity, but it should be remembered that the phrase 'A is not dependent on B' will mean 'A is not functionally dependent on B', rather than 'A is independent of B'.

Question

1. Why, in Fig 6.7a, is the large box placed around {orderNo, itemNo} rather than {itemNo, orderDate}? (3 min)

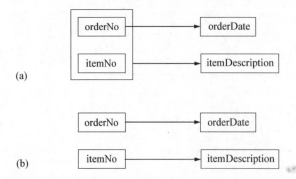

Fig. 6.7   The difference between non-functional dependency and no dependency
(a)   A single table. Non-functional dependency between orderNo and itemNo
(b)   Two independent tables. No dependency between orderNo and itemNo

Assignment

1.   Draw a determinancy diagram for the attributes in the Bilbo & Baggins invoice of Fig. 6.8. Omit both 'derivable' attributes, such as amountDue, and 'fixed' attributes, such as VAT(Value-added-tax)RegistrationNumber and promptPaymentDiscount, which are likely to be the same for all invoices. Assume plausible enterprise rules, and state your assumptions.

INVOICE			**BILBO & BAGGINS LIMITED**				

Hobbits Wharf
London

Customer no: 18723   Shipping address (if different)   Invoice no: 31477
                                                                                                                                                    Date: 1.2.2000
        A. Gandalf & Co Ltd.   VAT reg. no: 51226489
        Dragon Lane
        Mirkwood

Delivery instructions: Not Wednesday p.m.   Your ref: SM/AUG/1

Quantity per pack	Number of packs ordered	Part number	Description	Number of packs shipped	Price per pack	Amount due
1	3	PT210	Plasma torch	2*	76.00	152.00
25	10	DT400	Detonators	10	12.50	125.00
						277.00
					VAT @ 10%	27.70
*Part-filled order: balance to follow when available			Prompt payment discount: Deduct $2\frac{1}{2}$% if paid within TEN days of invoice date		TOTAL DUE	304.70

Fig. 6.8   Bilbo & Baggins invoice

6.8 Identifiers

The rule that no two rows in a table can have identical values throughout means that an individual row can always be identified by quoting the values of all its attributes. In many cases, however, some of the attribute values may never be needed to identify a row. For example, it may be known that an occurrence of the table type:

Employee (employeeNo, employeeName, salary)

will never contain two rows with the same value of employeeNo, so the value of employeeNo alone is sufficient to identify a row. In this example, employeeNo is a *row identifier* for the table. Although the value of the composite attribute {employeeNo, employeeName} would also identify a row, it will not be accepted as a row identifier because it contains a superfluous attribute. One further restriction, which will normally be applied, is that none of the component attributes of a row identifier may be null. In effect, a row identifier acts as a label for a row, and it seems reasonable to insist that the values on the label should be known, in the sense of being non-null. On some occasions, particularly where composite identifiers are concerned, there may be reasons for relaxing this rule.

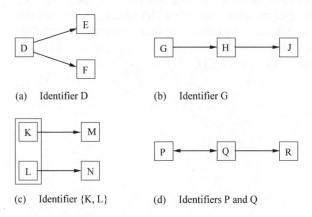

(a) Identifier D

(b) Identifier G

(c) Identifier {K, L}

(d) Identifiers P and Q

Fig. 6.9 Examples of identifiers

To summarise: a row identifier is an attribute (possibly composite) which can never have duplicate values within a table occurrence, and whose value is therefore always sufficient to identify a row. A composite identifier may not contain any superfluous attributes. None of the component attributes of an identifier may be null; this includes the special case where the identifier is a single attribute. In the context of the relational model, the row identifier for a table is often referred to as the table's primary key; we will refer to it simply as the *identifier*.

It is quite easy to recognise identifiers simply by inspecting a determinancy diagram. In Fig. 6.9a the identifier is attribute D. The diagram tells us that, given a value of D, we can determine (by inspection of a table occurrence) a single associated value for E and a single associated value for F. A value of D is therefore sufficient to identify a complete row in the table. Coupled with the fact that D does not contain any superfluous attributes (it obviously cannot, as it is a single attribute) this means that D must be an identifier. Notice that neither E nor F can be identifiers. If E were an identifier, a given value of E would by definition identify a row, and would therefore determine a single value of D, in which case there would be an arrowhead pointing from E to D to show that E is a determinant of D.

In Fig. 6.9b, a value of G is sufficient to determine the value of H which, in turn, determines the value of J; H does not determine G, and J does not determine anything; so G is the identifier.

In Fig. 6.9c, the identifier is the composite attribute {K, L}. K determines M, but is insufficient on its own to determine N.

In Fig. 6.9d, there are two identifiers. One identifier is attribute P (P determines Q directly and R directly[2]). The other identifier is Q (Q determines P directly and R directly). We say that there are two *candidate identifiers*. Usually, a table has only one candidate identifier (as in Figs 6.9a, 6.9b, and 6.9c) but it is quite possible for a table to have several candidate identifiers, in which case one of the candidate identifiers will be selected as the table identifier.

Questions

1. Write down the candidate identifier(s) for each of the determinancy diagrams in question 1 of section 6.6. Give a brief explanation of your reasoning for cases (d), (e), (f), (g), (k), (l), (n), (p), (q). Check your choice of candidate identifiers against the table occurrences written in answer to question 3 of section 6.6, to make sure that no two rows in a table have the same identifier value.   (15 min)

2. The determinancy diagram for table X(A, B, C) is:

An occurrence of the table is:

X	A	B	C
	a_1	b_1	c_1
	a_2	b_2	c_1
	a_3	b_2	c_2
	a_4	b_2	c_2

Suppose a fifth row, starting with a_2 as the value of A, were to be added. What must be the value of attribute B? What must be the value of attribute C? Why would the fifth row be illegal? Can attribute A contain duplicate values? Is attribute A a candidate identifier?   (2 min)

3. Every room in a building is identified by a roomNo and has precisely one telephone. Each telephone has its own distinct telephoneExtensionNo. There are two types of telephone, internal dialling only (type I), and external/internal dialling (type E). The rental charged depends only on the tariff. Type I telephones are charged on tariff T1, and type E on tariff T2. Information on rooms and telephones will be held in the table:

[2] See footnote to section 6.6.

Office (roomNo, numberOfOccupants, telephoneExtensionNo,
telephoneType, tariff)

Making any further plausible assumptions necessary:
(a)   draw a determinancy diagram for Office;
(b)   write down the candidate identifier(s).   (4 min)

4.   Repeat question 3, but with the addition of the attributes employeeNo and employeeName. Values of employeeNo identify individual employees. Each employee has only one name and occupies only one room.   (2 min)

5.   Repeat question 4, but allowing several telephones per room. All employees in a room share all the telephones in that room.   (3 min)

6.   The following table contains details of consultants and the projects to which they are currently assigned:

Assignment (consultantNo, consultantName, projectNo, projectTitle)

A consultant may currently be assigned to several projects, and several consultants may currently be assigned to the same project. The identifier of Assignment would be {consultantNo, projectNo} if it were not for the fact that it could contain nulls because some consultants are not currently assigned to any project, and some projects have not yet had any consultants assigned to them. However, every consultant has a number and name; likewise every project has a number and title.

Show how the table can be split into three, in a way which avoids the possibility of null occurrences in identifiers.   (2 min)

7.   A table is defined as:

Employee (employeeNo, fullName, dateOfBirth, address)

Candidate identifiers for this table are:

(a)   employeeNo
(b)   {fullName, dateOfBirth, address}

Which candidate identifier would you select as the table identifier? Why?   (2 min)

8.   Which of the following statements is true?
(a)   Every identifier is a determinant.
(b)   Every determinant is an identifier.   (1 min)

6.9   Determinancy diagrams and redundancy

Once a set of enterprise rules has been represented by a determinancy diagram, it becomes a simple matter to detect and eliminate table structures that could contain redundant data.

Figure 6.10 represents a situation in which each customerNo is associated with only one salespersonNo, but a salespersonNo may be associated with several different customerNo(s). In the real-world situation we may suppose that a salesperson services several customers, but each customer deals with only one salesperson. Inspection of the determinancy diagram makes it clear that salespersonNo may have duplicate values. If it were not so, salespersonNo would be an identifier and consequently a determinant of customerNo. Now, salespersonNo is a determinant of

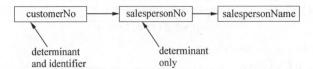

Fig. 6.10 Potential redundancy in values of salespersonName. Attribute salespersonNo is a determinant but not a candidate identifier

salespersonName, so each occurrence of a duplicated salespersonNo value will be associated with the same salespersonName value; therefore the table can contain redundant values of salespersonName. On the other hand, customerNo values cannot be duplicated (because customerNo is an identifier) so there cannot be redundant values of salespersonNo. The potential redundancy in the table arises because salespersonNo is a determinant but not a candidate identifier.

In Fig. 6.11, partNo may have duplicate values (otherwise it would be an identifier). As partNo is a determinant of partDescription, it follows that duplicated partNo values will be associated with the same partDescription value. Therefore the table can contain redundant values of partDescription. Once again, the potential redundancy in the table arises because there is a determinant (in this case, partNo) which is not itself a candidate identifier. The table can also contain redundant values of unitPrice.

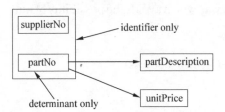

Fig. 6.11 Potential redundancy in values of partDescription and unitPrice. Attribute partNo is a determinant but not a candidate identifier

The above examples suggest the following simple rule (known as the *Boyce/Codd rule*) for detecting redundancy in a table:

'Every determinant must be a candidate identifier.'

A table which obeys this rule is said to be in *Boyce/Codd normal form* (BCNF). In this book we will use the term *well-normalised* to describe a table which obeys the Boyce/Codd rule, and *badly-normalised* to describe any other table.

6.10   Transformation into well-normalised tables

Call a determinant which is not a candidate identifier a *non-identifying determinant*. To transform a badly-normalised table into well-normalised tables, create new tables such that each non-identifying determinant in the old table becomes a candidate identifier in a new table. Each new table will also contain those attributes that are directly dependent on the new candidate identifier. The candidate identifiers of the old table and their directly dependent attributes will normally be left in the remnants of the old table (but see section 6.11, question 2(p), for one of the exceptions to this rule).

It is actually much easier to apply this procedure by inspecting a determinancy diagram than to follow a verbal description. In Fig. 6.10, salespersonNo is a non-identifying determinant, so create a new table which contains salespersonNo as its identifier and the attribute(s) directly dependent on salespersonNo, namely salespersonName. This leaves in the old table the identifier, customerNo, and its directly dependent attribute(s), salespersonNo. The resulting tables are shown in Fig. 6.12. Notice that salespersonNo forms the link between the tables, and that each of the new tables is well-normalised.

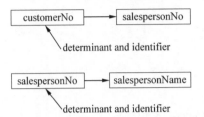

Fig. 6.12   The well-normalised version of Fig. 6.10. Every determinant is a candidate identifier

In Fig. 6.11, partNo is a non-identifying determinant, so create a new table containing partNo and its directly dependent attributes partDescription and unitPrice. This leaves {supplierNo, partNo} in the old table. The resulting well-normalised tables are shown in Fig. 6.13.

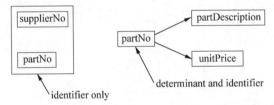

Fig. 6.13   The well-normalised version of Fig. 6.11. Every determinant is a candidate identifier

More complicated cases can be dealt with in stages if necessary. Figure 6.14 shows two routes to the same well-normalised solution; each route extracts one non-identifying determinant at each stage.

6.11   Notation

The identifier of a table type will be denoted by an underscore, as illustrated in the following table type definitions corresponding to Figs 6.10 to 6.14. Where there is a choice of candidate identifier, only the one chosen as the table identifier will be underscored.

Fig. 6.10:   CustSales (<u>customerNo</u>, salespersonNo, salespersonName)
Fig. 6.11:   SuppPart (<u>supplierNo, partNo</u>, partDescription, unitPrice)
Fig. 6.12:   Customer (<u>customerNo</u>, salespersonNo)
             Salesperson (<u>salespersonNo</u>, salespersonName)

Fig. 6.13:   SupplierPart (<u>supplierNo, partNo</u>)
              Part (<u>partNo</u>, partDescription, unitPrice)

In the tables for Fig. 6.12, salespersonNo in the Customer table is referred to as a *foreign key*, because it is the link to the identifier (or *primary key*) of the Salesperson table. Similarly, in the tables for Fig. 6.13, partNo in the SupplierPart table is a foreign key linking to the identifier (or primary key) partNo in the Part table.

Fig. 6.14:   (initial, badly-normalised table):
              TableBn (<u>A, B</u>, C, D, E, F, G)

Fig. 6.14:   (final, well-normalised tables):
              TableWn1 (<u>A, B</u>, F)
              TableWn2 (<u>A</u>, C)
              TableWn3 (<u>C</u>, D, E)
              TableWn4 (<u>F</u>, G)

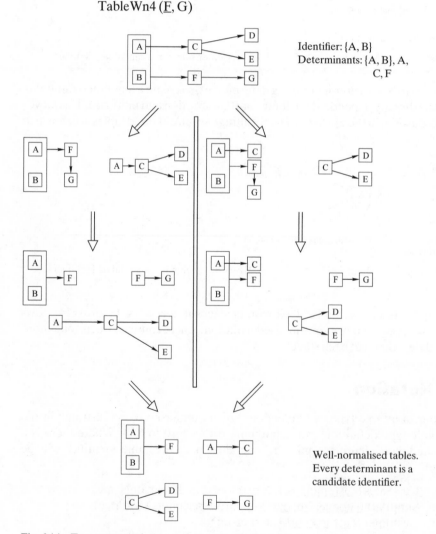

Identifier: {A, B}
Determinants: {A, B}, A,
              C, F

Well-normalised tables.
Every determinant is a
candidate identifier.

Fig. 6.14   Two routes to the same well-normalised solution

Questions

1. Write a typical table occurrence for the table shown in Fig. 6.10, including examples of redundant salespersonName values. Using the same data, write table occurrences for the well-normalised tables of Fig. 6.12, and explain why these tables do not contain redundant values of salespersonName. (3 min)

2. Derive a set of well-normalised tables for each of the determinancy diagrams in question 1 of section 6.6. Express each answer both as a determinancy diagram and in the form of table types with each table identifier underscored. (2 min each)

3. Can the functional dependency between attributes be deduced from a table type if it is known to be well-normalised? (2 min)

Assignment

1. Derive a set of well-normalised tables for the attributes in the Bilbo & Baggins invoice of Fig. 6.8. (Omit both derivable and fixed attributes; see assignment 1, section 6.7.)

Answer pointers

Section 6.2

1. Yes. Attribute quantityInStock cannot be a determinant of partNo because the value of 5000 is associated with more than one partNo (P2 and P1). Similarly, quantityInStock cannot be a determinant of partDescription because the value of 5000 is associated with more than one partDescription (nut and bolt).

2. Attribute quantityInStock cannot be a determinant of partNo (5000 is associated with P2 and P4), but it might be a determinant of partDescription (5000 is always associated with nut, at least in the table occurrence shown). If quantityInStock really is a determinant of partDescription, it would mean that there is a bizarre enterprise rule that all parts stocked in the same quantity must have the same partDescription.

Questions 1 and 2 illustrate that you may be able to tell by inspection of a table occurrence that an attribute is *not* a determinant, but you cannot tell that it *is* one.

3. Attribute employeeNo is a determinant of employeeName and also of salary. Neither employeeName nor salary are determinants of employeeNo. It is possible (although very unlikely) that employeeName is a determinant of salary, and/or that salary is a determinant of employeeName.

4. The answer to (b) depends on the answer to (a). Two possible combinations are:

(i) (a) Enterprise rule: 'All employees with the same name are paid the same salary.'
(b) Attribute employeeName is not necessarily a determinant of employeeNo.

(ii) (a) Enterprise rule: 'No two employees may have the same name.' Attribute employeeName must be a determinant of salary because employeeName is now just as good as employeeNo for identifying an employee, and each employee has only one salary. (b) Attribute employeeName is a determinant of employeeNo.

Section 6.4

1. (a)

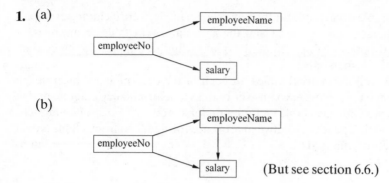

(b)

(But see section 6.6.)

2. (a) False. (b) True. (c) True. (d) False.
For (c) and (d) it is assumed that 'name' and 'salespersonName' are synonymous. Although, in this question, a salesperson has only one salespersonName, remember that the format of a salespersonName value has not been specified. It might, for example, be surname only (Doe), surname and initials (Doe J.A.), or full name (John Arthur Doe).

Section 6.5

1. Saying simply that supplierNo is a determinant of supplierName, but the determinant of packsize is the composite attribute {supplierNo, partNo}, is true, but begs the question: what are the underlying enterprise rules?
2.   A given supplierName may be associated with many packsizes, and a packsize with many supplierName(s), so neither attribute is a determinant of the other.
3.

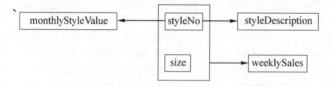

Section 6.6

1.

question	*determinant*	*attributes determined*
(a)	orderNo	orderDate
	{orderNo, itemNo}	quantity
(b)	orderNo	customerNo
	customerNo	address
(c)	orderNo	customerNo
	customerNo	address
(d)	orderNo	customerNo, orderDate
	{orderNo, itemNo}	quantity
(e)	{branchNo, customerSerialNo}	creditLimit, address

question	determinant	attributes determined
(f)	partNo	partDescription, stockLevel, unitCost, reOrderLevel
(g)	branchNo	branchAddress
	{branchNo, customerSerialNo}	creditCode, customerAddress
	creditCode	creditLimit
(h)	A	B, C
(i)	D	E, F
	E	G, H
(j)	{J, K}	L
	K	N
	L	M
(k)	{P, Q}	S
	Q	T
	{P, Q, R}	U
	U	V, W
(l)	none	
(m)	A	B
	B	A, C
(n)	D	E
	E	D, F, G
	F	E
(o)	{H, J}	K
	K	{H, J}
(p)	{L, M}	N
	N	M
(q)	{P, Q}	R
	{Q, R}	P

2. There are no transitive dependencies in (a), (d), (e), (f), (h), (l), (m), (n), (o).

(b), (c): address is transitively dependent on orderNo via customerNo.

(g) : creditLimit is transitively dependent on {branchNo, customerSerialNo} via creditCode.

(i) : G and H are transitively dependent on D via E.

(j) : M is transitively dependent on {J, K} via L.

(k) : V and W are transitively dependent on {P, Q, R} via U.

Some observations on (p) and (q) are given below. A decision on the presence or absence of transitive dependency in these examples would require a more thorough examination of the topic than is necessary for our treatment of data modelling.

(p) is a rather unusual case. The diagram shows that if you select a composite value of {L, M}, there is only one associated value of N, and hence only one associated value of M. Abbreviated, this means that if you know the value of {L, M} you can find M (by inspection of a table which the diagram represents). Abbreviated still further, this means that if you know the value of M, you can find the value of M, which hardly counts as news. However, the knowledge that {L, M} determines N, and N determines M, is significant.

(q) is another rather nasty piece of work. An example corresponding to the diagram is a table of results for track events at an athletics meeting. All events are run in lanes, and there are no relay races. For P, Q, R, read competitor, event, lane. Satisfy yourself that the determinancies shown in the diagram are correct. Why is Q not determined by {P, R}?

3.   Sample solutions. Many variations are possible.

(a) Order

orderNo	orderDate	itemNo	quantity
123	15.06.2001	R42	10
123	15.06.2001	A11	15
125	15.06.2001	R42	10
120	11.06.2001	D16	10
120	11.06.2001	A11	4
120	11.06.2001	A28	15
126	16.06.2001	R42	5

(j) Table_j

J	K	L	M	N
j_1	k_1	l_1	m_1	n_1
j_1	k_2	l_1	m_1	n_2
j_1	k_3	l_2	m_2	n_3
j_2	k_1	l_3	m_3	n_1
j_2	k_3	l_3	m_3	n_3
j_3	k_2	l_1	m_1	n_2
j_4	k_1	l_2	m_2	n_1
j_5	k_1	l_2	m_2	n_1

Section 6.7

1.   An order processing application will need to record which items are on which orders; this can be done by associating orderNo and itemNo values, as in Fig. 6.7a. Placing a large box around {itemNo, orderDate} instead, would associate each item with the dates of those orders that contain the item. Now, the determinancy arrow from orderNo to orderDate shows the association between order dates and orders, so there is a link between items and orders via order dates. However, if an item was ordered on a particular date, and an order was placed on the same date, it does not mean that the item was on that order, it may have been on a different order. (This type of situation is discussed further in Chapter 11 in the context of entity-relationship modelling.)

Section 6.8

1.   (a)   {orderNo, itemNo}
  (b)   orderNo
  (c)   {orderNo, itemNo}
  (d)   {orderNo, itemNo}
  (e)   {branchNo, customerSerialNo}
  (f)   partNo
  (g)   {branchNo, customerSerialNo}
  (h)   A
  (i)   D
  (j)   {J, K}
  (k)   {P, Q, R}
  (l)   {X, Y}

(m) A or B

(n) D, or E, or F

(o) {H, J} or K

(p) {L, M} or {L, N}

(q) {P, Q} or {Q, R}   (an example of overlapping identifiers)

2. A is a determinant of B, so wherever a given value of A appears it must be accompanied by the same value of B. Inspection of the table shows that a_2 is associated with b_2. Similarly, A is a determinant of C, and inspection shows that the value of C associated with a_2 is c_1. The fifth row would therefore be a_2, b_2, c_1, which would be illegal because it is identical throughout with row 2. It follows that A cannot contain duplicate values; therefore A is a candidate identifier.

3. (a)

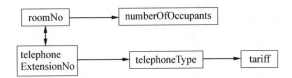

Assumptions made are that a roomNo has only one associated value for numberOfOccupants, and a roomNo is to be associated with the telephoneExtensionNo for that room only (and *vice versa*). It might have been true that each room has several associated values for numberOfOccupants, each applicable to a different usage (for example: use of senior executive, junior executive, classroom), although the presence of a usage attribute might then have been expected. The association between roomNo and telephoneExtensionNo might have been extended to include an alternative extensionNo to be used if no reply is obtained from the room extensionNo. Again, an attribute distinguishing between main and alternative extensionNo(s) might have been expected. Notice that the arrow from roomNo to numberOfOccupants could be replaced by one from telephoneExtensionNo to numberOfOccupants, since a telephone extension number identifies a room anyway. It does, however, seem more natural to relate numberOfOccupants to the roomNo. Similarly, telephoneType could be connected to roomNo rather than telephoneExtensionNo.

(b)   The candidate identifiers are roomNo and telephoneExtensionNo.

4. (a)

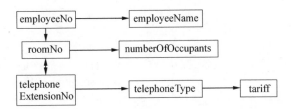

(b) The only candidate identifier is employeeNo. Neither roomNo nor telephoneExtensionNo is adequate because they cannot determine employeeNo, there being several employees per room and per extension.

5. (a)

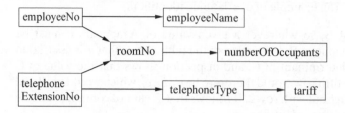

(b) The only candidate identifier is {employeeNo, telephoneExtensionNo}; employeeNo alone is no longer sufficient (compare 4(b)) because the same employeeNo may occur in several rows of the table, each occurrence being associated with a different telephoneExtensionNo.

6.   Consultant (consultantNo, consultantName)
     Project (projectNo, projectTitle)
     ConsultantProject (consultantNo, projectNo)
A consultant who is not assigned to any project will appear in Consultant but not in ConsultantProject. Similarly, a project that does not have any consultants assigned will appear in Project but not in ConsultantProject. The identifiers of Consultant, Project and ConsultantProject are, respectively, consultantNo, projectNo and {consultantNo, projectNo}.

7.   employeeNo has the advantages of brevity and stability. The other candidate identifier {fullName, dateOfBirth, address} is longer and will change in value if an employee changes name (by marriage, or deed-poll, say) or address. Furthermore, whereas one can guarantee that employeeNo really does identify an employee, there remains a nagging doubt that the other candidate identifier just might fail to be an identifier at all. There is a well-known law ('if something can go wrong, it will') which suggests that there really will be two employees with the same fullName, dateOfBirth and address.

It is not worth worrying overmuch as to whether some complex combination of attributes might be sufficient to act as a candidate identifier.

8.   Neither is true. Usually an identifier is also a determinant, but if an identifier comprises all the attributes in a table, then there are no attributes left for the identifier to determine.

Section 6.11

1.   CustSales

customerNo	salespersonNo	salespersonName
C2	S5	Smith
C4	S5	Smith
C3	S8	Jones
C6	S8	Jones
C8	S2	Smith

Table occurrence corresponding to Fig. 6.10. One value of Smith (in rows 1 and 2) and one value of Jones are redundant.

Customer

customerNo	salespersonNo
C2	S5
C4	S5
C3	S8
C6	S8
C8	S2

Salesperson

salespersonNo	salespersonName
S5	Smith
S8	Jones
S2	Smith

Table occurrences corresponding to the well-normalised tables of Fig. 6.12. The redundant values of salespersonName are eliminated because each value of salespersonNo occurs only once in the Salesperson table.

2. Selected answers:

(a)

OrderLine (<u>orderNo, itemNo</u>, quantity)
Order (<u>orderNo</u>, orderDate)

(e) Already well-normalised.
   Customer (<u>branchNo, customerSerialNo</u>, creditLimit, address)

(g)

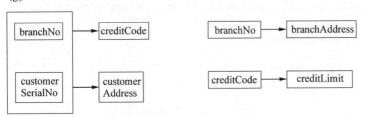

Customer (<u>branchNo, customerSerialNo</u>, creditCode, customerAddress)
Branch (<u>branchNo</u>, branchAddress)
CreditTable (<u>creditCode</u>, creditLimit)

(k)

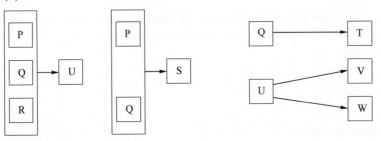

Table_k1 (<u>P, Q, R</u>, U)
Table_k2 (<u>P, Q</u>, S)
Table_k3 (<u>Q</u>, T)
Table_k4 (<u>U</u>, V, W)

(l)   Already well-normalised.
Table1 (<u>X, Y</u>)

(m)   Already well-normalised.
Table_m1 (<u>A</u>, B, C)   or   Table_m2 (A, <u>B</u>, C)

(o)   Already well-normalised.
Table_o1 (<u>H, J</u>, K)   or   Table_o2 (H, J, <u>K</u>)

(p)   This is a rather unusual and tricky table structure because the transitively dependent attribute M is itself part of the table's identifier. First, note that N is a determinant, but not a candidate identifier, so a separate table is required with the structure:

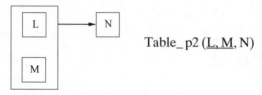

Table_p1 (<u>N</u>, M)

At first sight, it might be thought that this leaves behind a table with the structure:

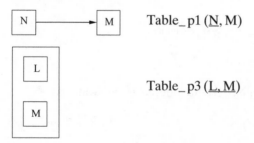

Table_p2 (<u>L, M</u>, N)

But Table_p2 is actually identical to the original badly-normalised table, except for the omission in the determinancy diagram of an arrow from N to M. Omission of this arrow does not, of course, get rid of the dependency of M on N, it simply means that the diagram is incorrectly drawn.

Another plausible, but wrong, solution is:

N ⟶ M   Table_p1 (<u>N</u>, M)

L

M   Table_p3 (<u>L, M</u>)

The problem here is that the original table cannot be reconstituted unambiguously from Table_p1 and Table_p3, because a given M value may be associated with several values of N. For example:

Table_p1

N	M
n_1	m_1
n_2	m_1

Table_p3

L	M
l_1	m_1
l_2	m_1

could be reconstituted into either:

Table_p4

L	M	N
l_1	m_1	n_1
l_2	m_1	n_2

or   Table_p5

L	M	N
l_1	m_1	n_2
l_2	m_1	n_1

The correct solution is found by recognising that the creation of Table_p1 should leave behind a table which contains only the attributes L and N, and these are non-functionally dependent on each other.

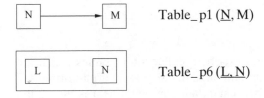

Table_p1 ($\underline{N}$, M)

Table_p6 ($\underline{L, N}$)

This solution is not ambiguous, because each value of N is associated with a single value of M. However, the dependency of N on {L, M} is no longer represented. Does this raise a consistency problem?[3]

(q)   Already well-normalised.[4]

Table_q1 ($\underline{P, Q}$, R) or Table_q2 (P, $\underline{Q, R}$)

3.   Yes, provided that all the candidate identifers are known. If, as is usually the case, there is only one candidate identifer, and this identifer is underscored, then the table type gives an unambiguous description of the functional dependencies. Every non-identifying attribute must be functionally dependent on the identifier, and there cannot be dependencies among the non-identifying attributes, otherwise the Boyce/Codd rule would be broken. A set of well-normalised tables conveys a lot of information about the enterprise rules.

[3,4] See *An Introduction to Database Systems* by C. J. Date (cited in the bibliography) for further discussion and examples of these table structures.

7

Fully-normalised tables

7.1   Introduction

The term *fully-normalised* will be used to describe a collection of tables which are structured so that they cannot contain redundant data. In most cases a well-normalised table (one in which every determinant is a candidate row identifier) is also fully-normalised, but there are some situations in which further normalisation is desirable.

7.2   Hidden transitive dependency

Figure 7.1 shows two well-normalised versions of the badly-normalised table Order. Version A is unexceptionable, but version B possesses some unsatisfactory features.

Order (orderNo, customerNo, customerName)

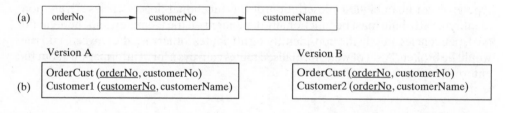

(a)

	Version A	Version B
(b)	OrderCust (orderNo, customerNo) Customer1 (customerNo, customerName)	OrderCust (orderNo, customerNo) Customer2 (orderNo, customerName)

Customer1	customerNo	customerName
	C1	Smith
	C2	Jones
	C3	Smith

OrderCust	orderNo	customerNo
	1	C1
	2	C2
	3	C1
	4	C1
	5	C2
	6	C3

Customer2	orderNo	customerName
	1	Smith
	2	Jones
	3	Smith
	4	Smith
	5	Jones
	6	Smith

(c)

Fig. 7.1   (a)   The badly-normalised table Order
        (b)   Two well-normalised versions of Order
        (c)   Typical occurrences for the well-normalised tables

Firstly, the grouping of attributes in version B is less logical than in version A. The latter version seems intuitively more sensible because there is one table which contains attributes of customers only, while the other table relates orders to customers. In version B, both tables relate orders to customers.

Secondly, version B can contain redundant data. Suppose the value Smith were deleted from row 1 of Customer2. The missing value could be deduced by using the orderNo (1) to find the corresponding customerNo in OrderCust (C1), then searching OrderCust for another orderNo placed by C1 (orderNo 3 or 4), and finally using one of these orderNo(s) to find the customer name from Customer2. As usual, the presence of redundancy introduces a consistency problem. Suppose the name of customer C1 is changed from Smith to Peters. In version A, only one row in Customer1 needs updating ('C1 Smith' becomes 'C1 Peters'). In version B, several rows need updating (one row for each order placed by C1). Version A, being free of redundancy, is fully-normalised; version B, although well-normalised, is not fully-normalised.

The basic error made in deriving version B was to associate in Customer2 a determinant, orderNo, with the transitively dependent attribute, customerName. In contrast, in version A each determinant is associated with directly dependent attributes only.

Question

1. With reference to the Order example above, compare the effect of a change in customerNo (e.g. C1 to C9) on versions A and B. Is a change of customerNo more, or less, likely than a change in customerName? Why?   (2 min)

7.3   Multi-valued determinancy

Suppose we want to show the authors and subject classifications of books. Each book has a unique bookNo, each author a unique authorNo, and each subject classification a unique subjectName. A bookNo value does not distinguish an individual copy of a book, rather it distinguishes an individual work. For example, all copies of the first edition of *How to Solve a Crossword* by Colin Parsons, published by Hodder & Stoughton, would have the same bookNo. A book may be written by several authors and be classified under several subjectName(s). An author may write several books. A subjectName may be applied to many books. In addition to bookNo, authorNo and subjectName, other attributes of interest are authorName and bookTitle.

The determinancy diagram is shown in Fig. 7.2a. This diagram is represented as a set of well-normalised tables in Fig. 7.2b. The AuthorBookSubject table will be of particular interest; a typical occurrence of this table is shown in Fig. 7.2c.

First convince yourself that the identifier of the AuthorBookSubject table is the composite attribute {authorNo, bookNo, subjectName}. Check that no single component attribute determines either of the others (e.g. does authorNo determine bookNo or subjectName?). Then check that no one component attribute is determined by the composite attribute formed from the other two attributes (e.g. does the composite attribute {authorNo, bookNo} determine subjectName?).

Now look at the AuthorBookSubject table occurrence in Fig. 7.2c where bookNo B15 is jointly authored by authors A2 and A5, and is classified under the subjectName(s)

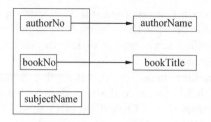

(a)

(b)
Author(<u>authorNo</u>, authorName)
Book(<u>bookNo</u>, bookTitle)
AuthorBookSubject (<u>authorNo, bookNo, subjectName</u>)

AuthorBookSubject

authorNo	bookNo	subjectName
A2	B15	biology
A2	B15	physics
A5	B15	biology
A5	B15	physics
A2	B18	physics

(c)

Fig. 7.2   An example of multi-valued determinancy
(a)   Determinancy diagram
(b)   Well-normalised tables
(c)   Table occurrence for AuthorBookSubject

biology and physics. This brings us to the crucial point. If it is true that every author of a given book is always associated with all the subjectName(s) under which the book is classified, then the attribute subjectName can contain redundant values. If the subjectName values biology and physics were deleted from rows 1 and 2, it would be possible to deduce the missing values from rows 3 and 4. The AuthorBookSubject table, although well-normalised, is therefore not fully-normalised. Full normalisation can be achieved by splitting the table into two parts, AuthorBook and BookSubject, as in Fig. 7.3.

AuthorBook

authorNo	bookNo
A2	B15
A5	B15
A2	B18

BookSubject

bookNo	subjectName
B15	biology
B15	physics
B18	physics

Fig. 7.3   Fully-normalised tables

The lack of full normalisation arises because the same set of subjectName(s) is associated with each author of the same book. The attribute bookNo is said to *multi-determine* authorNo and subjectName. The situation would be quite different if another enterprise rule were assumed, namely that subjectName refers to a subject area within a book for which an individual author was responsible. Under this rule there would not be any redundancy in the AuthorBookSubject table. For example, if the subjectName value biology were deleted from row 3, it would not be possible to deduce the missing value from elsewhere in the table. Conceivably, authors A2 and A5 were jointly responsible for the physics content of book B15, with A2 having sole responsibility for the biology content, and A5 having sole responsibility for the chemistry content. If so, the missing value from row 3 would have been chemistry. There is no way of deducing from the table that the missing value was in fact biology.

Questions

1. The table SupplierPart (<u>supplierNo, partNo</u>) is subject to the enterprise rules:
(a)   a supplier may supply many parts;
(b)   a part may be supplied by many suppliers;
(c)   every supplier must supply parts P1 and P2.
Explain why SupplierPart will contain redundant data. Suggest a table structure which avoids redundancy.   (3 min)
2. The table Supply (<u>supplierNo, partNo, projectNo</u>) shows which suppliers supply which parts to which projects. State an enterprise rule such that Supply could contain redundant data.   (3 min)

7.4   Advantages of full normalisation

So far, the argument presented in favour of full normalisation has emphasised the importance of eliminating redundancy, the advantages being a simpler data model and the avoidance of potential inconsistency in redundant data values. There are two further benefits of full normalisation; these relate to deletion and insertion operations.

Deletion side-effects
The CustomerSalesperson table in Fig. 7.4a is not fully-normalised, nor even well-normalised. Suppose customer C2 is deleted from the table. One might suppose that the values C2 and Carter could be replaced by nulls, but this would break the rule that the identifier (customerNo) may not contain a null. A single row with a null identifier might be tolerated, as each row in the table would still be distinguishable. However, if two or more customerNo(s) were deleted there would be two null identifiers, so the identifier would no longer identify a row (it would no longer be an identifier). The only way of deleting a customer from the table is therefore to delete the whole row, but this has the unfortunate side-effect that information about a salesperson's number and name may also be lost. By deleting customer C2, we lose the information that there is a salesperson S7 called Samson.

In contrast, the fully-normalised version of CustomerSalesperson (Fig. 7.4b) does not suffer from a deletion side-effect. Row C2 Carter S7 can be deleted from the Customer table without affecting row S7 Samson in the Salesperson table.

Insertion side-effects
These are the converse of the deletion side-effects. If one wants to add to the Customer Salesperson table (Fig. 7.4a) the information that there is a salesperson S3 with name Hall, one cannot do so until that salesperson is associated with a customer, otherwise the identifier (customerNo) will be null.

The fully-normalised version of CustomerSalesperson (Fig. 7.4b) does not suffer from an insertion side-effect. Row S3 Hall can be inserted in the Salesperson table even though salesperson S3 is not yet associated with any customer.

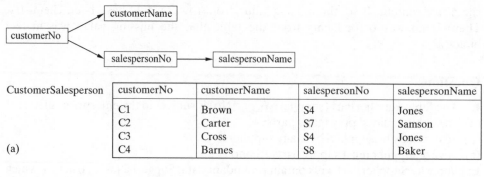

CustomerSalesperson	customerNo	customerName	salespersonNo	salespersonName
	C1	Brown	S4	Jones
	C2	Carter	S7	Samson
	C3	Cross	S4	Jones
(a)	C4	Barnes	S8	Baker

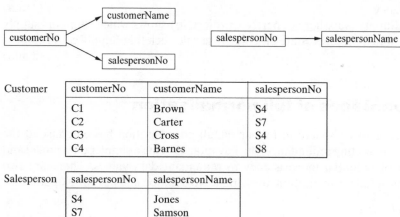

Customer	customerNo	customerName	salespersonNo
	C1	Brown	S4
	C2	Carter	S7
	C3	Cross	S4
	C4	Barnes	S8

Salesperson	salespersonNo	salespersonName
	S4	Jones
	S7	Samson
(b)	S8	Baker

Fig. 7.4   (a)   The badly-normalised table CustomerSalesperson
          (b)   The fully-normalised version of CustomerSalesperson

Questions

1.   With reference to the Order example of section 7.2, compare the fully-normalised version A and the well-normalised version B with respect to deletion and insertion side-effects.   (3 min)

2.   With reference to the Book example of section 7.3, compare the well-normalised version of Fig. 7.2 and the fully-normalised version of Fig. 7.3 with respect to deletion and insertion side-effects.   (3 min)

3.   (a)   A company requires a database which contains details of orders placed with suppliers. What are the side-effects of using the following table structure, in which orderNo is a determinant of supplierNo, itemNo is a determinant of price, and supplierNo is a determinant of supplierName and supplierAddress?   (3 min)

Order (<u>orderNo, itemNo</u>, price, supplierNo, supplierName, supplierAddress)

(b)   Assume that most orders are for only one item, that most suppliers have only one outstanding order at a time, and that details of an order can be deleted once an order has been delivered. Does the badly-normalised table have any advantages over a fully-normalised version?   (2 min)

7.5 Normal forms

The normalisation process is often described in terms of stages known as *first, second, third, fourth* and *fifth normal forms* (1NF–5NF). Although we have not adopted this approach in the present text, the terminology is sufficiently prevalent in the literature to warrant a brief explanation. The general idea is that at each successive stage of normalisation certain undesirable features are eliminated from the initial unnormalised table. First normal form is obtained by eliminating repeating groups, second normal form is obtained by eliminating non-identifier attributes that are not functionally dependent on the whole of the identifier, and third normal form is obtained by eliminating functional dependency between non-identifier attributes. (Third normal form is similar to Boyce/Codd normal form, but does not deal satisfactorily with overlapping candidate identifiers.) Fourth normal form deals with multi-valued determinancies, and fifth normal form deals with a rather unusual situation known as join dependency which is of little practical significance. For further details of this approach to normalisation, see the bibliography.

Assignments

1. Discuss the derivation of a fully-normalised version of the determinancy diagram shown in answer pointer 5(a) for section 6.8.
2. A set of fully-normalised table types encapsulates some of the enterprise rules which apply to the data. Give examples of enterprise rules which are not captured by full-normalisation, and discuss how such rules could be enforced in order to preserve the integrity of a database.
3. Write a dissertation on the historical development of the idea of normalisation. The bibliography provides a starting point for a literature search.
4. Design and implement a computer program which will convert a badly-normalised table into a set of well-normalised tables. Assume:
(a)   that the badly-normalised table has a single candidate identifier;
(b)   that the input to the program is the identifier plus a list of determinancies;
(c)   that transitive determinancies are absent from the input.
5. Investigate extensions to your design for Assignment 4, such as:
(a)   the ability to handle more than one candidate identifier;
(b)   automatic extraction of candidate identifiers;
(c)   detection of transitive determinancies;
(d)   generation of fully-normalised tables.
Implement one or more of these extensions.

Answer pointers

Section 7.2

1. Suppose customerNo C1 is changed to C9. For the fully-normalised version A, changes will be necessary in both Customer1 and in OrderCust. For the well-normalised version B, only OrderCust needs changing. In contrast to the effect of a change in a customerName value, the well-normalised version is actually easier to update than the fully-normalised version. In defence of version A, note that customerNo is much less likely to be changed than customerName, because an important criterion for the selection of an identifier is that it should be stable. Thus, even if it is known that no two customers will ever have the same name, the attribute customerName would be a poor choice for an identifier as it is more likely to change.

Section 7.3

1.   For each supplierNo value there will be one row in SupplierPart for partNo P1, and another row for partNo P2. These rows are redundant because the information in them can be deduced from the enterprise rule that every supplier must supply parts P1 and P2. It would be more economical to have one table MustSupply (partNo) which merely contains a list of mandatory partNo(s) (P1, P2), and another table AlsoSupplies (supplierNo, partNo) which contains the rest of the information. This solution ensures consistency in the list of mandatory partNo(s), but does entail processing two tables rather than one.

2.   There are several possibilities. For example:

(a)   All suppliers supply all parts to all projects.

(b)   All suppliers supply the same parts, but not necessarily to the same projects.

(c)   If a supplier supplies a project, then all the parts which that supplier is capable of supplying are supplied to that project.

Section 7.4

1.   The fully-normalised version A does not suffer from deletion or insertion side-effects. Deletion of an order does not affect the customerNo, customerName information. Details of a new customer can be inserted in Customer1 prior to the placing of an order by the customer. There may be problems of consistency between the two tables OrderCust and Customer1 if there are enterprise rules such as 'a row may not be deleted from Customer1 if the customer has any orders outstanding in OrderCust', or 'details of a new customer are not recorded until the customer has placed an order.'

Version B, which is well-normalised but not fully-normalised, does suffer from deletion and insertion side-effects. Deletion of an order affects both OrderCust and Customer2, and causes loss of customer information if there are no other orders outstanding from the customer (for example, deletion of orderNo 6 causes loss of information about C3 Smith). Details of a new customer cannot be inserted prior to the placing of an order by the customer. There is also a consistency problem if, as seems likely, an orderNo should not appear in one table without also appearing in the other.

2.   AuthorBookSubject will have a null component in its identifier if it is used:

(a)   to insert bookNo and subjectName for a book with no authors;

(b)   to insert authorNo and bookNo for a book which is not classified under any subject Name.

Several other examples of insertion side-effects can be devised.

Conversely, deletion of up to two attributes implies deletion of a row with consequential loss of information.

3. (a)   Item and supplier details cannot be inserted unless an order is outstanding. Deletion of an order may cause loss of item and supplier information.

(b)   The badly-normalised table has the advantage that it automatically enforces the enterprise rules that item and supplier details are not stored until an order is placed and should be deleted when the order is deleted. It is probably better, being more flexible, to use fully-normalised tables, with the enterprise rules being built into the conceptual schema elsewhere rather than in the table structure itself.

Part 3

Entity-relationship modelling

Part 3 discusses the development of a conceptual data model via a *top-down* approach which starts by identifying *entity* and *relationship types*, and then uses these to construct a framework into which the attributes may be slotted.

Chapter 8 considers the limitations of *bottom-up* data modelling, and defines the components—*entity, relationship* and *attribute*—of an alternative *top-down, entity-relationship modelling* approach. The diagrammatic convention used to represent an entity-relationship model is introduced.

Chapter 9 describes two important properties of relationships, namely *degree* and *participation*. The diagrammatic convention is extended to cater for both these properties.

Chapter 10 prepares the ground for aspects of Chapter 11 by showing how a relationship of degree many:many can always be decomposed into relationships of degree 1:many.

Chapter 11 explains how an entity-relationship model may contain features which prevent it from representing data in the way the designer intended. The detection and elimination of these *connection traps* is discussed.

Chapter 12 develops criteria for deciding how relationships may best be represented in the form of *skeleton tables*, that is tables which contain only entity or relationship identifiers. The distinction between relationship and table row identifiers is drawn out, and examples are given to illustrate the design of skeleton tables for the special case of recursive relationships.

Chapter 13 uses the concepts developed in Part 2 as guidelines for the assignment of attributes into the framework provided by the skeleton model. The need to extend a model which proves to be incomplete, and opportunities to trim superfluous parts of the model, are considered.

Chapter 14 draws together the ideas developed in the previous chapters into a general procedure for designing a preliminary, or *first-level* entity-relationship model. An example of the application of this procedure to a library loans system is given.

Chapter 15 shows how a first-level design may be *flexed* in order to improve its performance. The flexing techniques are applied to the library loans model designed in the previous chapter.

Chapter 16 extends the discussion of flexing to *distributed databases*, in which the database is spread across several geographically distinct sites. The library loans example is extended to a branch library system.

8

Introduction to entity-relationship modelling

8.1 Bottom-up data modelling

The data modelling procedure described so far adopts the following sequence of operations:

(a) select the attributes of interest to the enterprise;
(b) combine these attributes into fully-normalised tables.

This approach will be described as a *bottom-up* procedure, since its starting point is at the elementary level of attributes.

Although the bottom-up procedure works well in relatively simple situations, it does suffer from some problems when applied to more realistic circumstances, where there may be a large number of attributes to consider, or where there is more than one relationship between the same attributes.

If there are many attributes to consider, it can be difficult to sort out all the functional dependencies correctly, particularly where composite determinants exist. As a conceptual data model typically contains several hundred, or even several thousand, attributes it is necessary in practice to find some way of simplifying the design procedure. A more fundamental problem is that in the early stages of data analysis the data administrator will not usually be aware of all the attributes which will eventually be included in the data model. He or she is more likely to know that there will be attributes about, say, customers, parts and suppliers, than to know exactly what those attributes will be.

An example where there is more than one relationship between the same attributes is as follows. Suppose an employee may be assigned to only one project at a time, but many employees may be assigned to the same project. An employee may lead several projects (a project leader is not regarded as being 'assigned' to a project), but each project has only one project leader. Different projects may have different project leaders. The attributes of interest are employeeNo, employeeName, projectTitle, projectBudget. In the determinancy diagram of Fig. 8.1a, there are two arrows between employeeNo and projectTitle because there are two distinct relationships between these attributes, namely 'EmployeeLeadsProject' and 'EmployeeIsAssignedToProject'. At first sight it might have been thought that, since employeeNo determines projectTitle and *vice versa*, the two arrows could be replaced by one double-headed arrow, as in Fig. 8.1b. However, according to Fig. 8.1b, projectTitle always determines employeeNo, but in fact this should be true only for the relationship 'EmployeeLeadsProject' and not for the relationship 'EmployeeIsAssignedToProject'. Similarly, employeeNo should determine projectTitle only when assignments to projects, rather than the leadership of projects, is considered.

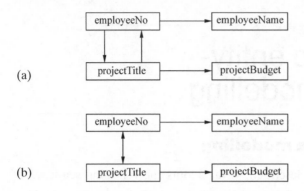

Fig. 8.1   Correct (a) and incorrect (b) representations of the relationships between employeeNo and projectTitle
(a)   Two relationships between employeeNo and projectTitle
(b)   One relationship between employeeNo and projectTitle. Not equivalent to part (a)

8.2   Entity-relationship modelling

The above problems can be avoided by adopting a *top-down* approach. In the particular top-down approach to be described in this book (known as entity-relationship modelling) the sequence of operations is:

(a)   select the entities (such as Customers, Parts and Suppliers), and the relationships between them (such as Customer Orders Parts, and Supplier Supplies Parts), which are of interest to the enterprise;
(b)   assign attributes to these entities and relationships in such a way that a set of fully-normalised tables is obtained.

The basic concepts used by the entity-relationship model are therefore those of *entity, attribute* and *relationship*. Some (rather circular) definitions of these concepts, in the context of entity-relationship modelling, are given below:

Entity
An entity is a thing (object, concept) which the enterprise recognises as being capable of an independent existence in the sense that it can be uniquely identified. For example, Customer, Machine, Contract, might be regarded as being entities.

Attribute
An attribute is a property of an entity. For example, attributes of a Customer entity might be customerNo, customerName; attributes of a Contract entity might be dateOfContract, valueOfContract.

Relationship
A relationship is an association between two (or more) entities. For example, an entity Department may be associated with an entity Employee via a relationship Employs.

These definitions are necessarily imprecise, for it will become apparent that there is no absolute way of classifying data into entities, attributes and relationships, although one classification may be in better accord than another with the enterprise's own view of its data. A useful clue for distinguishing between entities and relationships is that an enterprise often uses nouns to describe entities, and verbs to describe relationships.

8.3   Type vs occurrence

Suppose warehouses stock products, as shown in Fig. 8.2. The diagram shows two *entity types* (Warehouse, Product). There are two Warehouse *entity occurrences* (the warehouses identified by the warehouseNo(s) W1 and W2), and five Product *entity occurrences* (the products identified by the productNo(s) P2, P7, P4, P8, P6). There is one *relationship type* (Stores) and five Stores *relationship occurrences* (the five lines connecting the warehouse and product entity occurrences).

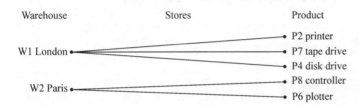

Fig. 8.2   Entity and relationship types and occurrences

As was the case with the terms table type and table occurrence, the terms entity and relationship used on their own may refer to either a type or an occurrence, or both, depending on context.

8.4   Identifiers

By definition, an entity occurrence must be uniquely identifiable. An attribute, possibly composite, whose value identifies an entity occurrence is called an *entity identifier*. In the preceding example, warehouseNo and productNo identify the entities Warehouse and Product respectively.

An entity may have more than one candidate identifier. For example, a sales area may have a unique salesAreaName (e.g. Midlands, North-West) and also, for the sake of brevity, a unique salesAreaCode (e.g. 01, 02). There is then a choice of candidate identifiers for a SalesArea entity type, and one of these candidates must be selected as the entity identifier. The choice may be completely arbitrary, but will often be swayed by considerations of brevity and the certainty of uniqueness. Thus salesAreaCode would usually be preferred to salesAreaName.

An entity identifier is, of course, essentially the same thing as the row identifier of a table. Similarly, an entity occurrence can be represented by a row in the table.

A relationship occurrence can be identified by the entity occurrences which it associates. A *relationship identifier* is therefore a composite of the identifiers of the entities which are associated via the relationship. For example, the fact that there is a relationship occurrence between warehouse W1 and product P2 can be stated by quoting the value {W1, P2} of the composite relationship identifier {warehouseNo, productNo}. An exception to this general rule for constructing relationship identifiers is discussed in section 12.7, and the connection between relationship identifiers and table row identifiers is examined in section 12.8.

8.5   Entity-relationship diagrams

Figure 8.2 is an example of an *entity-relationship occurrence diagram*, that is a diagram which shows individual entity occurrences and their relationships. (In future, non-identifying attributes such as warehouseLocation and partDescription will usually be omitted from diagrams of this kind.) Just as it was more convenient to work with table types rather than table occurrences, so it is easier to use an *entity-relationship type diagram* (Fig. 8.3) rather than the corresponding occurrence diagram.

Fig. 8.3   An entity-relationship type diagram

The conventions which will be used in drawing an entity-relationship type diagram are that entity types will be represented by rectangles and relationship types by connecting lines that show which entity types are associated by each relationship type. Each entity type and relationship type is named. Names of entity types are usually written in the singular (e.g. Product rather than Products) but remember that an entity type typically represents many entity occurrences (see Fig. 8.2). Entity type and relationship type names will be written in the same way as for table names, that is with initial capitals for each word in the name (e.g. ProductType). Attribute names will continue to be written with initial capitals except for the first word in the name (e.g. partDescription).

The naming of relationship types does pose a slight problem. If, in Fig. 8.3, one looks at the relationship type in the direction Warehouse to Product, then Stores is a perfectly reasonable relationship name since a warehouse stores a product. Looked at in the opposite direction the name is less reasonable, since a product is not normally thought of as storing a warehouse; a more meaningful name would be 'IsStoredIn'. Sometimes a less 'directional' name can be found (Stocks?). Sometimes a name such as WarehouseProduct will be used, if there is only one relationship between the entity types, but it would be equally appropriate to use ProductWarehouse. In Fig. 8.3 an optional solid arrowhead is used to show the direction in which the name of the relationship is to be read. Note that the arrowhead does not mean that the relationship is, in any sense, only a one-way relationship. If a warehouse stores a product, then it is equally true that a product is stored in a warehouse. If desired, a relationship type can be named in both directions, as in Fig. 8.4, but this makes diagrams more cluttered and has the drawback that there is no longer a unique name for each relationship type.

Fig. 8.4 A relationship type with both directions named

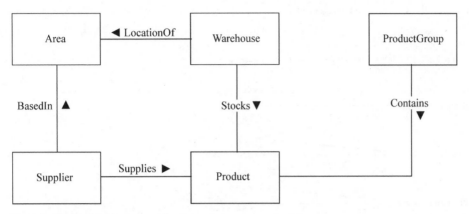

Fig. 8.5 Examples of relationship name placement

Usually, the meaning of a relationship name is clear, even without an arrowhead, so these arrowheads are normally omitted from entity-relationship diagrams. It is often either impossible or inconvenient to draw all relationship lines horizontally. Only straight line segments (no curves) are used for relationships. Relationship names may be written in any convenient position near, or across a gap in, the line as in Fig. 8.5.

Questions

1. Draw an entity-relationship type diagram, and a sample entity-relationship occurrence diagram, for the example shown in Fig. 8.1a. Assume entity types Project and Employee, and relationship types Leads and IsAssignedTo. The identifiers of Project and Employee are projectTitle and employeeNo, respectively. In the occurrence diagram distinguish between the two relationships by using solid lines for occurrences of IsAssignedTo, and dashed lines for occurrences of Leads (or, better still, use different colours).   (5 min)

2. A conceptual data model will contain the attributes propertyAddress, numberOfRooms, rateableValue, surnameOfOwner, initialsOfOwner. The data model structure should be capable of showing (a) who owns a given property, and (b) which property an owner occupies. An owner does not necessarily occupy a property which he or she owns. Suggest two entity types which might be recognised in an entity-relationship model, and suggest two possible relationship types between these two entities. Draw an entity-relationship type diagram.   (2 min)

3. Is an entity merely the sum of its attributes?   (2 min)

4. The definition of an entity (section 8.2) used the phrase 'independent existence'. The examples given of typical entities included Customer and Contract. Could a Contract entity occurrence exist independently of a Customer entity occurrence?   (3 min)

Answer pointers

1.

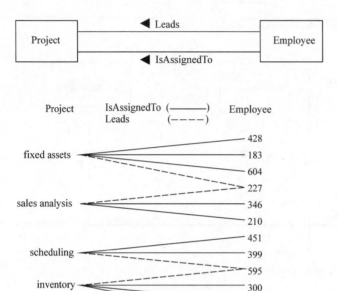

2.   Entity types: Owner, Property.
Relationship types: Owns, Occupies.
Entity-relationship type diagram:

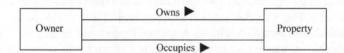

3.   Consider whether adding or deleting an attribute necessarily changes the nature of an entity, and whether different entities could have identical sets of attributes.

4.   A database that supports a typical contract application will usually need to associate each Contract entity occurrence with the Customer entity occurrence to which the contract relates. However, if the application is only concerned with, say, the values and completion dates of contracts, not details (such as name and address) of customers, then there would be no need for a Customer entity. In either case, a Contract entity would have an entity identifier (e.g. contractNo, or perhaps {customerNo, contractSerialNo} if contracts are numbered serially within customer) so Contract would satisfy the section 8.2 definition of 'being capable of an independent existence in the sense that it can be uniquely identified'. Although the participation conditions to be considered in Chapter 9 may require every occurrence of an entity to be associated with another entity occurrence (e.g. every Contract occurrence to be associated with a

Customer occurrence) this does not alter our insistence that every entity must have its own identifier.

Some data models (including the original Chen entity-relationship model) permit entities that do not have their own identifiers. We will not permit such entities, as it is simpler to integrate entity-relationship modelling with relational modelling if every entity occurrence can be uniquely identified independently of any other entity occurrence.

9

Properties of relationships

9.1 The degree of a relationship

An important property of a relationship is its *degree*. Suppose there is a relationship Teaches between the entities Lecturer and Course; a lecturer is identified by lecturerName, and a course by courseNo. There are three possible kinds of relationship degree, each corresponding to different pairs of enterprise rules for the relationship.

1:1 relationship
Enterprise rules:

> 'A lecturer teaches, at most, one course.'
> 'A course is taught by, at most, one lecturer.'

   This pair of enterprise rules defines Teaches as being a *1:1 relationship*. (Read 1:1 as 1-to-1.) A typical occurrence diagram is shown in Fig. 9.1a. Notice that a 1:1 relationship may, in general, include 1:0 and 0:1 relationships; that is, a lecturer does not have to teach a course, nor does a course have to be taught by a lecturer. (Perhaps the assignment of lecturers to courses has not been completed, or some lecturers are on study leave, or some courses are taught by persons who are not classified as lecturers.) However, the relationship's degree would still be 1:1 even if lecturers or courses could not exist independently, as would be the case for the enterprise rules:

> 'A lecturer teaches exactly one course.'
> 'A course is taught by exactly one lecturer.'

1:many relationship
Enterprise rules:

> 'A lecturer may teach many courses.'
> 'A course is taught by, at most, one lecturer.'

   This pair of enterprise rules defines Teaches as being a *1:many relationship* (often written 1:N). A typical occurrence diagram is shown in Fig. 9.1b. Notice that a 1:many relationship may, in general, include 1:1, 1:0 and 0:1 relationships, although some, or all, of these possibilities could be excluded from a 1:many relationship by more restrictive enterprise rules; for example:

> 'A lecturer must teach more than one course.'
> 'A course is taught by exactly one lecturer.'

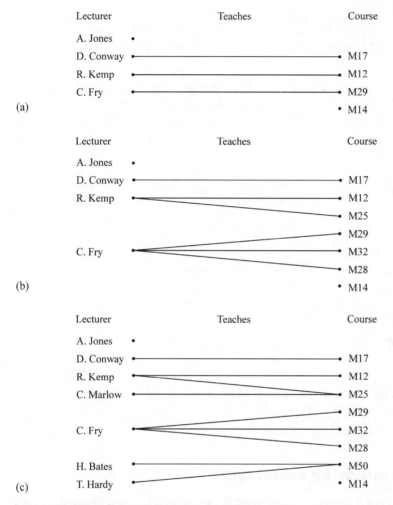

Fig. 9.1   Typical occurrence diagrams for 1:1, 1:many and many:many relationships
(a)   Typical occurrence diagram for 1:1 relationship
(b)   Typical occurrence diagram for 1:many relationship
(c)   Typical occurrence diagram for many:many relationship

The 'direction' of a 1:many relationship is significant. In this example the 1:many direction is from (one) Lecturer to (many) Courses. A 1:many relationship in the direction (one) Course to (many) Lecturers would require a different pair of enterprise rules.

Many: many relationship
Enterprise rules:

'A lecturer may teach many courses.'
'A course may be taught by many lecturers.'

This pair of enterprise rules defines Teaches as being a *many:many relationship* (often written M:N). A typical occurrence diagram is shown in Fig. 9.1c. Notice that a many:many relationship may, in general, include 1:many (in either direction), 1:1, 1:0 and 0:1 relationships, although some, or all, of these possibilities could be excluded from a many:many relationship by more restrictive enterprise rules.

Notation
Figure 9.2 shows how the degree of a relationship is represented on an entity-relationship type diagram. Answers to questions which ask for an entity-relationship type diagram should always show the degree of each relationship if the information is available.

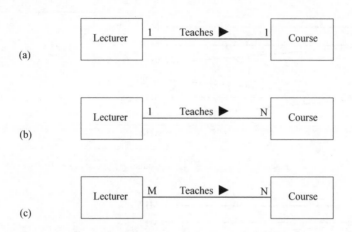

Fig. 9.2   Representation of relationship degree on an entity-relationship type diagram
(a)   Representation of 1:1 relationship
(b)   Representation of 1:many relationship
(c)   Representation of many:many relationship

9.2   Determinancy constraints

A more precise way of defining the degree of a relationship is in terms of determinancy constraints between the identifiers of the entity types concerned.

For the 1:1 relationship of Fig. 9.1a:

lecturerName is a determinant of courseNo.
courseNo is a determinant of lecturerName.

For the 1:many relationship of Fig. 9.1b:

lecturerName is not a determinant of courseNo.
courseNo is a determinant of lecturerName.

For the many:many relationship of Fig. 9.1c:

lecturerName is not a determinant of courseNo.
courseNo is not a determinant of lecturerName.

Our previous definition of a determinant was that attribute x is a determinant of attribute y if each value of x has precisely one (possibly null) associated value of y. In the present context 'null' is to be interpreted as meaning 'non-existent'. For example, the course taught by lecturer A. Jones is 'non-existent', as is the lecturer for course M14.

The definition of relationship degree in terms of determinants is summarised in Fig. 9.3. X and Y are entity types with identifiers x and y respectively. In the examples of typical occurrence diagrams, values of x and y are written in the form $x_1, x_2, \ldots, y_1, y_2, \ldots$

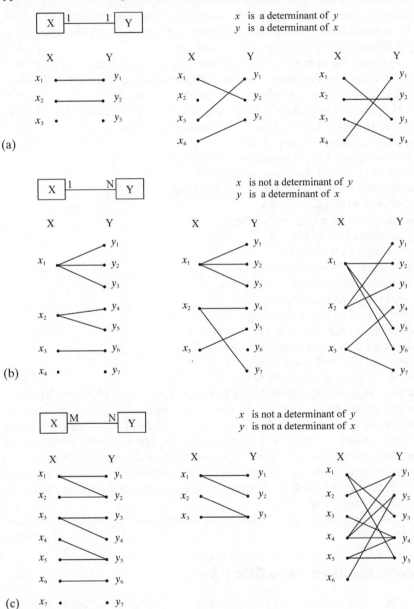

(a)

(b)

(c)

Fig. 9.3   Type diagrams and sample occurrence diagrams for 1:1, 1:many and many:many relationships
(a)   1:1 relationship
(b)   1:many relationship
(c)   many:many relationship

Questions

1. (a) Write down a pair of enterprise rules which would define a 1:many relationship 'TaughtBy', in the direction Course to Lecturer.
(b)   Express your rules in the form of determinancy constraints, assuming Course and Lecturer have identifiers courseNo and lecturerName, respectively.   (1min)
2. What is the minimum number of relationship occurrences which must be deleted from Fig. 9.1b to make the resulting diagram consistent with a 1:1 relationship? Does the resulting diagram necessarily imply a 1:1 relationship?   (1 min)
3. What is the minimum number of relationship occurrences which must be deleted from Fig. 9.1c to make the resulting diagram consistent with a 1:many relationship? Does the resulting diagram necessarily imply a 1:many relationship?   (1 min)
4. For each of the following pairs of enterprise rules, identify two entity types and one relationship type. State the degree of the relationship in each case.
(a)   A department employs many persons.
       A person is employed by, at most, one department.
(b)   A manager manages, at most, one department.
       A department is managed by, at most, one manager.
(c)   An author may write many books.
       A book may be written by many authors.
(d)   A team consists of many players.
       A player plays for only one team.
(e)   A lecturer teaches, at most, one course.
       A course is taught by exactly one lecturer.
(f)   A flight-leg connects two airports.
       An airport is used by many flight-legs.
(g)   A purchase-order may be for many products.
       A product may appear on many purchase-orders.
(h)   A customer may submit many orders.
       An order is for exactly one customer.   (5 min)
5. In a group medical practice, each doctor has many patients on his or her list, but a patient can register with only one doctor at a time. If the conceptual data model includes only current patient registrations, what is the degree of the DoctorPatientRegister relationship between the entity types Doctor and Patient? Draw an entity-relationship type diagram, and a sample entity-relationship occurrence diagram assuming that a doctor is identified by doctorName and a patient by patientNo.   (3 min)
6. How does the answer to question 5 change if the model is extended to include both present and past registrations?   (2 min)
7. How does the answer to question 5 change if a patient may simultaneously register with several doctors?   (1 min)

9.3   Participation conditions

In section 9.1 there are examples of two different ways in which an entity type can participate in a relationship. Some of the enterprise rules insist that every occurrence of an entity participates in the relationship, other enterprise rules allow occurrences of an entity to exist independently. The terms *obligatory* and *non-obligatory* will be used to distinguish between these situations.

Suppose the enterprise rules for an Employs relationship between Department and Employee are:

> 'Every employee must be employed within a department.'
> 'A department may exist even if it has no employees.'

(The second rule would allow information to be held about a new department, even though it does not yet have any employees.) We will say that the participation of Employee in the Employs relationship is obligatory, in other words an Employee occurrence must participate in (at least one) Employs relationship occurrence. Conversely, the participation of Department in the Employs relationship is non-obligatory, in other words a Department occurrence can exist without participating in an Employs relationship occurrence.

For a relationship between two entity types, there are then four possible combinations of participation conditions, as illustrated in Fig. 9.4. The diagrams also show the notation which will be used to represent participation on an entity-relationship type diagram. A blob inside a stripe on an entity symbol means that the entity's participation is obligatory; a blob outside an entity symbol means that the entity's participation is non-obligatory. Knowledge of the participation conditions of entities is important, as it may influence the design of data models and schemas.

A department must employ at least one employee
(a)   An employee must be employed by at least one department

A department need not employ any employees
(b)   An employee need not be employed by any department

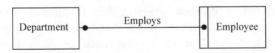

A department need not employ any employees
(c)   An employee must be employed by at least one department

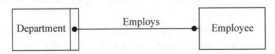

A department must employ at least one employee
(d)   An employee need not be employed by any department

Fig. 9.4   Possible combinations of participation conditions
(a)   Department participation obligatory; Employee participation obligatory
(b)   Department participation non-obligatory; Employee participation non-obligatory
(c)   Department participation non-obligatory; Employee participation obligatory
(d)   Department participation obligatory; Employee participation non-obligatory

Questions

1. Decide on plausible participation conditions for the entity types in each of the following: (2 min)

	Entity types	*Relationship*
(a)	House, Person	Ownership
(b)	House, Tenant	Occupation
(c)	Order, OrderLine	Contains (An order may contain several order-lines, each referring to a different item on the order.)
(d)	SalesArea, Customer	HasAssigned
(e)	BankClient, ClientAccount	Possesses
(f)	Employee, Skill	Has

2. Draw an entity-relationship type diagram and a sample entity-relationship occurrence diagram for each part of question 1. Represent each entity occurrence by a dot. There is no need to show entity identifiers.   (5 min)

3. What practical difficulty might be encountered when storing Department and Employee data in a database governed by the enterprise rules in Fig. 9.4a?   (2 min)

9.4   Multiplicity

Suppose there is a relationship type AB between the entity types A and B. The degree of the relationship AB specifies the maximum number of occurrences (1 or many) of A associated with an occurrence of B, and the maximum number of occurrences of B associated with an occurrence of A. For example, in Fig. 9.2b, the maximum number of Course occurrences associated with a Lecturer occurrence is 'many', and the maximum number of Lecturer occurrences associated with a Course occurrence is '1'.

Just as the degree of a relationship specifies maximum numbers, so the participation condition specifies minimum numbers. If the participation of A in relationship AB is obligatory, then each occurrence of A is associated with a minimum of one occurrence of B. Conversely, if the participation of A in relationship AB is non-obligatory, then each occurrence of A is associated with a minimum of zero occurrences of B. Similar statements apply to the participation of B in AB.

Degree is concerned with maxima (upper bounds) and participation with minima (lower bounds). An alternative *multiplicity* notation is often used, particularly in an object-oriented context. A *multiplicity* specifies the number of occurrences of an entity that can participate in a relationship with another entity, usually just by specifying a lower bound and an upper bound. Fig. 9.5 compares the equivalent multiplicity notation with the degree/blob notation for some of the possible combinations of degree and participation condition. Note that the participation condition of entity type A, represented by a blob at the A end of the relationship, is shown in the multiplicity notation as a lower bound at the B end of the relationship. Similarly, the participation

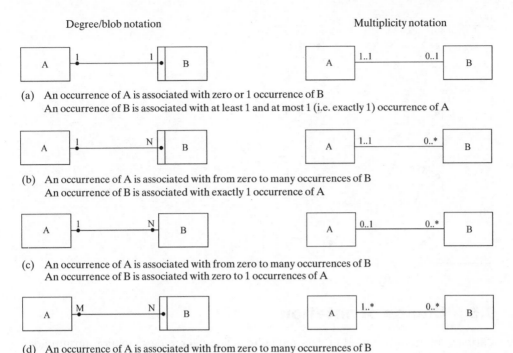

Fig. 9.5   Comparison of degree/blob notation with multiplicity notation

condition of entity type B, represented by a blob at the B end of the relationship, is shown in the multiplicity notation as a lower bound at the A end of the relationship. The asterisk (*) in the multiplicity notation represents an unlimited upper bound (i.e. many).

An upper bound cannot be less than the lower bound of its range. A multiplicity range of 1..1 (i.e. exactly 1) is often written simply as 1. A multiplicity range of 0..* is often written simply as *. The values used in multiplicities are usually 0, 1, *, but other values can be used where appropriate, for example as in 2..* or 10..20. Although very unusual in practice, a multiplicity could comprise several ranges as in 2, 5..8, 12 which would mean that 2, 5, 6, 7, 8 or 12 occurrences may be involved with a single occurrence of the other entity.

Questions

1.   Why would a multiplicity of 0..0 never be required?   (1 min)

2.   A multiplicity of 1..1 is often written as just 1. Similarly, 0..* is often written as just *. Why is this practice ambiguous?   (2 min)

3.   Convert each of the following entity-relationship diagrams from degree/blob to multiplicity notation.   (2 min)

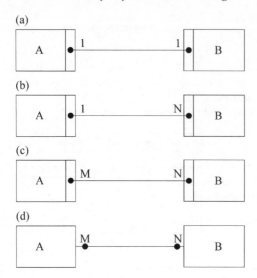

(a)

(b)

(c)

(d)

9.5 Choice of notation

Various notations are used in data modelling. The degree/participation terminology and the associated degree/blob notation are convenient for explaining the entity-relationship modelling approach, so they will be used in the next few chapters. The multiplicity notation has become generally accepted as the standard for object-oriented modelling, so it will be used in Chapter 20.

Answer pointers

Section 9.2

1. (a) A course may be taught by many lecturers.
A lecturer teaches, at most, one course.

There are other, equally valid, solutions. For example:

A course must be taught by many lecturers.
A lecturer teaches exactly one course.

(b) courseNo is not a determinant of lecturerName.
lecturerName is a determinant of courseNo.

2. Three relationship occurrences must be deleted, one for R. Kemp and two for C. Fry. The resulting diagram does not necessarily imply a 1:1 relationship, it is also consistent with a 1:many or many:many relationship. It is the enterprise rules which determine the relationship degree, not the occurrences which happen to exist at any one time.

3. Two relationship occurrences must be deleted, for example:

{R. Kemp, M25} and {H. Bates, M50}

The resulting diagram is consistent with a 1:many relationship in the direction Lecturer to Course. The resulting diagram is consistent with either a 1:many or many:many relationship, but not with a 1:1 relationship.

4.   The answers are written in the format:

> entity type 1, entity type 2, relationship type, degree

In the case of 1:many relationships, the degree is written in the direction entity type 1 to entity type 2.

(a)   Department, Person, Employs, 1:many
(b)   Manager, Department, Manages, 1:1
(c)   Author, Book, AuthorBook, many:many
(d)   Team, Player, PlayingStaff, 1:many
(e)   Lecturer, Course, Teaches, 1:1
(f)   FlightLeg, Airport, Connects, many:many (or many:2)
(g)   PurchaseOrder, Product, PurchaseOrderProduct, many:many
(h)   Customer, Order, Submits, 1:many

5.   1:many from Doctor to Patient.

6.   many:many. In deciding what degree a relationship should have, it is important to consider whether current data only, or a historical record, is required. How would a 1:1 relationship between Manager and Department be affected if historical records are required?

7.   many:many. The occurrence diagram for question 6 could be re-used here, although the meaning of the relationship would be changed to 'current registration'.

Section 9.3

1.   There is no one set of right answers. Possible participation conditions are suggested below, with brief reasons for the choice.

(a)   House obligatory. A house must have an owner. This might be true for an estate agent's database but would not be true for a register of houses whose owners are not known.
Person non-obligatory. A person does not have to own a house. This assumes that Person is not defined as 'an owner of a house'.

(b)   House non-obligatory. A house can be empty.
Tenant obligatory. Assumes a person who does not occupy a house is not classified as a tenant.

(c)   Order obligatory. An order must contain at least one order-line.
OrderLine obligatory. An order-line must belong to an order.

(d)   SalesArea non-obligatory. A sales-area need not contain any customers.
Customer obligatory. Every customer is assigned to a sales-area.

(e)   BankClient obligatory. Every client must have an account.
ClientAccount obligatory. An account must be associated with a client.

(f)   Employee non-obligatory. An employee might not have any skills.
Skill non-obligatory. Assumes a skill may be of interest even if it is not possessed by any employee. If the only skills of interest are those possessed by employees represented in the database, then Skill would have obligatory participation.

2. Each entity-relationship type diagram should be similar to one of those shown in Fig. 9.4, but with the relationship degree included. Your choice of relationship degree will depend on the enterprise rules you assume (e.g. can a tenant occupy more than one house?) and on whether historical, or only current, data is to be stored. The entity-relationship occurrence diagrams should be similar to those in Fig. 9.3.

3. The Department data cannot be stored until the Employee data is stored, but the Employee data cannot be stored until the Department data is stored. So neither can be stored. How would you resolve this problem?

Section 9.4

1. A multiplicity of 0..0 would mean that exactly zero entity occurrences participate in the relationship. Therefore the entity does not participate in the relationship and there is no point in including this relationship in the entity-relationship diagram.

2. It is not clear whether the 1 represents 1..1, or whether it represents only one of the bounds (lower or upper) with the other bound not yet specified. Similarly for *. Unspecified values could be represented by, say, a question mark, e.g. 1..?, which would make it clear that the lower bound is 1 and the upper bound is, as yet, unspecified.

3. The multiplicities (A end first) are: (a) 1..1 and 1..1; (b) 1..1 and 1..*; (c) 1..* and 1..*; (d) 0..* and 0..*.

10

Decomposition of many:many relationships

10.1 Decomposition

A many:many relationship between two entity types can be *decomposed* into two 1:many relationships. Knowing how to perform this trick is important for two reasons. Firstly, as shown in Chapter 11, it will make it easy to spot certain unsatisfactory features which may be present in an entity-relationship type diagram; secondly, some database management systems are not capable of representing many:many relationships directly, so all such relationships must be broken down into 1:many relationships.

It is often assumed that the decomposition can be done as shown in Fig. 10.1, but such an assumption is fallacious. The fact that the relationship in Fig. 10.1a is many:many means that there is no functional dependency in either direction between Project and Employee. In Fig. 10.1b, however, the PE relationship implies a functional dependency of Project on Employee, while the EP relationship implies a functional dependency of Employee on Project. Clearly, Figs 10.1a and 10.1b are not equivalent. Another way of looking at the error is to observe that PE and EP are really trying to express the same relationship (i.e. which employees work on which projects) and it is wrong to express this single relationship as two separate relationships. It is, of course, perfectly legitimate for a diagram to have the form of Fig. 10.1b, provided that PE and EP are distinct relationship types (see, for example, question 1, section 8.5).

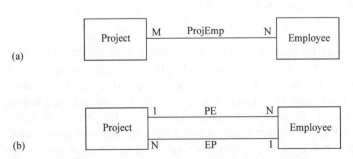

(a)

(b)

Fig. 10.1   Fallacious decomposition of many:many relationship
(a)   Relationship showing which employees work on which projects
(b)   This diagram is not equivalent to part (a)

To see how the decomposition should be done, look first at Fig. 10.2a. Each relationship occurrence corresponds to the assignment of an employee to a project; by treating each assignment as an entity occurrence, Fig. 10.2b is obtained. It is easy to see that the relationship between Project and Assignment is 1:many, and that the relationship between Employee and Assignment is 1:many. Converting the entity-relationship occurrence diagram to a type diagram yields Fig. 10.2c, and shows that the many:many relationship of Fig. 10.1a can be decomposed into two back-to-back 1:many relationships with their 'many' ends pointing towards each other.

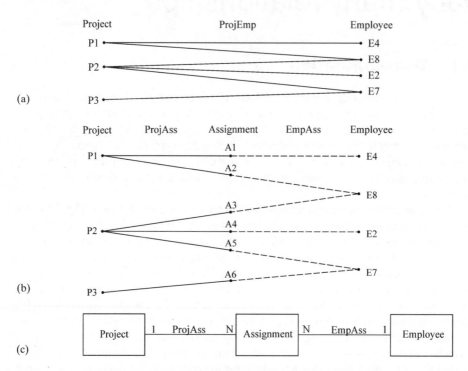

Fig. 10.2   Decomposition of many:many relationship into 1:many relationship
(a)   Single many:many relationship ProjEmp
(b)   ProjEmp decomposed into two 1:many relationships ProjAss(——) and EmpAss (----)
(c)   Entity-relationship type diagram corresponding to part (b)

A relationship can always be treated as an entity, although an entity so created may not necessarily be one which the enterprise would otherwise have recognised. If there is no obvious name for the new 'linker' entity it is convenient to use the name of the relationship which it replaces (ProjEmp in this example). Similarly, the linker entity could be given an entity identifier such as assignmentNo, but it may be more convenient to identify it by the former relationship identifier, namely {projectNo, employeeNo}. Using this notation, the decomposition of Fig. 10.2a is as shown in Fig. 10.3. Each occurrence of the ProjEmp linker entity in Fig. 10.3a necessarily links a Project occurrence to an Employee occurrence. Consequently, the participation of the ProjEmp entity type in its relationships with Project and Employee must

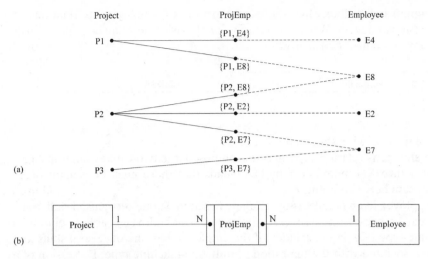

Fig. 10.3   A possible naming scheme for a linker entity type

be obligatory, as shown in Fig. 10.3b. The linker entity created by the decomposition of a many:many relationship always has obligatory participation in each of its relationships.

Questions

1.   The following table shows which suppliers supply which parts.

supplierNo	partNo
S1	P15
S1	P29
S1	P32
S2	P12
S2	P15
S3	P12
S3	P32

(a)   Draw an entity-relationship type diagram showing a single relationship between entity types Supplier and Part.
(b)   Decompose your diagram into an equivalent diagram containing only 1:many relationship types.
(c)   Draw an entity-relationship occurrence diagram showing the above data as two 1:many relationships.   (3 min)
2.   A college runs many evening classes (e.g. metalwork, pottery, art, local history). Each class may be taught by several teachers, and a teacher may teach several classes. A particular class always uses the same room (e.g. pottery always uses room R12). Because classes may meet at different times or on different evenings it is possible for different classes to share a room (e.g. pottery and art both use room R12).
(a)   Draw an entity-relationship type diagram showing the entity types Teacher, Class, Room and the relationship types TeacherClass and RoomClass.
(b)   Re-draw your type diagram, decomposing any many:many relationship into 1:many relationships.   (3 min)

3. The diagram below looks like the decomposition of a many:many relationship between Division and Dept. Would the relationship DivisionContainsDept necessarily be many:many, or could it be 1:many?   (2 min)

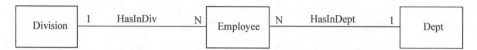

4. Which of the following statements is true?
(a) Any many:many relationship can be decomposed into two 1:many relationships.
(b) The structure X(1:many)Y(many:1)Z means that there must be a many:many relationship between X and Z.   (1 min)

5. Each employee in an engineering company has at most one recognised skill, but a given skill may be possessed by several employees. An employee is able to operate a given machine-type (e.g. lathe, grinder) if the employee has one of several skills, but each skill is associated with the operation of only one machine type. Possession of a given skill (e.g. mechanic, electrician) allows an employee to maintain several machine-types, although maintenance of any given machine-type requires a specific skill (e.g. a lathe must be maintained by a mechanic).

(a) Draw an entity-relationship type diagram, using the following entity and relationship types only:

Entity type	Relationship type	Entity type
Skill	PossessedBy	Employee
Machine-type	NeedsForOperation	Skill
Skill	AllowsMaintenanceOf	MachineType

(b) Re-draw your diagram with the NeedsForOperation and AllowsMaintenanceOf relationships combined into a single (many:many) OpOrMaint relationship.
(c) Re-draw your part (b) diagram with the many:many OpOrMaint relationship decomposed into 1:many relationships.
(d) Why is it not possible to reverse the above process, that is, given the part (c) diagram to convert it into the part (a) form?   (10 min)

6. Suppliers sell and service equipment, as illustrated in the type diagram and table occurrences below. A supplier may service equipment sold by other suppliers.

Sells	supplierNo	equipmentNo
	S1	E1
	S1	E2
	S2	E3
	S2	E4

Services	supplierNo	equipmentNo
	S1	E1
	S1	E3
	S2	E4

(a) By deriving a new table occurrence which shows which equipment each supplier sells or services, show that the result of combining the two 1:many relationships, Sells and Services, into a single SellsOrServices relationship yields a many:many rather than a 1:many relationship.

(b) Suggest a change to the enterprise rules which, without altering the entity-relationship type diagram, would make SellsOrServices a 1:many relationship.

(3 min)

Answer pointers

1. (a) Similar to Fig. 10.1a. (b), (c) Similar to Fig. 10.3.

2.

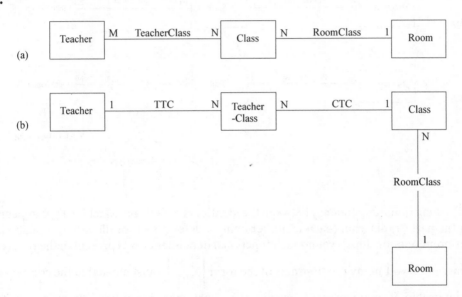

(a)

(b)

The entity name 'Class' illustrates nicely the ambiguity of language. For example:

(i) Is pottery Monday 7–8 p.m. a different class to pottery Wednesday 8–9 p.m.?

(ii) Is pottery Monday 7–8 p.m. in week 1 a different class to pottery Monday 7–8 p.m. in week 2?

(iii) Suppose there are enough students to allow two distinct pottery groups to be run. Is there one pottery class, or two?

In designing a conceptual model it is vital to know just what each entity (and relationship) type represents. An important step in defining an entity type is to define its identifier. Is it, for example, className, or {className, time}, or {className, time, weekNo}, or {className, groupNo}? A constant danger is that the meaning attached to a word may vary with context or user. (Question: 'How many classes have you taught this year?' Answer 1: 'Two. Pottery and metalwork.' Answer 2: 'Forty-six. Twenty pottery and twenty-six metalwork.')

3. DivisionContainsDept could be 1:many. The structure shown could support a many:many relationship, or a 1:many or 1:1 since the latter are special cases of the more general many:many. In practice, the enterprise rules would probably not allow a department to belong to more than one division. Try drawing an occurrence diagram, assuming the latter restriction applies. How could the diagram be rearranged so as to enforce a 1:many relationship between Division and Dept?

4. (a) True. (b) False, as exemplified by question 3.

5.

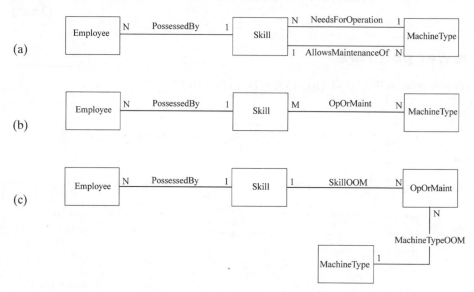

(a)

(b)

(c)

(d) Functional dependency between the identifiers of Skill and MachineType appears in the part (a) diagram (each identifier being a determinant of the other, though via different relationships), yet no such functional dependency was present in the part (c) diagram. Two 1:many relationships of the form $\begin{Bmatrix} 1:N \\ N:1 \end{Bmatrix}$ must mean that the combined relationship is many:many (consider the functional dependency between entity identifiers), so you need no information beyond that shown on the part (a) diagram to know that it can be converted into the part (b) form. Similarly the many:many relationship in part (b) can be decomposed into the part (c) form, given only the information shown on the part (b) diagram. However, you would need further information about the enterprise rules in order to (i) combine skillOOM and MachineTypeOOM into OpOrMaint (see question 3), or (ii) split OpOrMaint into NeedsForOperation and AllowsMaintenanceOf.

Try drawing occurrence diagrams for parts (a) and (b) (omit Employee and PossessedBy, and use different colours to distinguish occurrences of NeedsForOperation and AllowsMaintenanceOf). Can you tell by inspection of your part (c) diagram which of its relationship occurrences belong to NeedsForOperation and which to AllowsMaintenanceOf? (The answer should be no. But what if OpOrMaint could have an attribute attached ... ? Now read on ...)

6. (a)

SellsOrServices	supplierNo	equipmentNo
	S1	E1
	S1	E2
	S1	E3
	S2	E3
	S2	E4

Inspection of the table shows that a supplier may sell-or-service many items of equipment, and an equipment item (e.g. E3) may be sold-or-serviced by many suppliers, so the relationship is many:many.

(b)   'Equipment is serviced by the supplier who sells it.' This rule would eliminate row {S1, E3}.

11

Connection traps

11.1 Introduction

This chapter examines several pitfalls which the designers and users of a conceptual model must take care to avoid. In each case the problem arises because of a misinterpretation of the meaning of certain relationships. The term *connection trap* will be used to describe any such interpretation error; the terms *fan trap* and *chasm trap* will be applied to particular cases to indicate the cause of the problem. Any conceptual model will contain potential connection traps. Many of these may be of no significance to the enterprise; others can be avoided by restructuring the conceptual model. Either way, their existence must be recognised so that they can be eliminated or else given a clean bill of health. We will start with some trivial cases, and progress to those that are rather less obvious.

11.2 Misinterpretation

The meaning of any relationship type must be carefully defined, and thoroughly understood, in order to avoid errors of misinterpretation. For example, the relationship Tutors in Fig. 11.1 could refer to subject-tutorship, personal-tutorship, or both of these.

Fig. 11.1   What does Tutors mean? Subject-tutorship? Personal-tutorship? Both of these?

An error in the interpretation of the meaning may cause the database to be incapable of storing certain information (e.g. personal as distinct from subject tutorships), or may mean that information retrieved from the database is interpreted incorrectly (e.g. a list of tutors might be interpreted as being a list of personal tutors when it is actually a list of subject tutors).

Question

1.

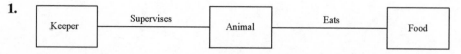

The above entity-relationship structure can represent:

(a)   which keeper supervises which animal;
(b)   which food an animal eats;
(c)   which food a keeper supervises;
(d)   which food a keeper eats;
(e)   which animal likes which food;
(f)   which animal is fed by which keeper.
Which of the above statements are true? You may wish to qualify a simple true/false
decision with some additional comment.   (5 min)

11.3   Fan traps

A relationship fan exists where two or more relationship occurrences of the same type fan
out from the same entity occurrence. Some of the more deceptive connection traps are
associated with structures where fans belonging to different relationship types can emanate
from the same entity occurrence, in other words the structure is of the form many:1/1:many.

    Looking at Fig. 11.2a, it might be thought that the existence of a connection from
Department to Employee via Division means that it would always be possible to deduce
which employees belong to which departments. Figure 11.2b demonstrates that this is
not so, there being no way of knowing which of employees 1, 2, 3 belong to department
1, and which to department 2. Similarly, employee 4 could belong to department 3 and
employee 5 to department 4, or *vice versa*. It is also conceivable that some employees,
for example technical advisers, may be regarded as belonging to divisions but not to
departments.

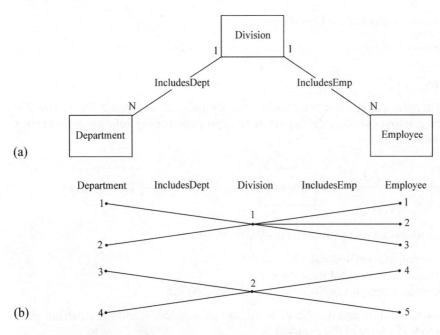

Fig. 11.2   Connection trap between Department and Employee
(a)   Type diagram
(b)   Occurrence diagram

Figure 11.3 shows another attempt at an entity-relationship structure for the Division/Department/Employee problem, and one which better reflects the natural hierarchy which usually exists among divisions, departments and employees. This structure eliminates the ambiguity about which employees belong to which department and, furthermore, there is no doubt as to which employees belong to which division (provided that all employees in a department are regarded as belonging to that department's division). The problem of employees who belong to divisions but not departments is examined in the next section.

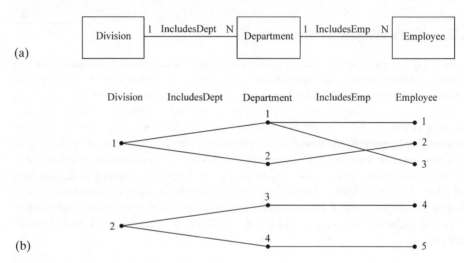

(a)

(b)

Fig. 11.3   Revised entity-relationship structure
(a)   Type diagram
(b)   Occurrence diagram

Questions

1.   Each department in a company has its own company car which may be used only by authorised employees within the department. A proposed entity-relationship structure is shown below:

The attributes associated with each entity are:

>   Car: registrationNo, make
>   Department: deptName, location
>   Employee: employeeNo, employeeName, jobTitle

(a)   If you know the employeeNo of an authorised employee, will the structure allow you to find details of the car used?

(b)   If you know the registrationNo of a car, will you be able to find which employees are authorised to use the car?

(c) How could the type diagram be extended, by the addition of a further relationship, so that it can represent authorised users?

(d) How could authorised users be represented if a further attribute were allowed?

(e) Assess the merits of replacing the UsedBy relationship between Car and Department with a UsedBy relationship between Car and Employee.

(f) Suggest a change to the enterprise rules which leaves the type diagram unaltered, but which eliminates the potential connection trap between Car and Employee.

(10 min)

2. With reference to Fig. 11.2 suggest a pair of (rather unlikely) enterprise rules which would make the association of employees with departments unambiguous. (1 min)

3. Suppose the identifiers of Division, Department, Employee, are divisionName, departmentName, employeeNo, respectively. Other attributes of interest are divisionLocation, departmentBudget, employeeName, and employeeSalary. Assuming plausible enterprise rules, and ignoring possible complications (e.g. employees who work for divisions but not departments), draw a determinancy diagram and derive a set of fully-normalised tables. Compare your answer with the structure shown in Fig. 11.3a. (5 min)

11.4   Chasm traps

A chasm trap occurs where a type diagram suggests the existence of a relationship between entity types, but where a path might not actually exist between certain entity occurrences. Suppose some employees are attached to divisions as technical advisers, but are not regarded as belonging to a department. The structure of Fig. 11.3 would be unsuitable as it does not allow an employee to be linked directly to a division, but only via a department. One solution would be to invent a dummy department for each division which has technical advisers. However, if the conceptual model is to mirror the real-world situation accurately, it should not contain dummy departments which do not exist in the real world. An alternative solution would be to add a third relationship type linking Division and Employee directly.

The basic problem is once again one of faulty interpretation. The implied relationships DivisionIncludesEmployee and DivisionIncludesDepartmentWhichIncludesEmployee are equivalent for most employees, but not for those who are technical advisers. The non-obligatory participation of Employee in IncludesEmp means that some employees cannot be connected to a division via a department.

Questions

1. Explain why the structure below contains a potential chasm trap.

(1 min)

2. Assess the merits of adding a third 1:many relationship to:

(a) Fig. 11.3a to connect Division and Employee directly;

(b)   Fig. 11.2a to connect Department and Employee directly;
(c)   the type diagram in question 1 above, to connect Division and Department
       directly.   (5 min)

11.5   Further fan traps

Our final example is of a situation which cannot be resolved merely by adding an
additional relationship type. Suppose any supplier can supply any part to any customer.
An attempt at an entity-relationship diagram is shown in Fig. 11.4a. By decomposing
the many:many relationships into 1:many relationships (Fig. 11.4b) it can be seen that
the diagram conceals a many:1/1:many structure, and should therefore be regarded
with particular caution. A fairly obvious connection trap in this case is that we cannot
show unambiguously which supplier supplies which customer (unless there are special
restrictions in the enterprise rules). However, we shall see that this is not the only
connection trap lurking within this example.

   Suppose the arrangements for supplying customers are as shown in Table 11.A.
Putting this data on an occurrence diagram gives Fig. 11.4c. The only relationship types
available are SuppPart and PartCust, so the data that can be represented on the
diagram is actually that shown in Table 11.B. It is not possible to tell from Fig. 11.4c
which supplier supplies which customer. Notice that the diagram is consistent with
supplier S1 supplying part P1 to customer C2, although we know from Table 11.A that
S1 does not, in fact, supply C2.

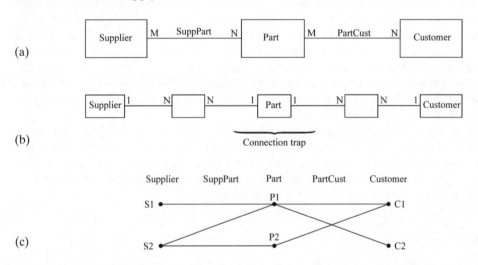

Fig. 11.4   Connection trap
(a)   Type diagram
(b)   Decomposition of type diagram
(c)   Occurrence diagram

   So far the problem is similar to that illustrated in Fig. 11.2. In the present case, the
ambiguity in the relationship of suppliers to customers can be resolved by adding a new
relationship, SuppCust (Fig. 11.5). By following the SuppCust relationship occurrences

Table 11.A

S1 supplies P1 to C1
S2 supplies P1 to C2
S2 supplies P2 to C1

Table 11.B

S1 supplies P1 | P1 is supplied to C1
S2 supplies P1 | P1 is supplied to C2
S2 supplies P2 | P2 is supplied to C1

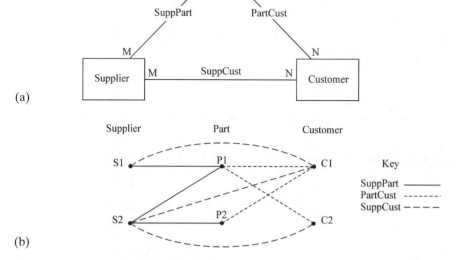

(a)

(b)

Fig. 11.5 Addition of SuppCust relationship
(a) Type diagram
(b) Occurrence diagram

in Fig. 11.5b, it can be seen that supplier S1 does supply customer C1, but does not supply customer C2. There is still, however, a further connection trap. We can tell which supplier supplies which parts, which parts are supplied to which customers, and which suppliers supply which customers; but we still cannot be certain about which suppliers supply which parts to which customers. For example, Fig. 11.5b is consistent not only with the data in Table 11.A, but also with supplier S2 supplying part P1 to customer C1. Once again, the root of the problem is the many:1/1:many double-fan structure. Inspection of Fig. 11.6, which represents the 1:many decomposition of Fig. 11.5a, shows that it is impossible to get between Supplier and Customer via Part without crossing a many:1/1:many structure, and the same is true for routes Part-Customer-Supplier and Customer-Supplier-Part.

The clue to an entity-relationship structure which will avoid this connection trap lies in an examination of Tables 11.A and 11.B. The data in Table 11.B relates entities in pairs, whereas Table 11.A shows the relationship between all three entities simultaneously. This suggests the solution, namely that all three entity types should be associated via a single relationship type, as in Fig. 11.7. A relationship type that involves three (or more) entity types is represented by a diamond (Fig. 11.7a). Each relationship occurrence appears as a three-armed 'starfish' (Fig. 11.7b).

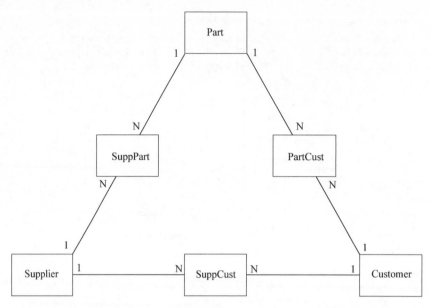

Fig. 11.6   Addition of SuppCust eliminates one connection trap, but leaves another

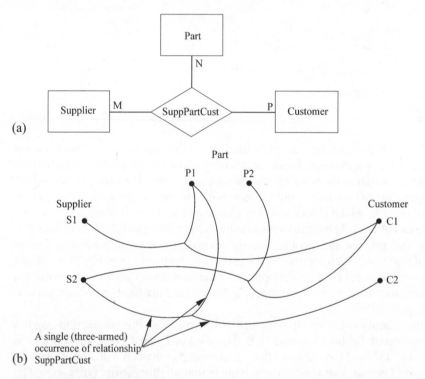

(a)

(b)   SuppPartCust

Fig. 11.7   Three-way relationship
(a)   A single relationship type connecting three entity types
(b)   Occurrence diagram for part (a) (using the data in Table 11.A, and showing the three occurrences of relationship SuppPartCust)

In general, any number of entity types may participate in the same relationship, but in practice it is unusual to find a need for relationships which involve more than three or four entity types. Relationships between two entity types are adequate for most purposes, so take care not to complicate conceptual models through the unnecessary inclusion of more complex relationships.

Questions

1. There may be many parts in a supplier's catalogue which are not currently the subject of a contract with a customer. Similarly, a supplier may be granted approved-supplier status by a customer, even though no contract is in force. Assuming that SuppPartCust in Fig. 11.7a represents only current contractual arrangements between suppliers, parts and customers, suggest how the type diagram could be extended to represent the non-contractual information as well.   (3 min)

2. The identifiers of Supplier, Part, Customer, are supplierNo, partNo, customerNo, respectively. Any supplier may supply any part to any customer. The conceptual model needs to represent who supplies what to whom. Assuming plausible enterprise rules, draw a determinancy diagram which includes the entity identifiers together with supplierName, partDescription, unitPrice, customerName and creditStatus. Derive a set of fully-normalised tables, and compare these with Fig. 11.7a.   (5 min)

3. Investigate the application of the bottom-up approach of question 2 to the problem posed in question 1.   (5 min)

11.6   Decomposition of complex relationships

The terms *binary* and *complex* will be used to distinguish relationships involving two entities from those involving more than two entities. It is sometimes helpful in interpreting an entity-relationship diagram, or necessary in view of constraints imposed by a DBMS, to treat a complex relationship as an entity. Any complex relationship can be broken down into a number of binary relationships, in much the same way as a binary many:many relationship is decomposed into 1:many relationships. The complex relationship is not really eliminated; it is more that it assumes a different form. The caveat about avoiding unnecessarily complex relationships still applies.

As an example of the decomposition of a complex relationship, compare Figs 11.7 and 11.8. The relationship type SuppPartCust in Fig. 11.7a is re-interpreted as the entity type Contract in Fig. 11.8a. The identifier of SuppPartCust, namely {supplierNo, partNo, customerNo}, is a candidate identifier for Contract (it might be worth inventing a new identifier, such as contractNo). In terms of occurrence diagrams, each relationship occurrence in Fig. 11.7b has become a Contract entity occurrence in Fig. 11.8b. (Imagine that each 'starfish' in Fig. 11.7b has a dot drawn on its body; each dot represents a Contract entity.)

11.7   Summary

The purpose of this chapter is to alert the reader to the possibility of connection traps, and to give examples of commonly occurring situations, rather than to offer an

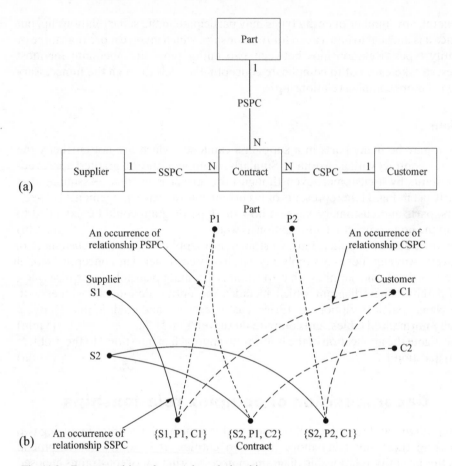

Fig. 11.8   Decomposition of a complex relationship
(a)   Type diagram
(b)   Occurrence diagram for part (a) (using the data in Table 11.A)

exhaustive classification. It is important to check that all the relationship types that a particular conceptual model must support are actually catered for by a proposed entity-relationship structure. A clear understanding of the semantics of relationships is essential; knowledge of a relationship's degree is important but is not the whole story: there may be other enterprise rules which affect the validity of a conceptual model. Remember to check that implied relationship types (those involving a path through more than one relationship type) really do mean what you think they mean.

Often, a potential connection trap does not matter because the enterprise is not interested in a particular relationship. Depending on circumstances, connection traps can be eliminated from entity-relationship structures by rearranging relationships, by adding further relationships, or by defining a complex relationship (or its equivalent decomposition). The temptation to smother an entity-relationship diagram with every conceivable relationship between the entity types should be resisted, as it will introduce redundancy and unnecessary logical complexity. For a first stage conceptual model the aim should be to minimise complexity. The inclusion of relationships which provide short-cuts between entities, but are not otherwise necessary, should be viewed in this light.

As hinted at by some of the questions and answer pointers, a bottom-up approach looking at the functional dependencies between identifiers can help in selecting appropriate relationship types.

Questions

1. The table below shows which lecturers lecture on which subjects to which students. Lecturers, subjects and students are identified by lecturerName, subjectName and studentNo, respectively.

lecturerName	subjectName	studentNo
Jones	Physics	S1
Jones	Physics	S2
Brown	Physics	S1
Brown	Physics	S2
Brown	Biology	S2

Assume an entity-relationship structure with three binary relationship types, LecturerSubject, SubjectStudent, LecturerStudent. By drawing an occurrence diagram for the data in the table, show that the structure contains a connection trap. Draw the type diagram of a more suitable structure.   (5 min)

2. Each subject is taught by only one lecturer, but a lecturer may teach many subjects. A subject may be attended by many students and a student may attend many subjects. Devise a suitable entity-relationship structure containing only two binary relationships.
                                                                        (5 min)

3. A conceptual model is to represent the authors and subject classifications of books. There are no functional dependencies between the identifiers of the entity types Author, Book, Subject, but an author is always associated with all the subject classifications applicable to a book he or she has written.

Assess the merits of each of the following structures. Which structure would you recommend, and why?   (5 min)

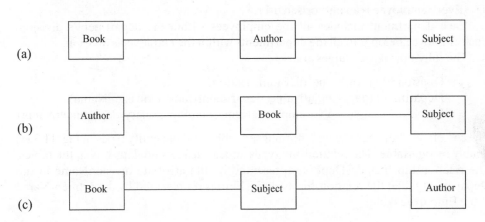

(a)   Book ——— Author ——— Subject

(b)   Author ——— Book ——— Subject

(c)   Book ——— Subject ——— Author

Answer pointers

Section 11.2

1. (a)   Probably true, although to assume automatically an anthropocentric view simply reveals one's prejudices. It may be that it is the animals which supervise the keepers.
(b)   Probably true.
(c)   The relationship implied between Keeper and Food is that of a KeeperSupervisesAnimalWhichEatsFood relationship, not a KeeperSupervisesFood relationship; the two can be equated only if there is some further enterprise rule such as 'a keeper who supervises an animal also supervises the food eaten by that animal'. If necessary, a SupervisesFood relationship could be added to the diagram.
(d)   A similar situation to (c). Why is it more obvious that (d) is false than that (c) is false?
(e)   False, unless there is an enterprise rule such as 'an animal eats only food that it likes'.
(f)   False, unless supervision includes feeding.

Section 11.3

1.   (a) Yes. (b) No. You cannot tell which branches of the Contains relationship fan should be used.
(c)   A relationship type AuthorisedUser could be added between Car and Employee, or between Department and Employee.
(d)   Associate an authorisedUser attribute with each Employee occurrence. The value of authorisedUser would be true or false.
   For solutions (c) and (d), what are the consequences of an employee being moved to another department?
(e)   The advantage is that a car can be associated with its authorised users. Disadvantages are that a car might erroneously be associated with several departments (e.g. if an employee changes department); that a department which temporarily has no authorised users will lose track of its car; and that access between Department and Car entails a search for an authorised user.
(f)   Every employee is an authorised user.
2.   Each department includes all the employees within the department's division. Each employee belongs to all the departments within the employee's division.
3.   The fully-normalised tables are:

> Division (<u>divisionName</u>, divisionLocation)
> Department (<u>departmentName</u>, departmentBudget, divisionName)
> Employee (<u>employeeNo</u>, employeeName, employeeSalary, departmentName)

The correlation between the well-normalised tables and the entity types in Fig. 11.3a is readily recognisable. The relationship types appear in a less obvious way in the tables. The relationship IncludesDept is represented by the attribute divisionName in the Department table; the relationship IncludesEmp is represented by departmentName in the Employee table.

Section 11.4

1. The association between a division and a department depends on there being at least one employee in the department.
2. (a) The extra relationship would cater for employees who belong to divisions as well as, or instead of, departments.
(b) and (c) yield the same structure as for (a).

Section 11.5

1. Extend Fig. 11.7a by inserting a CanSupply relationship between Supplier and Part, and an ApprovedSupplier relationship between Supplier and Customer. The latter assumes that approved-supplier status implies general approval, rather than approval for specific parts.
2. The fully-normalised tables are:

> Supplier (supplierNo, supplierName)
> Part (partNo, partDescription, unitPrice)
> Customer (customerNo, customerName, creditStatus)
> SuppPartCust (supplierNo, partNo, customerNo)

Given the above choice of table names, the correlation with Fig. 11.7a is obvious. Notice, in particular, that the relationship type SuppPartCust is represented by the SuppPartCust table type.
3. The relationship CanSupply could be shown by a box around supplierNo and partNo, similarly ApprovedSupplier could be represented by a box around supplierNo and customerNo. The resulting diagram is rather confusing compared with an entity-relationship type diagram.

Section 11.7

1. Occurrence diagram

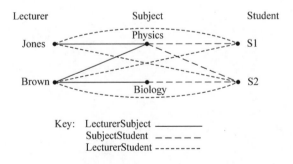

The diagram cannot show unambiguously whether Brown teaches Physics to student S2.

A suitable type diagram is shown below.

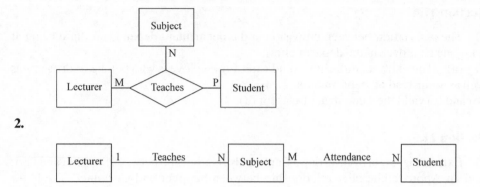

Any other linear arrangement suffers from a connection trap.

3. Every relationship is many:many. In each case, decomposition to 1:many relationships reveals a many:1/1:many connection trap. However, in (b) the connection trap does not matter because an author is to be associated with all the subject classifications applicable to his or her books.

12

Skeleton entity-relationship models

12.1   Introduction

Although an entity-relationship type diagram describes many of the important features of a conceptual model, it does not show the attributes associated with the entity and relationship types. This additional information can be represented conveniently in the form of a set of fully-normalised table types. In principle, one could define a table type for each and every entity and relationship type, but the number of table types so generated would often be unnecessarily large.

In practice, an entity type is almost always represented by its own table type, whereas most relationship types are not. On E-R type diagrams, we will use a suitable annotation within the symbols « » (known as guillemets) to indicate the exceptions. We will indicate the absence of a table for an entity type by the annotation «no table» and the presence of a table for a relationship type by «table». If preferred, every entity type or relationship type could be annotated with «table» or «no table», but we will annotate only the exceptions.

As a first step in deciding which table types are required in practice, it will be helpful to develop criteria for deciding how different kinds of relationship can best be represented. Keep in mind that the initial objective is to define a simple high-level, implementation-independent model which can be used as a basis for further refinement; decisions made at this stage are not irrevocable.

For the sake of brevity the term *entity-relationship* will be abbreviated to *E-R*. The combination of an E-R type diagram and its associated set of fully-normalised table types will be called an *E-R model*. It will be convenient to start by building a *skeleton E-R model*, that is one in which the table types contain only identifiers.

12.2   Representation of 1:1 relationships

Suppose company cars are assigned to company employees on a 1:1 basis, that is no car is shared between employees, and no employee has the use of more than one car. Employees and cars are identified by employeeNo and carNo (the vehicle registration number on the licence plate), respectively. This situation will be modelled by a 1:1 relationship Uses between the entity types Employee and Car. The way in which the Uses relationship is represented will depend, at this stage, purely on the participation conditions of the entity types.

12.2.1   Participation obligatory for both entity types (Fig. 12.1)

Suppose every employee has a company car and every company car is used by an employee. In this case, all the attributes of both entity types will be put into a single table type. Car attributes (such as carNo, make and model) can be regarded simply as additional attributes of Employee, and included in an Employee table type. The Uses relationship is represented implicitly by the presence of employeeNo and carNo in the same table type, rather than explicitly by a separate Uses table type; similarly there is no need for a separate Car table type. The Car attributes are said to be *posted* into the Employee table type.

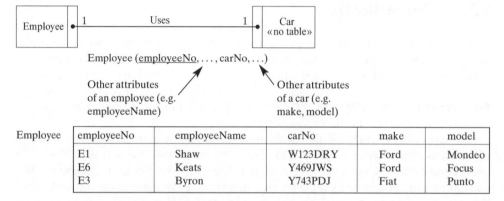

Employee	employeeNo	employeeName	carNo	make	model
	E1	Shaw	W123DRY	Ford	Mondeo
	E6	Keats	Y469JWS	Ford	Focus
	E3	Byron	Y743PDJ	Fiat	Punto

Fig. 12.1   1:1 relationship. Participation obligatory for both entity types. Strictly speaking, there is no distinction between 'other attributes of an employee' and 'other attributes of a car', since they are all attributes of the same Employee table

The E-R model could be redesigned at this point to show only an Employee entity type but, partly because it is a nuisance to re-draw the E-R diagram, and partly because having done so there might be reasons for re-instating Car and Uses at a later stage, it is simpler to take the view that Car and Uses still exist in the model even though they will not be represented explicitly by separate table types. In Fig. 12.1, the absence of a table type for Car is indicated by «no table». There is no need to annotate Uses, as the default for relationship types is «no table» (see section 12.1).

Questions

1.   Name two candidate identifiers for the Employee table type defined in Fig. 12.1.
(1 min)

2.   An alternative solution to the model of Fig. 12.1 would be to specify a Car table type and put the «no table» annotation in Employee, but not Car. Which solution, if any, is better?
(1 min)

12.2.2   Participation obligatory for only one entity type (Fig. 12.2a)

Suppose every company car is used by an employee, but not every employee has a company car. The fact that Employee has non-obligatory participation in Uses means that attributes of cars are not attributes of employees in general, but are attributes only of certain employees. In view of this, it is conceptually simpler to define separate table types for Car and Employee. To include all employee and car attributes in a single entity table type would have the drawback that for some entity occurrences (rows in the table) the car attributes would be null (Fig. 12.2b).

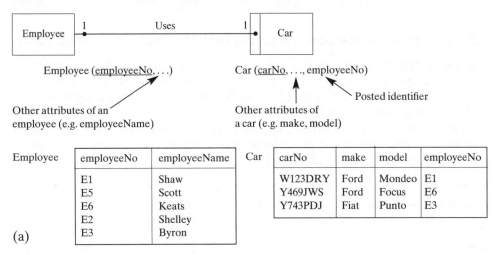

Employee (employeeNo, ...)

Car (carNo, ..., employeeNo)

Posted identifier

Other attributes of an employee (e.g. employeeName)

Other attributes of a car (e.g. make, model)

Employee

employeeNo	employeeName
E1	Shaw
E5	Scott
E6	Keats
E2	Shelley
E3	Byron

Car

carNo	make	model	employeeNo
W123DRY	Ford	Mondeo	E1
Y469JWS	Ford	Focus	E6
Y743PDJ	Fiat	Punto	E3

(a)

Employee (employeeNo, employeeName, carNo, make, model)

Employee

employeeNo	employeeName	carNo	make	model
E1	Shaw	W123DRY	Ford	Mondeo
E5	Scott	<null>	<null>	<null>
E6	Keats	Y469JWS	Ford	Focus
E2	Shelley	<null>	<null>	<null>
E3	Byron	Y743PDJ	Fiat	Punto

(b)

Fig. 12.2   1:1 relationship. Participation obligatory for only one entity type
(a)   Separate table types for Employee and Car. The Uses relationship is represented by a posted identifier
(b)   A single table type for all attributes contravenes the design rule that a posted identifier (carNo) must not be null

Should a separate table type be defined for Uses? In fact this is not necessary as the relationship can be represented most simply by posting the identifier of Employee (but not any of the other attributes of Employee) into the Car table type, as shown in Fig. 12.2a. Notice that the posted identifier employeeNo forms a logical link between an Employee occurrence and a Car occurrence, and also that it will never be null in Car because every car is used by an employee. The absence of a table type for Uses is implied by default (see section 12.1).

At the present design stage we will insist that a relationship is always represented by a posted identifier, provided that the table will remain normalised (no repeating group) and that the posted identifier can never be null. If either of these conditions would be violated, a separate relationship table will be used instead. Further examples of the application of this rule appear in the following sections.

Questions

1. Why, in Fig. 12.2a, is employeeNo posted to Car, instead of carNo being posted to Employee?   (2 min)

2. Why, in Fig. 12.2a, is employeeNo the only attribute posted into Car? Why not post other attributes of an employee, such as employeeName, as well?   (2 min)

12.2.3   Participation non-obligatory for both entity types (Fig. 12.3)

Suppose employees do not necessarily have company cars, and cars (for example those newly acquired) are not necessarily used by employees. It follows that the Uses relationship cannot be represented by posting employeeNo to Car, nor by posting carNo to Employee, since nulls would be necessary in either case. The solution is to represent Uses by a separate relationship table type. Just as an entity table type always contains the entity's identifier, so a relationship table type contains the relationship's identifier, in this case {employeeNo, carNo}.

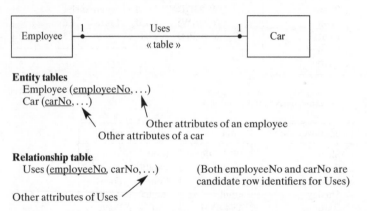

Fig. 12.3   1:1 relationship. Participation non-obligatory for both entity types

Question

1. In Fig. 12.3 the relationship identifier for Uses is {employeeNo, carNo}, but only employeeNo is underscored. Why?   (1 min)

12.2.4   Summary

For the initial high-level design the basic idea is to minimise the number of table types, subject to the rule that tables must be normalised and posted identifiers may not be null. At a later stage this rule will be relaxed; its application to the initial design means that the design can begin to take shape without the process being cluttered by detailed considerations such as 'what proportion of entity occurrences participate in the relationship?'.

For a 1:1 relationship the rules are as follows.

(a)   If participation is obligatory for both entity types, put all attributes into a single table type.

(b) If participation is obligatory for only one entity type, define two table types, one for each entity. Post the identifier of the non-obligatory entity into the obligatory entity's table type.

(c) If participation is non-obligatory for both entity types, define three table types, one for each entity and one for the relationship.

12.3   Representation of 1:many relationships

Consider the assignment of patients to hospital wards. The relationship Contains between entity types ward and Patient is 1:many (if current assignments only are considered) since a ward may contain many patients but a patient cannot be assigned to more than one ward. The identifiers of Ward and Patient are assumed to be wardName and patientNo, respectively. The participation condition of Ward (the entity at the '1' end of the relationship) is not important for the present discussion, but the participation condition of Patient (the entity at the 'many' end of the relationship) is crucial.

12.3.1   Participation of 'many' entity type obligatory (Fig. 12.4)

Suppose every patient must belong to a ward. In other words, the data is purely about in-patients. The simplest way to represent the Contains relationship is to post the identifier of Ward (i.e. wardName) into the Patient table type. Each Patient entity occurrence will contain precisely one non-null occurrence of wardName, since every patient belongs to precisely one ward. Only two table types are needed in all, one for Ward and one for Patient.

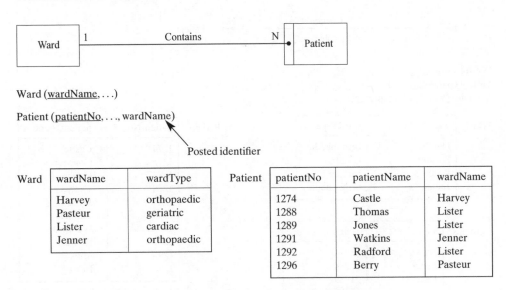

Fig. 12.4   1:many relationship. Participation obligatory for 'many' entity type

Notice that the identifier of the '1' entity type is posted into the table type for the 'many' entity type, and that posting a 'many' identifier to a '1' table type would be unsatisfactory. For instance, if patientNo were posted to Ward, each Ward entity occurrence, as identified by wardName, would then contain a repeating group of patientNo values. Although the repeating group could be eliminated by splitting the table into two, a superfluous table would be created in the process (see question 1 below).

Question

1.   Suppose patientNo were posted into Ward, so creating a repeating group, as shown below:

Ward (<u>wardName</u>, wardType, Patient (patientNo))

Each ward is of only one ward-type (e.g. orthopaedic). Eliminate the repeating group by splitting the Ward table, and comment on the result.   (3 min)

12.3.2   Participation of 'many' entity type non-obligatory (Fig. 12.5)

Suppose some patients do not belong to a ward. That is, there may be data about both in-patients and out-patients. In this situation it is not possible to post wardName into the Patient table type without introducing a null wardName occurrence for every out-patient. The preferred solution at this stage is therefore to define a separate table type for the Contains relationship, in addition to the table types for Ward and Patient. As usual, the skeleton relationship table contains just the relationship's identifier. For each in-patient only, there will be one row in the Contains relationship table.

Ward (<u>wardName</u>, ...)
Patient (<u>patientNo</u>, ...)
Contains (wardName, <u>patientNo</u>, ...)

Ward	wardName	wardType
	Harvey	orthopaedic
	Pasteur	geriatric
	Lister	cardiac
	Jenner	orthopaedic

Patient	patientNo	patientName
	1274	Castle
	1275	Conway
	1283	Hughes
	1288	Thomas
	1289	Jones
	1290	Thomas
	1291	Watkins
	1292	Radford
	1295	Mills
	1296	Berry

Contains	wardName	patientNo
	Harvey	1274
	Lister	1288
	Lister	1289
	Jenner	1291
	Lister	1292
	Pasteur	1296

Fig. 12.5   1:many relationship. Participation non-obligatory for 'many' entity type

Questions

1. Draw a determinancy diagram for the attributes wardName, wardType, patientNo, patientName, patientBloodGroup. Each ward is of only one wardType, and a patient has only one patientName and one patientBloodGroup. Only current assignments of patients to wards are of interest. Derive a set of fully-normalised tables. How is the relationship between the entity types Ward and Patient represented in your tables? How are out-patients distinguished from in-patients? (5 min)

2. Why, in Fig. 12.5, does the Contains table have patientNo underscored, but not wardName? (1 min)

12.3.3 Summary

For a 1:many relationship the rules for the initial high-level design are as follows.

(a) If the participation of the 'many' entity type is obligatory, define two table types, one for each entity. Post the identifier of the '1' entity into the 'many' entity's table type.

(b) If the participation of the 'many' entity type is non-obligatory, define three table types, one for each entity and one for the relationship.

12.4 Representation of many:many relationships

Figure 12.6 shows a many:many relationship between Lecturer and Student. Suppose Lecturer is identified by lecturerName and Student by studentNo. Posting studentNo into the Lecturer table type would create a repeating group of studentNo values. Similarly, posting lecturerName into the Student table type would create a repeating group of lecturerName values. The relationship should therefore be represented by a separate Tutorship table type.

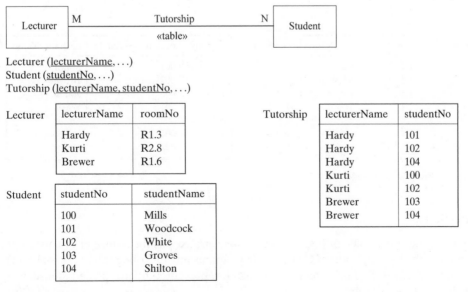

Lecturer (<u>lecturerName</u>, ...)
Student (<u>studentNo</u>, ...)
Tutorship (<u>lecturerName, studentNo</u>, ...)

Lecturer	lecturerName	roomNo
	Hardy	R1.3
	Kurti	R2.8
	Brewer	R1.6

Tutorship	lecturerName	studentNo
	Hardy	101
	Hardy	102
	Hardy	104
	Kurti	100
	Kurti	102
	Brewer	103
	Brewer	104

Student	studentNo	studentName
	100	Mills
	101	Woodcock
	102	White
	103	Groves
	104	Shilton

Fig. 12.6 Many:many relationship

The general rule for representing a many:many relationship between two entity types is as follows.

'Regardless of participation conditions, define three table types, one for each entity and one for the relationship.'

If there is one relationship between N entity types, define N entity table types and one relationship table type.

12.5   Pre-posted identifiers

Where an identifier is a composite attribute it may include as one of its components the identifier of another entity. In Fig. 12.7, SalesArea is identified by areaNo, and Customer is identified by the composite attribute {areaNo, customerSerialNo}. Customers in different areas may have the same customerSerialNo, but there are never duplicate values of customerSerialNo within the same area. It is apparent that a consequence of the way the identifiers have been chosen is that areaNo is, in effect, already posted from SalesArea into the Customer table. The Contains relationship is therefore already represented by this *pre-posted* identifier. Not surprisingly, a corollary of having chosen these identifiers is that Customer must have obligatory participation in Contains, so a posted identifier is, in any case, the natural choice for representing the relationship.

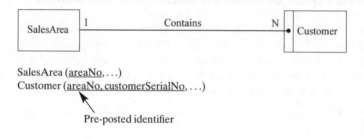

SalesArea (<u>areaNo</u>, ...)
Customer (<u>areaNo, customerSerialNo</u>, ...)

Pre-posted identifier

SalesArea	areaNo	areaName
	1	East
	2	West
	3	North
	4	South

Customer	areaNo	customerSerialNo	customerName
	1	001	Smith
	1	002	Brown
	1	003	Jones
	2	001	Ward
	2	002	Smith
	4	001	Harding
	4	002	Niven

Fig. 12.7   Pre-posted identifier

Questions

1.   Why does the choice of {areaNo, customerSerialNo} as the identifier of Customer mean that the participation of Customer in Contains must be obligatory?   (1 min)
2.   In what sense is a many:many relationship represented by pre-posted identifiers? Use Fig. 12.6 as an example.   (1 min)

12.6   Skeleton tables

As explained previously, the first step in extending an E-R type diagram into an E-R model is to decide how the relationship will be represented in terms of identifiers. Other attributes can be omitted from the model at this stage. A table type that contains only its (entity or relationship) identifier, together with any posted identifiers, will be called a *skeleton table*. The combination of an E-R type diagram and its associated set of skeleton table types will be called a *skeleton E-R model*. A table type may be either an *entity table type* or a *relationship table type*. A row in a table will represent either an entity occurrence or a relationship occurrence.

12.7   Relationship identifiers

Usually, a relationship identifier is constructed simply by concatenating the identifiers of the entities which participate in the relationship. An exception to this rule arises where the same entity occurrences can be connected by more than one occurrence of the same relationship. Figure 12.8 represents the appointments made by patients to see doctors. It is assumed that a doctor is identified by his or her name, and a patient by a patientNo, and that an historical record of appointments is to be kept. Because a patient may have more than one appointment with the same doctor, an occurrence of Appointment cannot necessarily be identified by the concatenation of the entity identifiers, namely {doctorName, patientNo}. One, or more, additional attributes must be included. In this example, assuming that a patient cannot make more than one appointment with the same doctor on the same day, a suitable choice of relationship identifier would be {doctorName, patientNo, appointmentDate}.

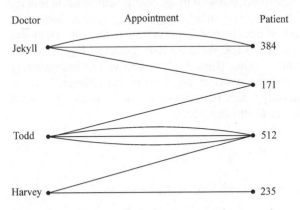

Fig. 12.8   Multiple relationship occurrences between the same entity occurrences

Questions

1.   Suppose a patient can make more than one appointment with the same doctor on the same day. Suggest two possible choices for an identifier of Appointment.   (1 min)
2.   Suppose more than one patient may arrange to see a doctor at the same time. For example, partners may arrange a joint consultation with their doctor. Also assume that

patients may make several appointments on the same day. Would {doctorName, patientNo, appointmentDate, appointmentTime} be suitable as a relationship identifier for Appointment?   (3 min)

3. Every student must enrol on a course at the start of each academic year. A record of all enrolments for the past ten years is kept. A student may not enrol on more than one course in any one year, but a course may last up to four years. Suggest an identifier for the relationship Enrolment.   (1 min)

12.8   Relationship vs row identifiers

Although an entity identifier is the same as the row identifier of its associated entity table type, a similar correspondence does not necessarily hold true for relationship identifiers. For example, in Fig. 12.5 the relationship identifier of Contains is {wardName, patientNo}, but the row identifier of Contains is patientNo on its own, since a patientNo value is sufficient to identify a row in the table.

For a 1:1 or 1:many relationship there will always be a difference between the relationship and row identifiers because at least one of the entity identifiers contained in the relationship identifier will be a determinant of the other entity identifier. In most many:many relationships the row and relationship identifiers are one and the same thing.

The distinction between row and relationship identifiers is important. You need the relationship identifier to construct a skeleton relationship table, but it is the row identifier that matters when the Boyce/Codd rule is used to check that the table will remain well-normalised after any further attributes are added, a procedure which is discussed in the next chapter.

If you are given the value of a relationship identifier you immediately know not only the relationship occurrence being described, but also its associated entity occurrences. However, given the value of a relationship row identifier, you may need to look up a relationship table occurrence (or an E-R occurrence diagram) first to find out about one of the associated entity occurrences. If, for the skeleton E-R model of Fig. 12.5, you were given the relationship identifier's value {Lister, 1289} you would immediately know which ward and which patient were involved. By contrast the relationship row identifier value 1289 would tell you only which patient was involved; to find the ward you would need to consult the Contains table occurrence.

12.9   Review

(i)   In the interests of achieving a simple skeleton E-R model the following rules are applied.

(a)   Do not define tables in which posted identifiers can be null.
(b)   Do not post an identifier if doing so would create a repeating group.
(c)   Do not represent a relationship by a separate table unless this is necessary to avoid violation of rules (a) and (b).

Application of these rules means that a separate relationship table type is needed for:

(a)   Any many:many relationship.

(b)   A 1:many relationship where the 'many' entity has non-obligatory participation.
(c)   A 1:1 relationship where both entities have non-obligatory participation.

(ii)   A relationship identifier is usually formed by combining the associated entity identifiers, but may occasionally require additional attributes.
(iii)   A relationship identifier may differ from the associated row identifier.

Questions

1.   Company employees may optionally be members of the company's sports club. An employee is identified by an employeeNo and a sports club member is separately identified by a membershipNo. Draw up a skeleton E-R model showing the relationship between entity types Employee and Member. How is the relationship between the entities represented?   (3 min)
2.   With reference to question 1, suppose sports club members are identified by employeeNo, not membershipNo. What difference would this make to your answer?
                                                                                    (2 min)
3.   Suppose a conceptual model of a monogamous society contains entity types Man and Woman related by a Marriage relationship showing marriages currently in force. Each individual is identified by a personalId. What is the degree of the Marriage relationship? What are the membership classes of Man and Woman in Marriage? Write down the skeleton table types.   (5 min)
4.   There is a 1:many HasOnRegister relationship between doctors and registered patients. How would you represent this relationship in terms of skeleton table types?
                                                                                    (1 min)
5.   A breed society keeps historical records of the owners of registered ponies. How would you represent the relationship between the entity types Owner and Pony in terms of skeleton table types?   (1 min)
6.   A shoe manufacturer identifies a style by a styleNo and a shoe by {styleNo, shoeSize}. How would you represent the relationship between entity types Style and Shoe in terms of skeleton table types?   (1 min)

12.10   Recursive relationships

It is not uncommon for an entity type to have a relationship with itself. The rules for representing the relationship are the same as before, but care is needed in distinguishing between the different roles played by the entity's identifier.

12.10.1   1:1 relationship

Figure 12.9 is a conceptual model for marriages currently in force in a monogamous society. The entity type Person has non-obligatory participation in the Marriage relationship since a person need not be married, so the relationship is represented by a separate table type. An occurrence of the Marriage relationship is identified by the personalId of the husband coupled with the personalId of the wife. Consequently the Person entity has two different roles in Marriage, namely Person-in-the-role-of-husband and Person-in-the-role-of-wife. To distinguish between these two roles the

E-R diagram is annotated (using guillemets) to show the roles played by Person in each side of the relationship. Also, in order to show which role is being played by each of the two personalId(s) which appear in the relationship table, the role prefixes 'husband' and 'wife' are used.

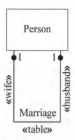

Person (<u>personalId</u>, ...)
Marriage (<u>wifePersonalId</u>, husbandPersonalId, ...)

Both wifePersonalId and husbandPersonalId are candidate keys of Marriage

Fig. 12.9   1:1 relationship of an entity type with itself; participation non-obligatory

12.10.2   1:many relationship

Figure 12.10 represents a hierarchical organisation structure. An employee may play the role of supervisor and/or the role of subordinate. Some employees do not supervise others, and the most senior employee is regarded as being self-supervised. Because the participation of Employee at the 'many' end of the relationship is obligatory, the Supervises relationship has been represented by posting the identifier of Employee-in-the-role-of-supervisor into the Employee table type. Each Employee occurrence therefore contains two employeeNo values, one identifying the employee, the other being the employeeNo of the employee's supervisor. The role prefix 'supervisor' is used to distinguish between the two roles of employeeNo.

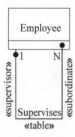

Employee (<u>employeeNo</u>, ..., supervisorEmployeeNo)

Fig. 12.10   1:many relationship of an entity type with itself; 'many' participation obligatory

12.10.3   Many:many relationship

Manufactured parts are often made by assembling other parts. Figure 12.11 shows the structure of two items, partNo(s) X and Y, made by a manufacturing company. Suppose partNo X (an improved mousetrap) is made by assembling partNo R (frame), partNo S

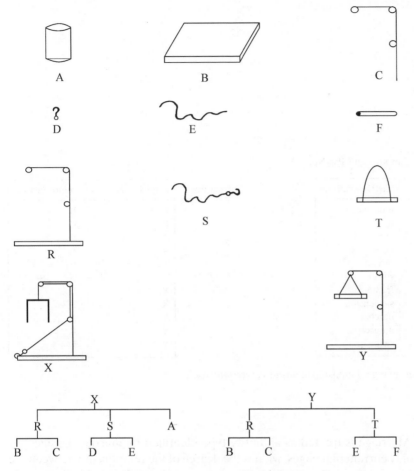

Fig. 12.11   Structure of improved mousetrap and budgerigar perch

(suspension), and partNo A (mouse-can). Suppose partNo R is, in turn, made from partNo(s) B (base) and C (arm), and partNo S is made from partNo(s) D (hook) and E (thread). To activate the mousetrap the purchaser impregnates the lower end of the thread with cream cheese (not supplied). Suppose partNo Y (a budgerigar swing) is constructed from two sub-assemblies (partNo(s) R and T) which themselves are constructed from components (partNo(s) B, C and E, F respectively).

In the E-R model of Fig. 12.12 the Part entity plays two roles. A part plays the role of a 'major' part when it is thought of as being made from other parts, for example partNo R in its role of major part is thought of as being made from partNo(s) B and C. Conversely, a part plays the role of a 'minor' part when it is thought of as being used in the making of other parts, thus partNo R in its role of minor part is thought of as being used on partNo(s) X and Y.

A part as a major part may be related to many minor parts, and a part as a minor part may be related to many major parts. The Structure relationship is therefore many:many and is represented by a separate relationship table type. The role of each partNo in the relationship table is shown by the role prefixes 'major' and 'minor'.

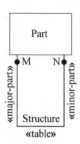

Part (partNo, ...)
Structure (majorPartNo, minorPartNo, ...)

Part	partNo	partDescription
	A	mouse-can
	B	base
	C	arm
	D	hook
	E	thread
	F	rod
	R	frame
	S	suspension
	T	perch
	X	mousetrap
	Y	swing

Structure	majorPartNo	minorPartNo
	R	B
	R	C
	S	D
	S	E
	T	E
	T	F
	X	R
	X	S
	X	A
	Y	R
	Y	T

Fig. 12.12   Many:many relationship of an entity type with itself

Questions

1. Suppose Marriage is treated as an entity type identified by marriageLicenceNo. Considering only current marriages, what is the degree of the relationship between the entity types Marriage and Person in a monogamous society? Define skeleton table types.   (3 min)

2. Draw up a skeleton E-R model, for current marriages only, of a polyandrous society. Use an entity type Person, identified by personalId, and a relationship type Marriage.   (5 min)

3. Would the answer to the previous question be changed if, instead of Person, you used the entity type MarriedPerson?   (3 min)

4. Why, in Fig. 12.12, is the participation of Part non-obligatory for both major and minor roles?   (1 min)

5. What additional rows should be entered into the table occurrences of Fig. 12.12 if:

(a)   the company makes a Christmas gift pack (partNo Z) which contains one improved mousetrap and one budgerigar swing;

(b)   cream cheese is supplied as part of each mousetrap? A pot of cheese (partNo V) is made from a carton (partNo G), a foil lid (partNo H) and a portion of cheese (partNo I).

The gift pack packaging is not regarded as being a part.   (5 min)

6. The concept of role has been introduced in the context of relationships between an entity type and itself. Is the concept more widely applicable?   (5 min)

Answer pointers

Section 12.2.1

1. employeeNo, carNo.
2. The attributes in the Car table type would be the same as those in the Employee table type in Fig. 12.1, so the only difference is that an entity would be thought of as a car with employee attributes, rather than an employee with car attributes. Most people would prefer the latter view.

Section 12.2.2

1. Because the participation of Car is obligatory, but that of Employee is non-obligatory. Consequently, if carNo were posted to Employee, some employee occurrences would contain nulls. Posting employeeNo to Car does not suffer from this disadvantage because every car is used by an employee, so the posted employeeNo will never be null.
2. There would be nowhere to post the attributes of an employee who does not use a car. The only employeeNo values posted to Car in Fig. 12.2a are those of car users.

Section 12.2.3

1. Because the underscore denotes a row identifier, not a relationship identifier. See also section 12.8. The attribute carNo could have been underscored instead, as it is also a candidate row identifier. Remember also that superfluous attributes are not allowed in an identifier.

Section 12.3.1

1. Ward1 (<u>wardName</u>, wardType)
   Ward2 (wardName, <u>patientNo</u>)
Ward1 corresponds to the original concept of the Ward entity. Ward2 corresponds to a Contains relationship table type and is therefore superfluous since it can be replaced by posting wardName into Patient. However, if the repeating group had included both patientNo and the other patient attributes, then Ward2 would itself correspond to a Patient table type containing the posted identifier wardName.

Section 12.3.2

1. The fully-normalised tables are:

> Ward (<u>wardName</u>, wardType)
> Patient (<u>patientNo</u>, patientName, patientBloodGroup, wardName)

The relationship between Ward and Patient is represented by the posted identifier wardName. Out-patients are distinguished from in-patients by the fact that wardName will be null. Bottom-up analysis always represents a 1:many relationship by a posted identifier regardless of participation conditions.

2. The underscore denotes a row identifier, not a relationship identifier (see section 12.8). The only candidate row identifier for Contains is patientNo, as the same wardName may appear on many rows.

Section 12.5

1. The identifier of Customer automatically contains an areaNo value. This attribute cannot be null, since by definition an identifier cannot contain a null (customerSerialNo on its own would not be sufficient to identify a Customer). Therefore each customer must have a non-null value of areaNo, and so must belong to a SalesArea.

2. The usual method of constructing a relationship identifier results in lecturerName and studentNo being pre-posted into the Tutorship relationship table. If an 'independent' identifier had been chosen for Tutorship, e.g. tutorshipNo, the simplest approach would have been to decompose the many:many relationship into two 1:many relationships. Tutorship then becomes an entity type, and the rules of section 12.3.1 apply, yielding the same Lecturer and Student tables as in Fig. 12.6, but changing the Tutorship table to:

Tutorship (tutorshipNo, lecturerName, studentNo, ...)

In this example, both tutorshipNo and {lecturerName, studentNo} are candidate identifiers for Tutorship.

Section 12.7

1. {doctorName, patientNo, appointmentDate, appointmentTime}. It may be sufficient to replace appointmentTime by an appointmentSequenceNo, or even a sessionNo, where the latter indicates, say, morning, afternoon or evening surgery. A unique appointmentNo could be used; if so, how would you show the connection between appointmentNo, doctorName and patientNo?

2. Yes, but note that a joint consultation would constitute several appointments. For example, with reference to Fig. 12.8, if patients 384 and 171 consult Dr Jekyll simultaneously, that constitutes two appointments that happen to coincide in time. An alternative approach would be to consider an appointment as being an event that takes place at a particular date and time involving one or more patients and one (or possibly more) doctors. A joint consultation would then be regarded as a single appointment. It is simpler to treat complicated relationships as entities. In this case, make Appointment an entity and write down its precise meaning (e.g. does an occurrence involve only one patient, or could it involve several?). Choose a suitable entity identifier. An invented entity identifier, such as appointmentNo, may be easier to deal with than a lengthy composite identifier. You can then consider the relationships that Appointment has with Patient and Doctor.

3. {studentNo, courseNo, year} where year could be the final digit of the calendar year. (Looking ahead to section 12.8, the row identifier of Enrolment would be {studentNo, year}.)

Section 12.9

1. The E-R type diagram should show a 1:1 relationship between Employee and Member. Employee has non-obligatory participation. Member has obligatory participation (assuming membership is restricted to employees). The skeleton table types are:

> Employee (<u>employeeNo</u>, ...)
> Member (<u>membershipNo</u>, ..., employeeNo)

The relationship is represented by the posted identifier employeeNo.

2. The skeleton table types would be:

> Employee (<u>employeeNo</u>, ...)
> Member (<u>employeeNo</u>, ...)

The identifier of Employee is pre-posted into Member.

3. 1:1 relationship. Non-obligatory participation. Table types:

> Man (<u>personalId</u>, ...)
> Woman (<u>personalId</u>, ...)
> Marriage (<u>wifePersonalId</u>, husbandPersonalId, ...)

The attribute husbandPersonalId is also a candidate identifier of Marriage. As there is a separate relationship table, the model (with suitable adjustment of the relationship identifier) could also hold details of previous marriages, the relationship degree then being many:many.

4. Participation of a patient in the 1:many relationship is obligatory, so post the identifier of Doctor into the Patient table type.

5. The relationship is many:many, so define a relationship table type containing the relationship's identifier. Allowing for the fact that an owner may acquire the same pony on more than one occasion, a suitable identifier could be {ownerMembershipNo, ponyRegistrationNo, dateAcquired}.

6. It is represented by the pre-posted identifier styleNo.

Section 12.10

1. 1:many. More precisely 1:2. The skeleton table types are:

> Marriage (<u>marriageLicenceNo</u>, ...)
> Person (<u>personalId</u>, ...)
> Involves (marriageLicenceNo, <u>personalId</u>, ...)

As the many end of this relationship is restricted to the small, fixed value of 2 there is a strong case for replacing Involves by two posted personalId(s) in Marriage, as follows:

> Marriage (<u>marriageLicenceNo</u>, wifePersonalId, husbandPersonalId, ...)

(Incidentally, Marriage now has three candidate identifiers, the others being the wife and husband personalId(s).) Compare the two solutions suggested, in terms of ease of access to (a) marriage-licence details given a personalId, (b) personal details given a marriageLicenceNo.

2. The skeleton E-R model will be identical to Fig. 12.9 except that the relationship is 1:many (one wife to many husbands), and that the only candidate row identifier for Marriage is husbandPersonalId.

3. No. One might be tempted to think that, because a Married-person must participate in a Marriage relationship, the participation of MarriedPerson is obligatory on both sides of the relationship. In fact this argument is fallacious because it does not take into account the different roles of MarriedPerson. A Married-person-as-husband does not participate in the 'wife' side of the relationship, nor does a Married-person-as-wife participate in the 'husband' side, so participation is non-obligatory in each case. If a posted identifier were used, it would be null for every occurrence of a female MarriedPerson.

4.   Some parts (e.g. X, Y) are not used on any other part, and so do not play the role of 'minor-part'. Some parts (e.g. A, B, C, D, E, F) are not made from any other parts, and so do not play the role of 'major-part'.

5.   (a)   The Part table will include {Z, gift pack}. The Structure table will include {Z, X} and {Z, Y}. (b) The Part table will include {V, pot of cheese}, {G, carton}, {H, foil lid} and {I, portion of cheese}. The Structure table will include {X, V} and {V, G}, {V, H}, {V, I}.

6.   Yes. For example, if an Employee entity has a Services relationship with a Customer entity, it would be helpful to annotate the relationship line connecting Employee and Services with the role name 'salesperson' to show that it is only those employees who are salespersons who service customers via this relationship. Usually a role is indicated adequately by the relationship name; for this example a name such as SellsTo or AccountExecutive would indicate the role better than Services.

In any situation where the same attribute is used in different capacities, it will be worth differentiating between its roles by qualifying its name in some way. A particular case in point concerns the representation of dates, for it would be very confusing if different types of date (e.g. order-date, invoice-date, date-of-retirement) could not be distinguished. An interesting way of looking at this example is to consider Day (date) as an entity type which has a lot of 1:many relationships (e.g. OrderedOn, InvoicedOn, RetiredOn) with other entity types. Since occurrences of Day are unlikely to be of interest in themselves, the Day entity table will be deleted (see section 13.6). Each relationship will be represented by posting date into the other entity's table type, or by its presence in a table type for the relationship. For clarity, each appearance of date will be qualified by a role name to represent the nature of the relationship. Hence the date which represents the OrderedOn relationship becomes orderDate, and similarly for the other dates.

13

Attribute assignment

13.1 Assignment rules

The next step after setting up a skeleton E-R model is to assign to the skeleton tables any further attributes which the model is to contain. The basic idea is to assign attributes in such a way that the resulting set of tables is fully-normalised. To be fully-normalised the tables must, of course, be at least well-normalised, so an attribute must not be assigned to a table if doing so would violate the Boyce/Codd rule that every determinant must be a candidate identifier.

In applying the Boyce/Codd rule to the top-down approach adopted in E-R modelling, several points must be borne in mind. Firstly, the rule applies to the row identifiers of entity and relationship tables and, in the case of 1:1 and 1:many relationships, the row identifier of a relationship table is not the same thing as the relationship identifier (see section 12.8 for the distinction). Secondly, the candidate identifiers have already been defined in the skeleton E-R model, and may not be redefined unless the skeleton model is itself revised. Changing an identifier alters the meaning of the corresponding entity or relationship, and so may affect properties such as degree and participation which, in turn, affect the specification of the skeleton tables. Consequently, further attributes must not be assigned to a skeleton table if doing so would alter the table's identifier. The third point is that the assignment of an attribute will be ambiguous if there is more than one skeleton table whose identifier is a determinant of the attribute. As a guide for resolving such ambiguities we will invoke the rule that nulls should be avoided. The final point is a reminder that fully-normalised tables must not contain repeating groups.

The rules for assigning further attributes may be summarised as follows:

(1) The final set of tables must be fully-normalised. Necessary conditions for full normalisation are:
    (a) no repeating groups;
    (b) every determinant in a table must be a candidate row identifier of the skeleton table.
(2) If there is a choice of table types for the placement of an attribute, try to avoid placing it where it will have null occurrences.

The examples which follow illustrate the assignment of attributes to skeleton tables derived in Chapter 12, though the actual attributes assigned may differ from those shown in the table occurrences in that chapter. In trying to find a home for an attribute, it may turn out that no suitable table exists in the skeleton model, in which case the model must be extended by defining further entity or relationship types as appropriate.

If the meaning of each entity and relationship type is kept clearly in mind, most decisions on attribute assignment will be perfectly straightforward. The rules proposed here are an aid to commonsense, not a substitute.

13.2   1:1 relationships

Suppose the attributes employeeName, make, carTotalMiles, currentMiles, and employeeTotalMiles are to be added to the skeleton tables defined in section 12.2 for various 1:1 relationships between Employee and Car. An employee has only one employeeName, and a car is of only one make. The attribute carTotalMiles is the cumulative mileage recorded on a car's mileometer; currentMiles is the mileage travelled by an employee in the company car which the employee is currently using, the mileage being recorded from the start of the employee's current period of use. Attribute employeeTotalMiles is the cumulative mileage travelled by an employee in company cars. Every employee has one employeeName, and every car is associated with one make and one carTotalMiles value. A value of currentMiles is applicable to every current employee/car combination. Every car user is associated with one employeeTotalMiles value.

13.2.1   Participation obligatory for both entity types

There is only one skeleton table (Fig. 12.1). All the further attributes can be assigned to this table without breaking the assignment rules, the result being:

> Employee (<u>employeeNo</u>, employeeName, employeeTotalMiles, carNo, make,
>
> carTotalMiles, currentMiles)

13.2.2   Participation obligatory for only one entity type

Every company car is used by an employee, but not every employee has a company car. The two skeleton tables (Fig. 12.2a) are:

> Employee (<u>employeeNo</u>, ...)
> Car (<u>carNo</u>, ..., employeeNo)

Attribute employeeName should, fairly obviously, be assigned to Employee; it cannot be assigned to Car because there would be nowhere to store the names of employees who do not have company cars. The car make should be assigned to Car; it should not be assigned to Employee, even though employeeNo is a determinant of make, because it would be null for each employee who does not use a company car. Likewise, carTotalMiles and currentMiles should be assigned to Car to avoid nulls in Employee.

The assignment of employeeTotalMiles is slightly more of a problem because of the non-obligatory participation of Employee in Uses. If it is assigned to Car, its value will be lost whenever an employee's use of company cars is not continuous. If, instead, it is assigned to Employee, it will be null for each employee who has never been a car user. The best choice will depend on how the data will be processed, and on how many employees are car users. If the value of employeeTotalMiles is no longer required when an employee ceases, even temporarily, to be a car user, then the attribute could be stored in Car. On the other hand, assignment to Employee would cater for breaks in car use, without consequent loss of information. At this stage there may be insufficient information to justify either solution, in which case the attribute will be assigned to Employee on the grounds that it is more obviously a property of an employee than of a car. Decisions like this will be reviewed later in the design process. The completed tables are:

> Employee (<u>employeeNo</u>, employeeName, employeeTotalMiles)
> Car (<u>carNo</u>, make, carTotalMiles, currentMiles, employeeNo)

Questions

1. It might be argued that an employee who is not currently a user of a company car should be regarded as having a zero value for currentMiles, with the consequence that this attribute could be assigned to Employee instead of Car. Suggest two disadvantages of this solution.   (2 min)

2. Suppose that the Uses relationship (Fig. 12.2a) is represented by a separate table, instead of by a posted identifier. Write down a set of table types for Employee, Car and Uses, to show how you would assign the attributes.   (5 min)

3. Suppose most employees are never authorised to use company cars. Compare the merits of the following models:

Model A
> Employee (<u>employeeNo</u>, employeeName, employeeTotalMiles)
> Car (<u>carNo</u>, make, carTotalMiles, currentMiles, employeeNo)

Model B
> Employee (<u>employeeNo</u>, employeeName)
> Car (<u>carNo</u>, make, carTotalMiles, currentMiles, employeeTotalMiles,
> employeeNo)

Model C
> Employee (<u>employeeNo</u>, employeeName)
> CarUsingEmployee (<u>employeeNo</u>, employeeTotalMiles)
> Car (<u>carNo</u>, make, carTotalMiles, currentMiles, employeeNo)   (5 min)

13.2.3   Participation non-obligatory for both entity types

Employees do not necessarily have company cars, and cars are not necessarily used by employees. The skeleton tables (Fig. 12.3) are:

> Employee (<u>employeeNo</u>, ...)
> Car (<u>carNo</u>, ...)
> Uses (<u>employeeNo, carNo</u>, ...)

The assignment of employeeName and make is straightforward. Attribute carTotalMiles can only be assigned to Car, otherwise this information will be lost whenever a car is temporarily withdrawn from use. Null occurrences of currentMiles can be avoided by placing it in Uses; it is, in any case, logically an attribute of the employee/car relationship.

As before, if there is no clear evidence to the contrary, employeeTotalMiles will be assigned to Employee. The attribute assignments are therefore:

>   Employee (<u>employeeNo</u>, employeeName, employeeTotalMiles)
>   Car (<u>carNo</u>, make, carTotalMiles)
>   Uses (<u>employeeNo</u>, carNo, currentMiles)

Attribute assignment is often more difficult for 1:1 relationships than for 1:many or many:many relationships, because the fact that each identifier is a determinant of the other means that more assignment options are available. Particular care must be taken in defining the meaning and use of attributes. In practice, most relationships are 1:many. Moreover, a many:many relationship can always be decomposed into 1:many relationships, as discussed in Chapter 10.

13.3   1:many relationships

Suppose the attributes patientName, dateOfBirth, wardType, numberOfBeds and dateOfAdmission are to be added to the skeleton tables defined in section 12.3 for 1:many relationships between Ward and Patient. Every patient has one patientName and one dateOfBirth; every ward is of one wardType and has one numberOfBeds value. Attribute dateOfAdmission refers to the date on which a patient was last admitted to the hospital as an in-patient. Once a patient is discharged from hospital, the dateOfAdmission is no longer required, even if the patient continues as an out-patient.

13.3.1   Participation of 'many' entity type obligatory

Every patient is an in-patient. The skeleton tables (Fig. 12.4) are:

>   Ward (<u>wardName</u>, ...)
>   Patient (<u>patientNo</u>, ..., wardName)

Assignment of the further attributes is straightforward:

>   Ward (<u>wardName</u>, wardType, numberOfBeds)
>   Patient (<u>patientNo</u>, patientName, dateOfBirth, dateOfAdmission, wardName)

As every patient is an in-patient, dateOfAdmission need never be null. Although wardType and numberOfBeds are functionally dependent on patientNo, they should not be assigned to Patient as the tables would not be fully-normalised.

Question

1. The tables would not be fully-normalised if either wardType or numberOfBeds were to be assigned to the Patient table. Why not?   (3 min)

13.3.2   Participation of 'many' entity type non-obligatory

Patients may be in-patients or out-patients. The skeleton tables (Fig. 12.5) are:

>   Ward (<u>wardName</u>, ...)

Patient (<u>patientNo</u>, ...)
Contains (wardName, <u>patientNo</u>, ...)

As dateOfAdmission applies only to in-patients it cannot be assigned to Patient without incurring nulls. However, it can be assigned to Contains, since this table is restricted to in-patients only. The resulting set of tables is:

Ward (<u>wardName</u>, wardType, numberOfBeds)
Patient (<u>patientNo</u>, patientName, dateOfBirth)
Contains (wardName, <u>patientNo</u>, dateOfAdmission)

Question

1. A library keeps information about its books and borrowers, including a record of which books are currently on loan to which borrowers. Each copy is identified by an accessionNo, and each borrower by a borrowerNo. Other attributes required are title, acquisitionDate, acquisitionPrice, loanDate, borrowerName, borrowerLimit. A copy has only one title. The acquisitionDate and acquisitionPrice refer to the date the library acquired the copy and the purchase price at that time. The borrowerLimit, which is the maximum number of books a borrower may have on loan at any one time, is not necessarily the same for all borrowers. Design an E-R model using Copy and Borrower for the entity types. (5 min)

13.4 Many:many relationships

Suppose the attributes roomNo, studentName, lecturerHours, studentHours, attendanceHours are to be added to the skeleton tables for Lecturer, Student and Tutorship shown in Fig. 12.6. Every student has one name, and lecturers may share the same room. Attribute lecturerHours is the total tutorial hours on a lecturer's timetable, and may vary between lecturers. Attribute studentHours is the total tutorial hours on a student's timetable, and may vary between students. Attribute attendanceHours is the total hours a given student has actually been tutored by a given lecturer.

The assignment of attributes is straightforward:

Lecturer (<u>lecturerName</u>, roomNo, lecturerHours)
Student (<u>studentNo</u>, studentName, studentHours)
Tutorship (<u>lecturerName, studentNo</u>, attendanceHours)

Questions

1. Suppose lecturerHours is redefined as meaning the total hours a lecturer has actually tutored students, and studentHours is redefined as meaning the total hours a student has been tutored by lecturers. Would any of the attributes in the Lecturer, Student or Tutorship table types be redundant? (2 min)
2. Suppose all lecturers are always timetabled for exactly the same number of tutorial hours. Should lecturerHours be assigned to Lecturer? How else might it be included in the model? (2 min)

13.5   Extending the skeleton model

In trying to find a home for an attribute, it may turn out that no suitable table exists in the skeleton model. Sometimes it may be best to redefine some of the existing entities and relationships in the skeleton model, but often it is sufficient to extend the skeleton model by adding further entity or relationship types.

For example, suppose the Ward/Patient model of section 13.3.1 should also include the attributes operationCode and operationName, where operationCode is a determinant of operationName. A patient may undergo several operations and a ward is not restricted to one type of operation, so neither the Ward nor the Patient table can be used for the new attributes. The solution is to define a new entity OperationType and a new (many:many) relationship between OperationType and Patient. The resulting E-R model is shown in Fig. 13.1. If a patient may have the same operation more than once, the identifier of Operation will need to be qualified, say by including operationDate.

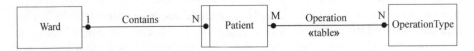

Ward (<u>wardName</u>, wardType, numberOfBeds)
Patient (<u>patientNo</u>, patientName, dateOfBirth, dateOfAdmission, wardName)
OperationType (<u>operationCode</u>, operationName)
Operation (<u>patientNo, operationCode</u>)

Fig. 13.1   Addition of OperationType entity and Operation relationship

As a second example, suppose a skeleton model contains only the table:

Patient (<u>patientNo</u>, . . .)

and that the attributes patientName, wardType, numberOfBeds and wardName are added to the model in that order. All patients are in-patients. Although patientName, wardType and numberOfBeds can be assigned to Patient without breaking the assignment rules, it would not be possible to complete the model by assigning wardName to Patient as well, since wardName would be a determinant (of wardType and numberOfBeds) without also being a candidate identifier of Patient. It is essential to check for such potential violations of the Boyce/Codd rule; if one is detected it implies that an entity type is missing. In this case, a Ward entity type is required with identifier wardName. The E-R diagram should be revised to include Ward and its relationship with Patient. The rules for constructing skeleton tables and for assigning attributes should then be re-applied. Consequently, wardName will be posted into Patient, and wardType and numberOfBeds will be re-assigned to Ward, giving:

Patient (<u>patientNo</u>, patientName, wardName)
Ward (<u>wardName</u>, wardType, numberOfBeds)

Notice that if the list of attributes had not included an identifier for a Ward entity, the other attributes of a ward (wardType and numberOfBeds) might remain in the Patient table type. Although there would be no redundancy, there would be considerable scope for inconsistency. For example, if the number of beds in a ward changes, the value of numberOfBeds would have to be updated for every patient who is in the ward, whereas only a single value will need updating if there is a separate Ward entity. The database designer must try to discern entities which exist in the enterprise by watching out for groups of attributes which describe possible entities, even if no identifier has yet been recognised. Once a potential entity has been detected, a suitable identifier can be chosen.

Questions

1. Would it be valid to assign either or both of the attributes consultantName, consultantSpecialty, to the following tables?

> Patient (<u>patientNo</u>, patientName, ..., wardName)
> Ward (<u>wardName</u>, wardType, numberOfBeds, ...)

Each patient is under the care of one consultant. Each consultant has only one specialty, and no two consultants have the same name. A consultant may be responsible for patients in any ward, and there are no restrictions on the association of consultants or specialties with wards.   (3 min)

2. Suppose entity types Patient and Ward have been selected, and that their relationship is represented by posting wardName into Patient. What potential is there for inconsistent updating of wardName when the name of a ward is changed? Is the situation any different to that which occurs for numberOfBeds if there is no Ward entity, as discussed in the last paragraph of section 13.5?   (3 min)

13.6 Superfluous entity tables

Suppose that, after all attributes have been assigned, an E-R model includes the tables shown in Fig. 13.2a, where qualificationName has values such as BA, BSc, MSc. The Qualification entity table is simply a list of qualificationName(s), and the question arises as to whether it is necessary to keep this list in the model at all, or whether the qualificationName(s) appearing in the QualOfEmp table are sufficient.

The decision rests on two criteria. Firstly, is it likely that the model will, in the forseeable future, need to include attributes which are functionally dependent on qualificationName (for example, qualificationName might be a determinant of a new attribute salaryIncrement)? If so, the set of tables will not be well-normalised unless Qualification is retained as an entity in its own right. Secondly, is the participation of Qualification non-obligatory? If so, the Qualification table may include the names of qualifications that are not currently held by any employee, and which could not therefore be stored in QualOfEmp. Such a situation would occur if the enterprise needs to keep a list of officially recognised qualifications. If it is unlikely that there will be any attribute functionally dependent on qualificationName, and if the only qualifications of interest are those held by employees, then the Qualification table can be deleted; otherwise it should be retained.

In general, an entity table which still contains only the entity's identifier, even after all the attributes have been assigned to the model, should be examined using the criteria illustrated above to see if the entity really does need to be represented by a separate table type. If it does not, either annotate the entity type's symbol to show that there is no corresponding table type (Fig. 13.2b), or else revise the E-R type diagram by deleting the entity type and converting its relationship(s) to entity types (Fig. 13.2c).

Employee (employeeNo, employeeName, homeAddress)
Qualification (qualificationName)
(a)   QualOfEmp (employeeNo, qualificationName)

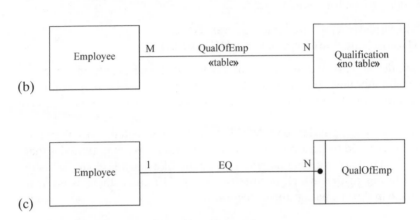

(b)

(c)

Fig. 13.2   E-R models for an Employee/Qualification problem
(a)   Qualification represented as a separate entity table
(b)   Annotation denoting absence of Qualification table
(c)   QualOfEmp as an entity type. Each occurrence of this entity represents the name-of-a-qualification-held-by-a-particular-employee, not just the name-of-a-qualification; hence the degree of the EQ relationship is 1:many. EQ is represented by the pre-posted identifier employeeNo in QualOfEmp

Question

1. For the Fig. 13.2a model, should the Qualification table contain all the qualifications recognised by the enterprise, or should it contain only those not present in the QualOfEmp table?   (2 min)

13.7   Entity subtypes

Suppose every employee has an employeeNo, employeeName, homeAddress, jobTitle, dateOfBirth and salary, but only those employees who are salespersons have associated values of salesQuota and salesBonus. A salesperson who exceeds his or her salesQuota receives the salesBonus payment in addition to his or her salary. Quota and bonus values are set individually for each salesperson.

A possible E-R model would have separate entity types for Salesperson and Non-salesperson employees:

Salesperson (employeeNo, employeeName, homeAddress, jobTitle,
                           dateOfBirth, salary, salesQuota, salesBonus)

Non-salesperson (<u>employeeNo</u>, employeeName, homeAddress, jobTitle,
dateOfBirth, salary)

If most of the processing of employee data is the same, whether an employee is a salesperson or not, it would be more convenient, as well as providing a more concise model, to have a single Employee entity type containing the data common to all employees. Now, salesQuota and salesBonus cannot be assigned to Employee without incurring nulls for those employees who are not salespersons, so it is worth considering the creation of an entity subtype Salesperson which contains those attributes which apply only to an employee in the role of salesperson. The set of tables for this version of the model is therefore:

Employee (<u>employeeNo</u>, employeeName, homeAddress, jobTitle,
dateOfBirth, salary)
Salesperson (<u>employeeNo</u>, salesQuota, salesBonus)

where the 1:1 relationship between Employee and Salesperson is represented by a pre-posted identifier. Just as Salesperson is referred to as an entity subtype, so Employee is referred to as an entity supertype.

The reason for thinking of Salesperson as an entity subtype, rather than as an entity type, is simply that the attributes associated with Salesperson must be supplemented by those in the parent entity type Employee in order to give a complete description of a salesperson. (We will encounter a similar idea in the context of object-oriented modelling, where it is referred to as inheritance.)

Fig. 13.3 shows how supertype and subtype can be represented on an E-R type diagram. Both Salesperson and Designer are subtypes of the supertype Employee. The Employs relationship involves employees in general; the ServicedBy relationship

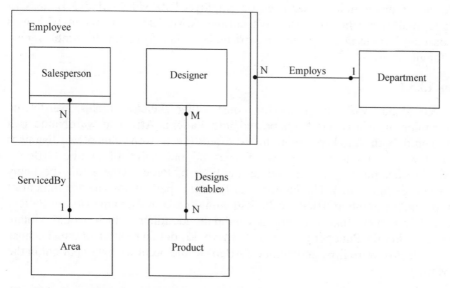

Fig. 13.3   E-R diagram showing Employee as an entity supertype with entity subtypes Salesperson and Designer

involves only those employees who are salespersons; the Designs relationship involves only those employees who are designers. It is usual to insist that the subtypes of a given supertype are disjoint, in which case Fig. 13.3 could not model a situation in which an employee could be both a salesperson and a designer.

Question

1. Which of the following restrictions do you think should apply to the use of the terms entity subtype and entity supertype?

(a)   an entity subtype must have the same identifier as its supertype;
(b)   an entity subtype must have obligatory participation in its relationship with its supertype;
(c)   an entity subtype must have non-obligatory participation in its relationship with its supertype.   (5 min)

Answer pointers

Section 13.2.2

1. Every employee will have a currentMiles value, not just those employees who are car users. A zero value of currentMiles might be taken to imply that the employee is a car user, although this is not necessarily the case.

2. It might be more natural to regard currentMiles as a property of an employee/car combination, and therefore to assign it to Uses (Fig. 12.3). The advantage of a more natural assignment must be weighed against the disadvantages of including an extra table type in the model.

3. Model A: many null occurrences of employeeTotalMiles. Model B: loss of employeeTotalMiles value if car usage discontinuous. Model C: no problems with nulls or discontinuous car usage, but needs an extra table containing duplicated employeeNo values for all car users.

Section 13.3.1

1. In accordance with the rules for constructing skeleton tables, wardName (the identifier of Ward) has been posted into Patient. Attribute wardName is a determinant of both wardType and numberOfBeds (i.e. a given value of wardName is associated with just one value of wardType and one value of numberOfBeds). However, wardName is not a candidate identifier of Patient (there may be many patients in the same ward). The identifier of Patient is patientNo. The assignment of wardType and/or numberOfBeds to Patient would make wardName (in the Patient table) a determinant that was not a candidate identifier, which would violate the Boyce/Codd rule. Put another way, Patient would contain redundant data because the same values of wardType and numberOfBeds would occur for every patient in the same ward.

Section 13.3.2

1.

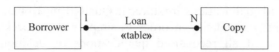

Borrower (<u>borrowerNo</u>, borrowerName, borrowerLimit)
Copy (<u>accessionNo</u>, title, acquisitionDate, acquisitionPrice)
Loan (<u>accessionNo</u>, borrowerNo, loanDate)

Section 13.4

1. A lecturer's lecturerHours could be derived by summing all the attendanceHours for that lecturer. The studentHours could be derived by summing attendanceHours for each student. The model contains redundancy if a value is derivable, but this may be acceptable in the interests of a faster response. In the early stages of design it is best to omit any derivable attribute unless it is already obvious that it would take too long to recompute its value each time it is required. This question again illustrates the importance of defining the meaning of an attribute very carefully.

2. If lecturerHours is assigned to Lecturer, it will contain redundant values. (The model will not be fully-normalised.) In this example, lecturerHours is an example of a parameter of the system for which only one value needs to be stored. As such, the simplest approach is to assign it to a separate list of such parameters.

Section 13.5

1. Neither consultantName nor consultantSpecialty can be assigned to Ward as they would be repeating groups. Either attribute could be assigned on its own to Patient, since a given patient is associated with only one consultant and one specialty, but both attributes cannot be assigned to Patient because consultantName is a determinant of consultantSpecialty but would not be a candidate identifier of Patient. A new entity type Consultant is required, the corresponding table type being Consultant (<u>consultant Name</u>, consultantSpecialty). The relationship of Consultant to Patient should be represented by posting consultantName into Patient.

2. The same problem occurs in that the wardName value for every patient in the ward will need updating, but there are some important differences. Firstly, if there are many attributes of a ward, there will be many opportunities for inconsistent updating if these attributes are assigned to Patient. Secondly, if wardName is likely to be changed it is not a good choice for an identifier anyway; perhaps a wardNo should be used. An entity identifier whose value is liable to change is not much use for identifying anything. Thus, the values of wardName as the identifier of Ward should not normally change, apart from additions and deletions. A value of wardName as a posted identifier in Patient will change whenever a patient is moved to another ward, but this affects only the one Patient occurrence[1] involved.

---

[1] In the context of an E-R model, a term such as 'Patient occurrence' refers to an individual Patient entity occurrence and hence to its associated *row* within the Patient table; it does *not* refer to a complete Patient *table* occurrence.

Section 13.6

1. To avoid redundancy, the same qualification names should not appear in both tables (assuming only recognised qualifications are stored in QualOfEmp), but it would usually be worth accepting this redundancy in order to simplify the processing of transactions, such as retrieval of all recognised qualifications or deletion of a QualOfEmp occurrence.

Section 13.7

1. (a) and (b) apply. An occurrence of a subtype is always associated with an occurrence of the supertype (e.g. a salesperson is necessarily an employee) so (c) does not apply.

14

First-level design

14.1 Introduction

The ideas developed in the previous chapters can now be drawn together into a general procedure for a *first-level* data model design. The description *first-level* is used because the design will need further work to transform it into a final implementation.

So far we have concentrated mainly on *data analysis* issues, that is on the properties of the data which exist independently of the transactions which may operate on the data. In addition to data analysis, the first-level design procedure involves *functional analysis*, where the latter term refers to the analysis of the transactions which the data model must support. In fact, although there is a difference in emphasis between data analysis and functional analysis, the two are interdependent. Data will not be included in a model unless there are likely to be transactions which will use the data, and transactions cannot be described without reference to the data on which they will operate.

In previous chapters there has often been at least an implicit appeal to functional analysis to guide the choice of entities and relationships, and the assignment of attributes. For example, the significance of potential connection traps depends very much on how the data will be used. As the design progresses further towards a physical implementation, so the importance of functional analysis will increase, with optimisation of internal schema design depending heavily on quantitative information such as the volume and frequency of transactions.

14.2 First-level design procedure

A discussion of an overall analysis methodology is beyond the scope of this book, so it will be assumed that a requirements specification has already been prepared in sufficient detail to form a basis for the first-level design. However, it is not assumed that all the necessary information is available at the outset. One of the great merits of data modelling is that it prompts the analyst to ask many pertinent questions about the enterprise rules with the result that the need for further information may become apparent during the modelling process.

The steps in the first-level design procedure are described below, followed by comments and examples.

(1) Get a feel for the problem by sketching E-R type diagrams. Diagrams drawn in this step are little more than doodles to help you start thinking about the data.

(2)   Prepare a preliminary list of transactions which the data model must support.

(3)   Prepare a preliminary list of attributes (the *attribute list*).

(4)   Write down a preliminary list of those entity types that you can confidently identify, and select the identifier of each of them. For each entity type, write down a table containing just its identifier.

(5)   Draw an E-R type diagram showing the known relationships between the entity types. Include relationship degree and participation details.

(6)   Make a preliminary check that your E-R type diagram will support the transactions, and amend the diagram if necessary. Although attributes have not yet been assigned to entities and relationships, it is still possible to get a reasonable idea whether the transactions can be supported at the entity/relationship level. In particular, look for potential connection traps and decide whether they can safely be ignored.

(7)   Using the rules given in Chapter 12, develop the (above) step 4 tables into skeleton tables corresponding to your E-R type diagram. Delete all attributes used in the skeleton table identifiers from the attribute list.

(8)   Add the attributes remaining on the attribute list to the table types, ensuring as you do so that the attribute assignment rules given in section 13.1 are obeyed. As each attribute is assigned to a table, delete it from the attribute list. If the assignment of an attribute to a table would create a determinant which is not also a candidate identifier of the table, return both the determinant and the attributes it determines to the attribute list.

(9)   If any attributes on the attribute list cannot be assigned to the existing set of tables, define further entity and/or relationship types as necessary to accommodate them (see section 13.5). Note that some previous attribute assignments may now violate the assignment rules, so repeat the design procedure from step 5.

(10)   Decide whether there are any other attributes or transactions that must be included in the model now, or that ought to be included to allow for future developments. If so, add them to the attribute and transaction lists; return to step 6 to deal with new transactions, and to step 8 to deal with new attributes.

(11)   Check that your choice of entities, relationships and attributes still seems appropriate. Check that the set of tables is fully-normalised. Check that all transactions can be supported at the attribute level. If changes are needed, repeat the procedure, if necessary from step 1.

(12)   Delete any superfluous entities (see section 13.6).

Comments on design procedure

Step 3   The transactions listed in step 2 will indicate many of the attributes that will be required. If there is a danger of being swamped by a large number of attributes, omit from your first attempt attributes that obviously have similar properties to others already on the attribute list. For example, if an employee's initials are likely to be treated in much the same way as an employee's surname, the former could be temporarily ignored.

If an attribute is composite, it is safer to break it down into its constituent parts. For example, suppose a customer code comprises a sales area code coupled with a customer serial number. The table Customer (customerCode, customerName, salesAreaCode) looks fully-normalised, but in fact it contains redundant duplication of salesAreaCode, one manifestation being explicit, and the other being concealed in customerCode. Likewise, the table Customer (<u>customerCode</u>, customerName, salesAreaName) also looks fully-normalised, but the salesAreaCode hidden in customerCode is a determinant of salesAreaName but not a candidate identifier of Customer. However, many attributes are potentially composite, and excessive zeal in decomposing them will cause an unnecessary proliferation of attributes. A price might be decomposed into {poundsPrice, pencePrice} or a date into {year, month, day}, but in most cases neither decomposition will be useful.

Step 4 Doubtful entity types should be omitted at this stage. The need for any further entity types will become apparent at step 9. If you have difficulty selecting an identifier, it can be helpful to invent an identifierNo, at least for temporary use. For example, an employee might be identified by {employeeName, address, dateOfBirth}, but it will be simpler to invent employeeNo if it does not already exist. In any case the value of the composite attribute would change if an employee's name or address changed, making it unsuitable as an identifier.

Step 5 If the degree of a relationship is in doubt, prefer many:many to 1:many, and l:many to 1:1, so that undesirable constraints are avoided. However, a 1:1 relationship will be simpler to process than a 1:many relationship, and a 1:many will be simpler than a many:many. Also, remember that a 1:many 'snapshot' view may correspond to a many:many long-term view. Likewise a 1:1 snapshot view may correspond to a 1:many or a many:many long-term view. If a relationship type seems unduly complex, consider whether it would be simpler to regard it as an entity type instead.

Steps 7 and 8 Deletion of attributes from the attribute list ensures that all the attributes are dealt with, and that no attribute appears more often than it should in the tables. In step 8, the return of a previously assigned attribute to the attribute list implies that a new entity type is going to be required.

Step 11 Obvious candidates for entity subtypes can be split off at this stage, but any decisions requiring detailed analysis should be deferred.

Step 12 Having got this far, you may find that your choice of attributes, entities and relationships is now suspect as an accurate representation of the enterprise. As you now understand the problem better, start again from step 1!

14.3 First-level design example

Scenario

A library keeps records of current loans of books to borrowers. Each borrower is identified by a borrowerNo, and each copy of a book by an accessionNo (the library may have more than one copy of any given book). The name and address of each borrower is held so that communications, such as overdue loan reminders, can be sent when necessary. The information required about books is the title, authors, publisher, publication date, international standard book number (ISBN), purchase price and current price, where purchase price is the price the library paid at the time of purchase, and current price is the current list price. There is a restriction on the number of books a borrower may have on loan at any one time, the limit depending on whether a borrower is classified as having junior or adult status. Books out on loan may be reserved by other borrowers pending their return. The library stocks only the hardback version of a book. If a new edition of a book is published, all copies of earlier editions are withdrawn from stock.

Design steps

Step 1   Draw your own doodles.

Step 2   A preliminary list of transactions is as follows. (Note that the purpose of the transaction is stated, rather than the detailed processing of attributes.)

    (1)   Store details of new borrower.
    (2)   Store details of new acquisition.
    (3)   Make loan.
    (4)   Record return of loan.
    (5)   Delete borrower.
    (6)   Delete acquisition.
    (7)   Reserve book.
    (8)   Delete reservation.
    (9)   Update current price.
   (10)   Send overdue loan reminder.

Step 3   A preliminary list of attributes is:

borrowerNo, accessionNo, borrowerName, borrowerAddress, title, authorName, publisherName, publicationDate, ISBN, purchasePrice, currentPrice, loanLimit, borrowerStatus, loanDate, reservationDate.

Several of these attributes might be regarded as composite. The attribute borrowerName may be split into surname and initials, and borrowerAddress may be split into several address lines, but neither of these is likely to be particularly significant for the structure of the data model. The attribute which will need watching most closely is ISBN. An ISBN contains four facets denoting the language of publication, the publisher, the serial number, and a check digit. For example, the ISBN 0-7131-2815-1 represents an English language publication (0), published by Edward Arnold (7131), serial number 2815, and check digit 1. Assuming that the library stocks English language books only, the first facet can be discarded. As check digits are for verification, rather than being an essential feature of the data structure, they are best omitted from the first-level design. The remaining two facets will be retained, with the attribute renamed ISBNX to indicate that it is not a full ISBN. To illustrate the pitfalls, ISBNX, rather than {publisherCode, serialNo}, will be used in the design procedure, but it would be safer to use the individual attributes to derive the fully-normalised tables, and then substitute ISBNX for {publisherCode, serialNo} if the former is more meaningful.

Step 4   The mention in the scenario of identifiers borrowerNo and accessionNo strongly suggests that Borrower and Copy are likely to be suitable choices for entity types. Other possible entity types could be selected at this stage, but for the time being we will work with just these two. At this stage the entity tables are simply Borrower (borrowerNo, ...) and Copy (accessionNo, ...).

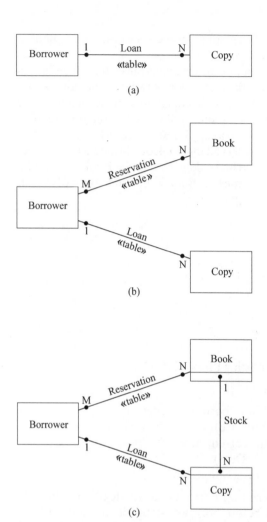

Fig. 14.1 Development of E-R type diagram; steps 5 and 6

Step 5 A borrower may have several copies currently on loan, but a copy cannot be currently on loan to more than one borrower. A copy is not necessarily on loan, nor does a borrower have to borrow copies. The E-R type diagram is shown in Fig. 14.1a.

Step 6 Transactions 1, 2, 5 and 6, as listed above, appear to be catered for by the creation and deletion of Borrower and Copy occurrences, and loans (transactions 3 and 4) can be processed via the Loan relationship. (In fact, the processing may not be quite as simple as this; a more detailed analysis is made in step 11.) The attribute currentPrice will probably be an attribute of Copy, so transaction 9 can be handled. The information needed for overdue loan reminders (transaction 10) can probably be found using Copy, Loan and Borrower. The only problem is with reservations (transactions 7 and 8). As a borrower may make many reservations, and the same book may be reserved by many borrowers, a model based on Fig. 14.1a would have to contain a repeating group. At first sight the solution is to add a many:many Reservation relationship between Borrower and Copy, but this would be unsatisfactory because a borrower does not reserve a particular copy, but a particular book. If there are several copies of the same book it does not matter which copy a borrower receives.

This failure of the E-R type diagram to support reservation transactions highlights a fundamental confusion in the scenario over the distinction between copies and books. It is not books which are loaned, but copies. The diagram can be amended by introducing a Book entity and a Reservation relationship (Fig. 14.1b), but this creates a connection trap between Copy and Book. When a copy is returned by a borrower, it will be necessary to check whether anyone has reserved the book of which this is a copy, so the connection trap must be eliminated. This can be done by relating Book to Copy via a relationship Stock (Fig. 14.1c). We will assume that Book is identified by ISBNX, but see questions 7 and 8 below, for possible complications.

Step 7   The skeleton tables are:

> *Entity tables*
> Borrower (<u>borrowerNo</u>, . . .)
> Copy (<u>accessionNo</u>, ISBNX, . . .)
> Book (<u>ISBNX</u>, . . .)

> *Relationship tables*
> Loan (<u>accessionNo</u>, borrowerNo, . . .)
> Reservation (<u>borrowerNo, ISBNX</u>, . . .)

The Stock relationship is represented by posting ISBNX into Copy.

Step 8   Assignment of the attributes gives:

> Borrower (<u>borrowerNo</u>, borrowerName, borrowerAddress)
> Copy (<u>accessionNo</u>, ISBNX, purchasePrice)
> Book (<u>ISBNX</u>, title, publicationDate, currentPrice)
> Loan (<u>accessionNo</u>, borrowerNo, loanDate)
> Reservation (<u>borrowerNo, ISBNX</u>, reservationDate)

Contrary to the assumption in step 6, currentPrice is not an attribute of Copy after all. Notice that, if loanLimit were assigned before borrowerStatus, it would have been assigned to Borrower but subsequently withdrawn following the attempted assignment of borrowerStatus, because the latter would be a determinant of loanLimit but not a candidate identifier of Borrower. For the same reason, these two attributes would also be returned to the attribute list if borrowerStatus were dealt with before loanLimit.

Assuming that only one publisherName is recorded for each book, it is tempting to assign publisherName to the Book table. However, concealed within ISBNX is the publisherCode, which would be a determinant of publisherName but not a candidate identifier of Book. The Copy table would not provide a suitable home either, even though accessionNo is a determinant of publisherName, because values of publisherName would be redundantly duplicated if there were several copies of the same book. Consequently, publisherName must be left on the attribute list for the time being.

Step 9   The attributes as yet unassigned are authorName, borrowerStatus, loanLimit and publisherName.

Attribute authorName has not been assigned to Book because it would be a repeating group. If there is no need to store any attributes of an author other than authorName, it is sufficient to split off the repeating group into an Authorship entity with the identifier

{ISBNX, authorName}. An alternative route to the same solution is to create an Author entity (identifier authorName) having a many:many Authorship relationship (identifier {ISBNX, authorName}) with Book. Assuming authorName is the only attribute of Author, the Author entity is superfluous. The Authorship relationship can then be replaced by an Authorship entity having a many:1 relationship with Book. (See also section 13.6.)

For the reason given in step 8, the attributes borrowerStatus and loanLimit cannot both be assigned to Borrower. A new entity type, Limit, is therefore required. If borrowerStatus had been overlooked as an attribute, loanLimit would at this stage be in Borrower. It would be necessary to detect that the same loanLimit will apply to all borrowers of the same status, and that this implies that borrowerStatus should be included in the model. Attribute loanLimit would then have to be withdrawn from Borrower and returned to the attribute list.

Attribute publisherName can be dealt with by creating an entity Publisher, identified by publisherCode. The most sensible way of inserting Publisher into the E-R type diagram is to relate it to Book via a Publishes relationship. This relationship is represented in the table types by the implicit pre-posting of publisherCode within ISBNX.

The model including Authorship, Limit and Publisher, is shown in Fig. 14.2. The membership class of Publisher in Publishes has been made obligatory, on the assumption that the only publishers about whom data will be stored will be publishers of books held by the library.

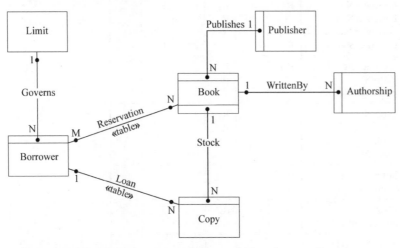

Borrower (borrowerNo, borrowerName, borrowerAddress, borrowerStatus)
Copy (accessionNo, ISBNX, purchasePrice)
Book (ISBNX, title, publicationDate, currentPrice)
Limit (borrowerStatus, loanLimit)
Authorship (ISBNX, authorName)
Publisher (publisherCode, publisherName)
Loan (accessionNo, borrowerNo, loanDate)
Reservation (borrowerNo, ISBNX, reservationDate)

Fig. 14.2   The completed first-level E-R model

Step 10   Other transactions which should be considered include:
   (1)   Store details of new book.
   (2)   Delete book.

(3) Notify borrower that reservation is now in stock.
(4) Change borrower's status.
(5) Find books written by a given author.
The model appears to be capable of supporting these transactions.

Step 11 A detailed analysis of each transaction must be made so that the adequacy of the model can be checked. For example, a loan might be recorded simply by storing a new Loan occurrence; alternatively the Borrower and Copy tables could be checked first to ensure that the accessionNo and borrowerNo are valid. Deletion of the last copy of a given book implies deletion of not only the Copy occurrence[1], but also the associated Book occurrence[1] and perhaps Publisher and Authorship occurrences[1] as well, plus a check on the Loan and Reservation tables in case they refer to the accessionNo or ISBNX of the copy.

A useful way of checking that all transactions can be supported at the attribute level is to draw up a transaction/attribute grid (Fig. 14.3). The codes used in the grid are:

D—delete   R—retrieve   S—store   U—update

Entity/ Relationship	Attribute	Transaction Loan		Return		Status	
Borrower	borrowerNo	R_1		R_4		R_1	
	borrowerName			R		R	
	borrowerAddress			R			
	borrowerStatus	R				R	U_2
Copy	accessionNo	R_2		R_2			
	ISBNX			R			
	purchasePrice						
Book	ISBNX			R_5			
	title			R			
	publicationDate						
	currentPrice						
Limit	borrowerStatus	R_3					
	loanLimit	R					
Authorship	ISBNX			R_6*			
	authorName			R			
Publisher	publisherCode						
	publisherName						
Loan	accessionNo		S_5	D_1			
	borrowerNo	R_4*	S_5	D			
	loanDate		S_5	D			
Reservation	borrowerNo			R	D_7		
	ISBNX			R_3	D_7		
	reservationDate			R_3	D		

Fig. 14.3 Transaction/attribute grid

[1] Remember that, in the context of E-R modelling, these refer to *row* occurrences, not complete *table* occurrences.

An asterisk indicates that access to several rows within a table may be necessary at a particular stage of the transaction. A numeric subscript shows the order in which a table is accessed. For retrievals and deletions the subscript is applied to the attribute(s) used as an entry point to the table. For storage and update the subscript is applied to all the attributes involved in the operation. A transaction that accesses the same table at different stages of the transaction will require more than one column. The actual physical mechanisms for processing the transactions are not significant at this stage, the only concern being whether the model can logically cope with the transactions. Thus, if a transaction is to check the status of a borrower, given a borrowerNo, grid entries are made for borrowerNo and borrowerStatus only, even though it may eventually turn out that a record containing all the borrower's details will have to be physically retrieved.

The following examples are illustrated in Fig. 14.3. The comments on the Loan transaction are more detailed than those for Return and Status.

Loan: Use borrowerNo as entry point to Borrower to check validity of borrowerNo and to find borrowerStatus. Use accessionNo as entry point to Copy to check that accessionNo is valid. Use borrowerStatus as entry point to Limit to find loanLimit. Use borrowerNo iteratively as entry point to Loan to find the number of copies the borrower has on loan. If borrower will not exceed loanLimit, store a new Loan occurrence.

Return: (It is assumed that this transaction will include, whenever applicable, notification that a reservation is now available.) Delete loan occurrence. Find ISBNX for this accessionNo. Find the borrower, if any, with the earliest reservationDate for the book. Find the borrower's name and address. Find the title and authors of the book. Delete the reservation.

Status: Use borrowerNo to find borrower's name (as a check on accuracy of borrowerNo) and to check the borrower's present status. If necessary, update the borrower's status.

Step 12 Each entity table contains at least one attribute in addition to its identifier, so none of the tables is superfluous. If Author, identified by authorName, had been chosen as an entity type, the Author table would probably have been deemed to be superfluous at this point, as it would contain only authorName.

Final comment
When working from a scenario, like the one at the beginning of this section, it is a good idea to underline possible choices for entities, relationships and attributes, using a different colour for each category.

Questions

These questions relate to the library data model shown in Fig. 14.2.

1. Why is purchasePrice an attribute of Copy rather than Book? (1 min)
2. Suppose the language code is omitted from the ISBN because it has a fixed value, as in the example, but that the check digit is retained. What determinancy exists between publisherCode, serialNo and checkDigit? Where will checkDigit appear in the fully-normalised table types? (4 min)

3.   Which links between table types are implied by posted identifiers, even though there is no direct connection on the E-R type diagram?   (2 min)

4.   Draw up a transaction/attribute grid for each of the following transactions:

(a)   List the ISBNX and title of all books written by a named author.   (2 min)

(b)   Delete all details of a borrower, given the borrowerNo, provided that the borrower has no copies out on loan. If the borrower is deleted, all reservations by that borrower should also be deleted.   (2 min)

(c)   Store details of a new acquisition. Some acquisitions may be additional copies of books already in stock.   (2 min)

5.   Redesign the library E-R model to include the following extensions:

Each book is classified as being fiction or non-fiction and is indexed under a single subject code, where each code denotes a particular subject heading (e.g. art, science, crime, romance). Some copies, being for reference only, are not available on loan. The date of birth of each author is required. The number of copies on loan to each borrower is stored to save deriving this figure every time a loan is made. A borrower may occasionally reserve several copies of the same book. A borrower's loan rights may be withdrawn, perhaps temporarily, because of an infringement of the library's rules.

(15 min)

6.   With reference to the revised data model of question 5, what changes should be made to the transaction/attribute grid of Fig. 14.3 for the Loan and Return transactions?   (3 min)

7.   Not all books, particularly older ones, have an international standard book number. How could this problem be solved?   (2 min)

8.   A book which is published jointly by two publishers may have two international standard book numbers. What problems does this pose for the library system? Assuming a maximum of two publishers, how would you amend the data model?

(3 min)

9.   From the data modelling viewpoint, the library has a convenient policy of stocking only a single edition of only the hardback version of a book. Suppose different versions (e.g. hardback, paperback) may be stocked, each in several editions. What further information would you need to redesign the data model?   (3 min)

10.   The publisher-code and serial number facets of an ISBN together occupy eight digits, but individually are of variable length. A prolific publisher has a short publisher-code to allow a large range of serial numbers; the larger number of low-volume publishers are catered for by giving them long publisher-codes and correspondingly small serial number ranges. What problem does this pose for computer system design and how might it be solved?   (2 min)

Answer pointers

1.   The purchasePrice may vary from one copy to another of the same book.

2.   {publisherCode, serialNo} is a determinant of checkDigit. Consequently, checkDigit will appear only in the Book table. Where {publisherCode, serialNo} appears in Copy, Authorship and Reservation, it will not be possible to verify the values by recomputing the check digit. Inclusion of the check digit in these tables, although technically introducing redundancy and potential inconsistency of check digit values, can be defended on the grounds that the whole purpose of the check digit is to permit verification of the internal consistency of an ISBNX. A check digit is an example of a derivable attribute.

3. By ISBNX: Copy to Authorship, Copy to Reservation, Authorship to Reservation. By ISBNX/publisherCode: Publisher to Copy, Publisher to Authorship, Publisher to Reservation.

4. (a) Use authorName as entry point to Authorship to find ISBNX values, then use ISBNX as entry point to Book to find title of each book. Notice that no distinction can be made between different authors who happen to have the same name. To do so, we could include an Author entity with identifier authorNo. The identifier of Authorship would become {ISBNX, authorNo}. The E-R model would then incorporate the tables:

> Author (<u>authorNo</u>, authorName)
> Authorship (<u>ISBNX, authorNo</u>)

(b) Use borrowerNo as an entry point to Loan. If borrower has no copies on loan, delete the occurrence of Borrower identified by borrowerNo, then use borrowerNo as entry point to Reservation to delete all occurrences of Reservation for this borrower.

(c) Store accessionNo, ISBNX and purchasePrice in Copy. Using ISBNX as entry point, check whether Book details for this ISBNX are already known; if not store these details and then store Publisher details, if any, plus Authorship details for each author, if any.

5. Add entity types Subject and Author (both with relationships to Book). The (many:many) relationship table linking Author to Book will be equivalent to the old Authorship table. Since different authors may have the same name, but different dates of birth, an authorNo attribute will probably be chosen as the identifier of Author. If not, the identifier should include at least authorName and authorDateOfBirth, in which case, authors with the same name and date of birth will still not be distinguishable, but this probably will not matter. Additional attributes required are: fnfFlag (fiction/non-fiction), subjectCode, subjectHeading, referenceOnlyFlag, noCopiesOnLoan, noCopiesReserved. Some thought is needed in deciding how to deal with a borrower who reserves further copies of a book which he or she has already reserved. Is it sufficient to update the value of noCopiesReserved, leaving reservationDate unchanged, or would this be considered unfair to other borrowers who have also reserved this book? If both new and old reservation dates are to be stored, how does this affect the choice of identifier for Reservation? Attribute borrowerStatus could be used to indicate withdrawal of loan rights.

6. The Loan transaction would check noCopiesOnLoan in Borrower (instead of counting Loan occurrences) and would update its value if a loan is made. The Return transaction would update noCopiesOnLoan and, if necessary, noCopiesReserved (in Reservation). The names of authors could still be found from Authorship (now a relationship table).

7. The library could invent its own pseudo-ISBNX, containing the standard ISBN publisherCode but the library's own serialNo. An attribute, ISBNXType, would indicate whether the ISBNX value is genuine or not. Alternatively, the library could use its own bookNo throughout. It is also possible that some publishers will not have publisher-codes within the ISBN system, so special provision may be necessary here as well. One should always check that an identifier will have a valid value for every occurrence of the entity it purports to identify. Incidentally, accessionNo could be replaced by a combination of the Book identifier and a copyNo, where copyNo takes the values 1, 2, 3, . . . for successive copies of the same book.

8.   Although an ISBNX still identifies a book, it is not entirely satisfactory as an identifier, since different ISBNX values may identify the same book. One way of amending the data model would be to choose one of the values as the main identifier (ISBNX1) and to store the other as an additional attribute (ISBNX2) of Book. A value of ISBNX2 quoted in a reservation would have to be converted into the corresponding ISBNX1 value. The retrieval of publisherName information would require a search of Publisher using the publisherCode implicit in ISBNX1 and also that in ISBNX2.

9.   How is an edition identified? Do different editions have different ISBNs, is the same ISBN used for all editions of the same book, or does ISBN policy vary between publishers? What is the policy about ISBNs and versions? What limit, if any, is there on the number of editions and versions? Is the current price required for each version? How will a reservation indicate that a specific version or edition is (a) required, (b) immaterial? How will reservation requests be processed in each case?

10.   If the publisherCode and serialNo are stored as variable length attributes, the boundary between them must be indicated somehow, and a program requiring publisherCode or serialNo will have to pick out the right string. The simplest solution is to make each facet fixed length by padding with, say, blanks, although some string manipulation will then be necessary to display an ISBN in the conventional format.

15

Second-level design

15.1   Introduction

The objective of first-level design is to develop a logically simple, redundancy-free model which will form a sound basis for subsequent stages of design. *Second-level design* is concerned with amending, or *flexing*, the model to improve its performance, at least to a level at which it is compatible with functional analysis constraints, notably storage requirements and transaction processing times. Flexing should also take account of the general design objectives. The first-level design might be left as it is if the main objective is flexibility, but substantial changes may be necessary if efficiency of performance is crucial.

The approach taken here is to do second-level design before the model is mapped into a form which satisfies the constraints of a particular database management system (DBMS). This design sequence has the merit that the issues are not clouded by concern over the detailed structure of the DBMS, but the disadvantage that features of the DBMS may subsequently turn out to have a marked effect on the justification of second-level design decisions. The latter is often particularly true of the mechanisms provided for representing relationships. In practice, it is often sufficient to keep an eye on just the main features of the target DBMS, but for some DBMS it may be better to defer second-level design until after the first-level model has been mapped into DBMS form.

The second-level design procedure discussed below takes a more quantitative approach than the first-level procedure, but any calculations required are restricted to relatively straightforward estimations of trade-offs in storage requirements and transaction processing times. It is best to concentrate on the critical constraints, such as those transactions which need the fastest response times, or those tables which occupy the most storage. Having flexed the model into a state which can satisfy these critical constraints, it can then be checked out against those that are less critical to see whether further flexing is necessary.

Transaction processing time can be estimated from the average number of accesses to table occurrences per transaction and the average access time of the probable storage device, making due allowance for the type of access (e.g. direct or sequential) which is likely to be used, and taking account of plausible blocking factors. Storage requirements can be estimated from table sizes, with some rule of thumb allowance for overheads such as overflow space or indexes which may be used in the physical design. The aim of making these estimates is not to come up with accurate figures, but to weed out designs that are clearly infeasible. In practice, second-level design decisions can often be made by inspection rather than by calculation.

Ideally, in terms of the three-level DBMS architecture discussed in Chapter 2, the first-level design would correspond closely to the conceptual schema, whereas the second-level design would be a step along the road towards internal schema design. This presupposes a DBMS which is clever enough to map an external schema via the conceptual schema into an internal schema, where each type of schema may have a markedly different view of the data (in the way that Fig. 15.2 differs from Fig. 14.2, for example). Few, if any, commercially available DBMS are capable of this degree of sophistication, so it may be more realistic to view the first-level design as the conceptual *model*, with the second-level design being the basis for conceptual *schema* design.

Various flexing techniques are described below and subsequently illustrated in the context of the library E-R model developed in section 14.3.

Question

1. The flexing of a data model has failed to produce a design which satisfies the system constraints. Suggest one solution.   (1 min)

15.2   Flexing by table elimination

15.2.1   1:1 relationships

Figure 15.1 shows a first-level E-R model for Project and Employee data. The annotation in the symbol stripes shows that 10 per cent of Employee occurrences, and 95 per cent of Project occurrences, participate in the IsOn relationship. In accordance with the rules of first-level design, a separate IsOn relationship table has been defined because both entity types have non-obligatory participation in the 1:1 IsOn relationship. The employeeNo attribute has been arbitrarily selected as the row identifier of IsOn, in preference to projectNo.

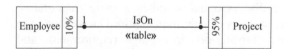

Employee (<u>employeeNo</u>, employeeName)
Project (<u>projectNo</u>, projectName, projectStartDate)
IsOn (<u>employeeNo</u>, projectNo)

Fig. 15.1   First-level E-R model

One way of flexing the model is to treat it as though one of the entity types has obligatory participation. For example, the IsOn relationship could be represented by posting employeeNo into Project at the expense of relatively few null occurrences for the posted identifier. There is likely to be a saving on storage, and faster access for a transaction needing access to both the Employee and the Project tables, since there is no IsOn relationship table to be stored or traversed. The result of the flexing is:

Employee (<u>employeeNo</u>, employeeName)
Project (<u>projectNo</u>, projectName, projectStartDate, employeeNo)

Another way of flexing the model is to treat it as though both entity types have obligatory participation, in which case the tables can be combined, giving:

EmpProj (employeeNo, employeeName, projectNo, projectName,
projectStartDate)

This structure is likely to need more storage space, since most employees are not on projects. Access to occurrences may be slower for some transactions (a) because the table will occupy a larger extent of a storage device, (b) because there may be more transfer of superfluous data by transactions, and (c) because it will no longer be possible to store the employee and project data in different physical sequences (e.g. Employee ordered on employeeNo, and Project on projectNo). Set against these disadvantages is the faster processing which may be possible for transactions which would otherwise have to access more than one table.

A third way of flexing the model is to post an identifier and some, but not all, of the other attributes from one entity table to the other. If the most important transaction retrieves employeeName and projectName, given employeeNo, but projectStartDate is rarely needed, then it may be worth grouping the attributes accordingly. For example:

Employee (employeeNo, employeeName, projectNo, projectName)
Project (projectNo, projectStartDate)

The penalty for this flex is that 90 per cent of the projectNo and projectName occurrences in the Employee table will be null.

The last two flexing techniques can also be applied to a first-level 1:1 relationship in which only one of the entity types has obligatory participation.

Questions

1. Compare the merits of flexing Fig. 15.1 by (a) posting employeeNo to Project, (b) posting projectNo to Employee.   (2 min)
2. State one transaction, involving both employee and project data, which should be faster if the IsOn relationship table is retained.   (1 min)
3. Assume that the size of each attribute is: employeeNo 5 bytes; employeeName 20 bytes; projectNo 3 bytes; projectName 15 bytes; projectStartDate 6 bytes. There are 950 employees. Ignoring complications, such as index space, calculate the storage requirement for the model of Fig. 15.1. Compare your answer with that obtained for a model in which the IsOn relationship table is replaced by posting employeeNo into Project.   (5 min)
4. Why, in the fully-combined EmpProj table, discussed above, is the table's identifier not underlined?   (2 min)
5. For the fully-combined EmpProj table, state one transaction which would probably be processed faster, and one which would probably be processed slower, compared with the model of Fig. 15.1.   (2 min)
6. Using the data in question 3, and ignoring overheads such as index space, compare the storage requirements of the Fig. 15.1 model with those of the fully-combined EmpProj table. What difference would it make if the participation of Employee in IsOn were 80 per cent instead of 10 per cent ?   (5 min)

15.2.2   1:many relationships

Suppose the relationship degree in Fig. 15.1 is changed to 1:many (one project to many employees). As the participation condition at the 'many' end is non-obligatory, the first-level rules dictate the inclusion of the separate IsOn relationship table in the model.

The most likely way of flexing the model is to treat it as though the participation condition of the 'many' entity, Employee, were obligatory; in other words post projectNo to Employee and delete the IsOn table. Other attributes of Project could also be posted to Employee to speed up the processing of certain transactions, but this advantage must be weighed against the disadvantage of introducing redundant data into Employee. A flex in which all the Project attributes are posted into Employee is likely to be worthwhile if a high proportion of the 1:many relationship occurrences are actually 1:1 and if both entity types have obligatory participation. In effect, the relationship is treated as though it were a fully-obligatory 1:1 relationship.

Alternatively, if the 1:many relationship is actually 1:few, employeeNo (and perhaps other Employee attributes) could be posted into Project. The advantage is that there would be faster access to the employeeNo(s) of the staff on a given projectNo. The disadvantage is that a repeating group would be created in Project, with all the ramifications which that entails; in particular, it is likely to be more difficult to access a given employeeNo if it is in a repeating group, so finding a given employee's project will be less straightforward. It may help to recast the repeating group into separate attributes, particularly when each attribute has a different role. For example, if each project is staffed by only two employees, one of whom is the project leader, then the relationship could be shown as follows:

> Employee (employeeNo, employeeName)
> Project (projectNo, projectName, projectStartDate, seniorEmployeeNo,
> juniorEmployeeNo)

A more accurate view of this model is that there are two 1:1 relationships between Employee and Project, namely SeniorStaff and JuniorStaff, each of which is represented by a posted identifier.

The creation of entity types to avoid repeating groups is a common source of 1:many relationships in a first-level design; these entities should be examined to see whether it would be better to eliminate them by accepting a repeating group in the parent entity table. For instance, an employee's qualifications may have been split off into an entity type EmployeeQual (employeeNo, qualificationName, dateAcquired). The qualification details could be re-incorporated into the Employee entity as a repeating group, giving:

> Employee (employeeNo, employeeName, Qual (qualificationName,
> dateAcquired))

If there is not a reasonably low upper limit to the number of repetitions in a repeating group, or if an attribute in the group is likely to be an important entry point, then the EmployeeQual entity type is best retained. Otherwise the model can be simplified by eliminating the entity type in favour of a repeating group, which not only reduces the number of tables but also often reflects one's normal view of the real world better. For example, it is more natural to view an employee's qualifications as being attributes of the Employee entity itself.

Questions

1. A project may be staffed by many employees, but an employee is assigned to at most one project. Attributes, and their sizes in bytes, are: employeeNo 5; employeeName 20; projectNo 3; projectName 15; projectStartDate 6. The percentage of employees on projects is P. Ignoring complications, such as index space, calculate the breakeven value of P at which the storage requirements are the same whether a separate relationship table or a posted projectNo is used.   (4 min)

2. With reference to question 1, what will be the effect on the breakeven value of P of an increase in size of (a) employeeName, (b) employeeNo, (c) projectNo?   (3 min)

3. Generalise the calculation in question 1 for entities X and Y with identifiers of length i_x and i_y, respectively. The direction of the relationship is X (1:many) Y. Derive a formula for the breakeven point P, where P is the fraction of Y occurrences which participate in the relationship.   (3 min)

4. Fast response is required for a display of employeeName(s) in alphabetical order within projectNo order, where the Project/Employee relationship is 1:many and participation conditions are non-obligatory. Comment on the suitability of the Fig. 15.1 table types. Suggest a flex which would improve the response time for this transaction.
                                    (3 min)

15.2.3   Many:many relationships

If a many:many relationship is known to be few:many, the relationship table can be dispensed with by posting the identifier (and perhaps other attributes) of the 'few' entity into the 'many' entity as a repeating group. The same kind of flexing can, of course, be applied to few:few relationships. The earlier comments on 1:few relationships apply equally to few:many and few:few relationships.

Another method of flexing is to put the attributes of one of the entity tables into the relationship table, to facilitate access for certain transactions. For example:

> Employee (employeeNo, employeeName)
> IsOn (employeeNo, projectNo, projectName, projectStartDate)

The penalty is the introduction of redundant projectName and projectStartDate values into the relationship table.

Questions

1. For the example immediately above, what problem, if any, arises with the identifier of IsOn if the participation condition is non-obligatory for (a) Project and (b) Employee?   (3 min)

2. Show that the assignment of projectName and projectStartDate to IsOn is equivalent to assigning projectNo, projectName and projectStartDate to Employee as a repeating group, followed by the removal of the repeating group into a separate entity.   (2 min)

3. There is a many:many OrderLine relationship between the entity types Item and Order. Identifiers are itemNo, orderNo; other attributes are itemName, itemPrice, orderDate. Show how the model can be flexed by (a) posting all the Order attributes into Item, (b) posting all the Item attributes into Order, (c) posting all the Order

attributes into OrderLine, and (d) posting all the Item attributes into OrderLine. Which attributes may contain redundant data in each case?   (10 min)
4.   There is a many:many relationship between Employee and Project in which each employee is assigned to exactly one major project and exactly one minor project. How could the relationship be represented without using a relationship table or a repeating group?   (1 min)

15.3   Flexing by splitting

Obvious candidates for entity subtypes will already have been split off in the first-level design. In second-level design, a more thorough check should be made for attributes that are often null, and groups of attributes that are simultaneously null, so that the nulls can be eliminated by splitting these attributes off into entity subtypes. It is also worth re-examining the transaction/attribute grid, used in first-level design, to see whether a table can be split into two or more parts in such a way that no transaction accesses more than one of the parts. Suppose a Machine entity table is defined as:

> Machine (machineNo, type, dateAcquired, workCentre, capacity,
>   serviceDate, lastFailureDate)

If there are two transaction types, one accessing machineNo, type, workCentre and capacity, and the other accessing machineNo, dateAcquired, serviceDate and lastFailureDate, then the entity table could usefully be split into the two parts:

> MachineLoading (machineNo, type, workCentre, capacity)
> MachineDetails (machineNo, dateAcquired, serviceDate, lastFailureDate)

Each table will occupy a smaller extent on a storage device, less data has to be transferred in accessing a row, more rows can be held in a buffer in main memory, and different storage media can be used for the two tables. The same split could be used even if some transactions accessed both tables, but processing of these transactions would probably be faster using the Machine table.

15.4   Derivable attributes

Access paths can be shortened by introducing additional attributes. Sometimes it is sufficient to set a flag in a table to indicate whether access to another table is necessary (see question 2, below); in other cases a derived value may be stored to avoid recalculating it every time it is required. For example, orderTotal values might be stored to save recalculating them from itemPrice and quantityOrdered values. The penalty, apart from the extra storage required, is the need to maintain consistency between the derivable attribute values and the rest of the database.

An attribute may need to be included in a model because, although at some stage its values are derivable, they cannot be derived throughout the whole of the period required. For example, values derived for orderTotal may be affected by price changes, thus necessitating the storing of orderTotal values (or conceivably itemPrice values) before a price change takes effect.

A special case of a derivable attribute is where an attribute type is redundantly duplicated, as in:

> Employee (<u>employeeNo</u>, employeeName, projectNo, projectName)
> Project (<u>projectNo</u>, projectName, projectStartDate)

Here, projectName is immediately available within either table.

Questions

1. An entity table is defined as:

> Machine (<u>machineNo</u>, type, location, contractorAddress, contractType, contractServiceDate, contractCharge)

Maintenance contracts apply to only 10 per cent of machines. Suggest how the table could be flexed into two tables to reduce storage requirements. (1 min)

2. With reference to question 1, both the tables generated by flexing would have to be accessed to be sure of finding all details of a machine. How could this retrieval be made faster by using a derivable attribute? What are the penalties? (2 min)

3. A first-level model may be altered substantially in flexing it into a second-level design. Why bother with the first-level model in the first place? (3 min)

Assignment

1. The following tables form part of an Admission E-R model:

> Student (<u>studentNo</u>, studentName, dateOfBirth, localAddress, homeAddress, nextOfKin)
> EntryQuals (<u>studentNo, qualificationCode</u>, dateAcquired)

Occurrences of localAddress will be null for students who have not yet found accommodation. The majority of students live at home, so homeAddress is often the same as localAddress. NextOfKin will be null for a student who has no living relatives or guardian. Occurrences of dateOfBirth will be null for those students who have failed to produce a birth certificate as yet. Up to six entry qualifications may be recorded for a student. Frequent access is required to qualificationCode for any given student, using studentNo as an entry point, but there is no need for access via qualificationCode. Information about a student is not normally required once the student has been notified of his or her final grade, but the data (except for localAddress) is retained indefinitely.

Suggest how the model might be flexed into a second-level design. State any assumptions made, and justify your decisions.

15.5 Second-level design example

For an example of second-level design we return to the library E-R model of Fig. 14.2. It will be assumed that the Loan and Return transactions are critical, and that they are processed on-line as shown in Fig. 14.3. Economy of storage is less important, but should be kept in mind. It would be an advantage if some batch jobs could be run as background processing during on-line working, so the less time taken by on-line processing the better.

For the sake of brevity the above specification and the discussion below are less complete and rather less quantitative than would normally be the case for second-level design. Examples of the kind of calculations which may be necessary are provided by several of the questions in this chapter. The discussion is organised under several headings, but it will be seen that flexing one part of the model may upset the justification offered for flexing some other part of the model.

Loan table   The only 1:many relationship table which exists is for Loan. The Loan table could be eliminated by posting borrowerNo and loanDate into Copy, giving:

Copy (accessionNo, ISBNX, purchasePrice, borrowerNo, loanDate)

If a high percentage of copies are on loan, then posting would reduce storage requirements because accessionNo is not duplicated in Copy or Loan, but if a low percentage are on loan the storage requirements would be increased because of the large number of null borrowerNo(s) and loanDate(s). Examination of Fig. 14.3 shows that a Loan will be processed slower because counting the number of copies the borrower already has on loan will now involve access to larger Copy occurrences. For the processing of a Return, the deletion of a Loan occurrence in the first-level model will be replaced by the updating of a Copy occurrence in the flexed model (to set borrowerNo and loanDate to null). A more detailed analysis would be necessary to see whether there is any worthwhile gain here. Assume that the decision is in favour of retaining the Loan table.

Authorship   Assuming that an upper limit of, say, three authorName values per book is acceptable, the Authorship entity could be consolidated into Book, a move which would streamline the processing of Returns. As the majority of books are written by a single author, there would probably be some increase in storage.[1] This could be avoided by assigning the name of the first author to Book, whilst leaving the names of any further authors in Authorship. A sole-author flag attribute in Book could be set to indicate whether access to the Authorship table is necessary. The splitting up of authors' names in this way would be particularly worthwhile if it were found to be sufficient to quote just the first author's name on a reservation notification, maybe with an '*et al*' to indicate any other authors. Assume that this is the case.

Limit   Access to a borrower's loanLimit could be simplified by putting loanLimit into Borrower. The Limit table could then be deleted, provided that each distinct borrowerStatus value is always associated with a different loanLimit value (i.e. loanLimit is a candidate identifier of Limit). Changing the loanLimit for a given borrowerStatus will take longer if loanLimit is in Borrower, but this change is not likely to happen very often and, as it can be done by batch processing, the response time will not be critical.

As the Limit table could easily be retained in main memory during processing, there is very little performance gain for this flex, but quite a substantial loss of flexibility, so the Limit table will be preserved.

---

[1] Variable length records are not considered at this stage, as they may be subject to constraints peculiar to whichever DBMS is used.

Book and Copy   For most books only one copy is stocked, so Stock is effectively a 1:1 relationship in most cases, which in turn suggests that the Book and Copy tables be amalgamated into:

> Copy (<u>accessionNo</u>, ISBNX, title, publicationDate, purchasePrice,
> currentPrice)

where title, publicationDate and currentPrice values would be redundantly duplicated whenever multiple copies of a book are stocked. Returns ought to be processed faster, since a separate access to Book to retrieve title is no longer necessary, but the increased size of Copy would adversely affect the speed of Loan processing. However, the size of Copy could be reduced by splitting off the infrequently used attributes purchasePrice, publicationDate and currentPrice, giving:

> Copy (<u>accessionNo</u>, ISBNX, title)
> CopyDetails (<u>accessionNo</u>, publicationDate, purchasePrice, currentPrice)

The earlier proposal to insert the first author's name in Book would have to be reconsidered if the Book table were deleted. The first author's name could be included in Copy instead; this would make Returns easier to process, but would adversely affect Loan transactions. Assume that all authors' names are returned to Authorship, and that Copy and CopyDetails are created as above.

Borrower   Access to borrowerName and borrowerAddress is not often required, even for Returns since most returned books will not be on reservation anyway, so these fairly lengthy attributes could be split off to speed up processing of Loan transactions, but at the cost of duplicating borrowerNo. Assume that this is done.

Derivable attributes   Much of the time taken in processing a Loan is spent on counting the number of copies a borrower already has on loan. This could be obviated by including a loanCount attribute in Borrower. Similarly, a reservationFlag attribute in Loan would speed up the processing of the many Return transactions for which the returned book is not on reservation.

Consolidated second-level model   The consolidated second-level E-R model is shown in Fig. 15.2. A thorough check is necessary to see if some changes to the first-level model have invalidated the arguments for or against other changes. The transaction/ attribute grid should be revised to reflect the new table structure, and the model should be checked out against the system specification to see if it is capable of satisfying all constraints. Because of the compromises made in deriving the second-level model, the correspondence between the E-R type diagram and the table types has become less straightforward. The Reservation table links borrowerNo not, as implied by the diagram, to accessionNo, but to ISBNX. To avoid confusion, the connecting line between Reservation and Copy has been labelled 'ISBNX' (the quote marks distinguish the label from a role or relationship name). Similarly, the connection between WrittenBy and Copy is also labelled to show that it is ISBNX, not accessionNo, which is posted into Authorship. There is also a problem with the degree of WrittenBy, which is now actually many:many. It would, however, be rather misleading to show it as many:many since an Authorship occurrence can relate only to the Copy occurrences for one book. The degree is therefore left as 1:many, with the ISBNX label serving as a warning that care is needed in interpreting the diagram.

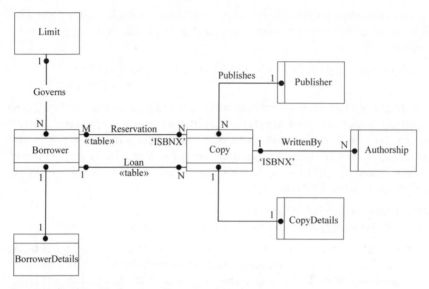

Borrower (<u>borrowerNo</u>, borrowerStatus, loanCount)
BorrowerDetails (<u>borrowerNo</u>, borrowerName, borrowerAddress)
Copy (<u>accessionNo</u>, ISBNX, title)
CopyDetails (<u>accesssionNo</u>, purchasePrice, publicationDate, currentPrice)
Limit (<u>borrowerStatus</u>, loanLimit)
Authorship (<u>ISBNX, authorName</u>)
Publisher (<u>publisher Code</u>, publisherName)
Loan (<u>accessionNo</u>, borrowerNo, loanDate, reservationFlag)
Reservation (<u>borrowerNo, ISBNX</u>, reservationDate)

Fig. 15.2   The completed second-level E-R model

Questions

1. Assess the merits of changing the definition of Authorship to Authorship (<u>ISBNX</u>, authorName1, authorName2, authorName3).   (2 min)
2.   In discussing the flexing of the Limit table, it was stated that a pre-condition for deleting the Limit table is that loanLimit should be a candidate identifier of Limit. Why should this be so?   (2 min)
3.   Suppose that an implementation using the Fig. 15.2 model would exceed the available secondary (e.g. disk) storage capacity. What solutions would you consider?   (3 min)
4.   Assess the merits of eliminating the Reservation table from the Fig. 14.2 model by posting ISBNX and reservationDate into Borrower as a repeating group.   (3 min)
5.   Which attributes in Fig. 15.2 may contain redundant data?   (3 min)
6.   Revise the transaction/attribute grid of Fig. 14.3 to make it consistent with the Fig. 15.2 model.   (10 min)
7.   Suggest how the transaction/attribute grid could be extended to include more quantitative information about transactions.   (10 min)
8.   Attribute sizes (in bytes) are: borrowerNo 3; borrowerName 20; borrowerAddress 80; borrowerStatus 1; accessionNo 4; ISBNX 6; purchasePrice 3; title 50; publicationDate 4; currentPrice 3; loanLimit 1; authorName 20; publisherCode 3; publisherName 25; loanDate 4; reservationDate 4; loanCount 1; reservationFlag 1.

There are 100000 borrowers, 200000 copies of 190000 different books, 4 borrower status values, 100 publisher codes, an average of 1.3 authors per book, a maximum of 100000 current loans and 10000 reservations. On-line disk storage available is 30 Mbytes. Estimate the storage requirements for an implementation of the first-level design (Fig. 14.2). How much storage is needed for the second-level design (Fig. 15.2)? Is there likely to be sufficient on-line disk storage for either of these designs?

(10 min)

9. The combination of hardware and software to be used for the library system provides an average direct access time of 20 msecs. The system specification states that a Loan transaction should be processed within 0.5 seconds, 95 per cent of the time, even if five Loan transactions arrive simultaneously from different library counter terminals. An active borrower has, on average, three books on loan when a further loan is requested. No borrower has more than ten books on loan. On average a borrower borrows two books at the same time. Compare the merits of the first- and second-level designs (Figs 14.2, 15.2).

(15 min)

Answer pointers

Section 15.1

1. Try harder. Discuss with another designer. Negotiate a relaxation of one or more constraints. For example, faster but more expensive hardware, or simplified transactions, might solve the problem.

Section 15.2.1

1. Because of the different participation rates (10%, 95%) (a) needs relatively few nulls in Project occurrences, but (b) needs a relatively large number of nulls in Employee occurrences. The size of employeeNo would have to be very much greater than that of projectNo to tip the balance in favour of (b) in terms of storage requirements, but (b) would be better for transactions needing access to both projectNo and employeeName.

2. Find the projectNo for a given employeeNo (or *vice versa*).

3. For Fig. 15.1: $950(5 + 20) + 100(3 + 15 + 6) + 95(5 + 3) = 26\,910$ bytes.
For posted employeeNo: $950(5 + 20) + 100(3 + 15 + 6 + 5) = 26\,650$ bytes.

4. There is no clear-cut candidate for an identifier. The employeeNo attribute will not always identify an occurrence because it will be null for every occurrence in which a project is not staffed by an employee. Similarly, projectNo will be null for every occurrence in which an employee is not on a project. In the circumstances {employeeNo, projectNo} seems the best choice as, although it may contain nulls, it will always identify an occurrence.

5. Possibilities are: Find the values of all the attributes, given employeeNo; Find employeeName given employeeNo.

6. At 10 per cent Employee participation there are 100 projects, 5 of which are unstaffed. For Fig. 15.1, size $= 26\,910$ bytes (see answer to question 3). For EmpProj table, size $= (950 + 5)(5 + 20 + 3 + 15 + 6) = 46\,795$ bytes. At 80 per cent Employee participation there are 800 projects, 40 of which are unstaffed. For Fig. 15.1, size $= 950(5 + 20) +$ $800(3 + 15 + 6) + 760(5 + 3) = 49\,030$ bytes. For EmpProj table, size $= (950 + 40)(5 + 20 + 3 + 15 + 6) = 48\,510$ bytes.

Section 15.2.2

1. Let number of employees be N. Using IsOn, storage (bytes) $= (5 + 20)N + (5 + 3)P.N +$ Project table size. Using a posted projectNo, storage (bytes) $= (5 + 20 + 3)N +$ Project table size. So $25N + 8P.N = 28N$, and $P = 37.5\%$.

2. (a) no effect. (b) P lowered (favours posting). (c) P raised (favours relationship table). These effects are most easily seen by inspection of the answer to question 3.

3. Let number of Y occurrences be N, and size of X and Y rows be r_x and r_y, respectively. $Nr_y + N.P\,(i_x + i_y) = N\,(r_y + i_x)$. So $P = i_x/(i_x + i_y)$. Notice that it is only the size of the identifiers which matters.

4. As it is not possible to access the Fig. 15.1 tables in employeeName within projectNo order, it would be necessary to generate for each project a workfile of employeeName(s) which could then be extracted in alphabetical order. This may be fast enough if the workfile can be held in main memory. Otherwise, the model could be flexed to place both projectNo and employeeName in the same table (IsOn would be the best choice) so that access can be provided (e.g. by an index) in the required order.

Section 15.2.3

1. (a) Some projects may not be staffed, in which case the employeeNo part of the identifier will be null. (b) No problem. If an employee is not on a project there will not be an IsOn occurrence containing that employeeNo.

2. Assignment of Project attributes to Employee gives:

Employee (employeeNo, employeeName, Project (projectNo, projectName, projectStartDate))

Notice that the Project attributes must form a repeating group in Employee. If they were assigned as a non-repeating group (by omitting Project and the inner brackets from the above table), the table's identifier would no longer be employeeNo, so it would no longer represent the same entity type. It would, in fact, be identified by {employeeNo, projectNo}, and would be a badly-normalised version of the IsOn relationship table. Having created the repeating group, it can be split off in the usual way into an entity subtype.

3. Attributes which may contain redundant data are underlined with dashes.

(a)   Item (itemNo, itemName, itemPrice, Order (orderNo, orderDate))

(b)   Order (orderNo, orderDate, Item (itemNo, itemName, itemPrice))

(c)   Item (itemNo, itemName, itemPrice)
      OrderLine (itemNo, orderNo, orderDate)

(d)   Order (orderNo, orderDate)
      OrderLine (itemNo, orderNo, itemName, itemPrice)

4. Employee (employeeNo, employeeName, majorProjectNo, minorProjectNo)

Section 15.4

1. Machine (<u>machineNo</u>, type, location)
   MachineContract (<u>machineNo</u>, contractorAddress, contractType,
                     contractServiceDate, contractCharge)

2. Put a contractFlag attribute into Machine. A minor penalty is the extra storage (in principle this could be a one-bit value per occurrence, in practice it might mean an extra byte or word). More significant is the need to maintain consistency between the flag setting and the presence or absence of a MachineContract occurrence for each machineNo.

3. The first-level design can be completed without bothering about second-level detail. The first-level design procedure encourages a critical analysis of the enterprise rules; the procedure is an aid to systems analysis as well as system design. It is easier to assess the justification for second-level design decisions when there is a first-level model to act as a reference point. The first-level model provides a baseline free of redundancy; if it is implemented unchanged, it is likely to be more robust and call for simpler procedures to maintain integrity.

Section 15.5

1. Simple, fast access to all authorName(s) for a given book. Cannot sequence occurrences on authorName. May not be easy to use authorName as an entry point. Storage may be increased or decreased depending on average number of authorName(s) per book.

2. Because, otherwise, the enterprise rules would allow the library to set the same loanLimit value for borrowers of different status. If borrowerStatus had been deleted from the model, it would not then always be possible to deduce a borrower's status from a loanLimit value. Thus, if juniors and adults are both given the same loanLimit value, it would be difficult to implement a subsequent change of library policy in which the limit is altered for, say, adult borrowers only.

3. Store a little-used table, such as CopyDetails, off-line on an exchangeable device or perhaps on a medium like microfiche. Consider use of a data compression technique. Find out what limits the available capacity and do something about it.

4. An upper limit on the number of reservations per borrower would have to be set in practice. If few borrowers make reservations there would be a lot of wasted storage in Borrower. Access to the ISBNX and reservationDate values for a given borrowerNo would be easier, but is probably not needed anyway.

5. title, publicationDate, currentPrice, loanCount, reservationFlag.

6. A Loan transaction does not retrieve any Loan or Limit occurrences, but must update loanCount if a loan is made. A Return transaction retrieves a Loan occurrence to check the reservationFlag and a BorrowerDetails occurrence if there is a reservation on this copy.

7. Include size of each attribute and each table, transaction rates, transaction mode (on-line/batch), mean and maximum response times.

8. For first-level design (in bytes): Borrower 10400000; Copy 2600000; Book 11970000; Limit 8; Authorship 6422000; Publisher 2800; Loan 1100000; Reservation 130000. Total 32624808 bytes.

For second-level design (in bytes): Borrower 500000; BorrowerDetails 10300000; Copy 12000000; CopyDetails 2800000; Limit 8; Authorship 6422000; Publisher 2800; Loan 1200000; Reservation 130000. Total 33354808 bytes.

On the face of it neither design will fit in 30 Mbytes, and the second-level design is the worse prospect. However, if the database can be partitioned so that, say, BorrowerDetails and CopyDetails are held off-line during library opening times, but are swapped with Copy after hours for further processing, then the on-line storage requirements will drop well below 30 Mbytes for the second-level design. This should leave enough room for index and overflow overheads, and for any temporary files which the database management system may use in processing the data. In this example database, there are only a few attributes, entities and relationships. The data storage requirement is quite small and may easily be exceeded by the storage taken up by the database management system, the operating system and the application programs. The situation would be very different if the library were to offer on-line access to text, audio, static images or video.

9.   The volume of data transferred in any one access is fairly small, so the data transfer time may be ignored. For the first-level design, the accesses and their estimated timings in milliseconds are: retrieve Borrower (20); retrieve Copy (20); retrieve Limit (0); retrieve Loans (40); store new Loan (10). Retrieve Limit is taken to be zero because Limit is a very small table which can be held in main memory by the application program. Retrieve Loans is estimated at 40 msecs because there are normally several loan occurrences to retrieve. It might very well take longer, but there is also the possibility of storing most of a given borrower's loan records in the same block so that they can be retrieved in one access; a more thorough analysis may be needed here. Store new Loan is taken to be 10 msecs because several Loan transactions (e.g. those issued at the same time to the same borrower) could be batched up and written to the storage device in one go. The total time to process five simultaneous transactions is therefore approximately $5(20 + 20 + 40 + 10) = 450$ msecs, on average, which is uncomfortably close to the 0.5 second upper limit. If there were reasons (e.g. freedom from redundancy) for pursuing the first-level design, a more detailed performance analysis, or benchmarking test, would be necessary.

For the second-level design, the access timings are: retrieve Borrower (20); retrieve Copy (20); store Loan (10); update loan-count in Borrower (20). Confidence in the estimates should be greater because there will be one (occasionally zero) update of Borrower, as opposed to a variable number of retrievals of Loan. The total time to process five simultaneous transactions is therefore approximately $5(20 + 20 + 10 + 20)$ $= 350$ msecs.

The second-level design offers a healthier safety margin. It is also likely to yield a more consistent response time, which is psychologically desirable. The smaller size of the Borrower occurrences may offer scope for further performance improvements, such as storing the whole of the Borrower table in main memory; the size might be reduced even further by crafty selection of physical formats, or if borrowerNo is a sequential numeric code lending itself to a relative file organisation, i.e. where records are self-indexed on borrowerNo. (Copy and CopyDetails might be better candidates for relative file organisation. Why?) Although one does not want to get bogged down in details of physical organisation at this stage, a design's potential for further tuning should not be completely ignored.

Remember that the access time quoted in the question was an average time. The maximum might be much greater. Also, the access times for input and output were taken to be equal, which is often not the case in practice. Actual access times will depend on the storage structures (e.g. hash, indexed sequential) used for each table. The figures used for access time calculations should allow for operating system and DBMS overheads, preferably obtained from measurements made on the actual hardware/software configuration to be used. A single application program command can trigger the execution of an alarming number of machine instructions in a DBMS.

Part 4

Further topics

Part 4 covers several topics related to data analysis.

Chapter 16 extends the entity-relationship modelling and flexing techniques of Part 3 to a distributed database system context, where the data is stored at geographically distinct locations and accessed over a communications network.

Chapter 17 introduces the idea of a relational data manipulation language for querying a database, using relational algebra as the vehicle.

Chapter 18 discusses the need to optimise query performance, reviews some important physical file structures, and gives examples of options available to a query processor in formulating an efficient query plan.

Chapter 19 introduces SQL, the standard language for accessing a relational database. This chapter is based on the SQL92 standard.

Chapter 20 reviews object-oriented concepts and outlines object-relational developments in the context of the SQL99 standard.

16

Distributed database systems

16.1 Introduction

The users of a database are often widely dispersed, for example, throughout a building, a city, nationally or internationally. They typically belong to departments or divisions located at geographically distinct sites. Such a physical organisation necessitates the linking of sites by a communications network if the users are to access a shared database. However, transmission speeds across a network are much slower than for local access to a database, and the extent and complexity of the network make it more vulnerable to failure. These disadvantages may be alleviated by distributing the database amongst the user sites. Users can have fast, reliable, local access to data that they frequently use while still being able to access data that is stored at remote sites.

A *distributed database (DDB)* is managed by a *distributed database management system (DDBMS)* which, as well as providing the usual DBMS functions, keeps track of how the data is distributed. Consequently, users and applications do not need to know where the data is stored. To them, the distributed database looks like a single, local database.

For a distributed database, the flexing methods discussed in the previous chapter can be extended to include consideration of where data should be located. Different tables can be located at different sites, the rows and/or columns of a table can be split between several sites, and copies of the same table (or part thereof) can be stored at several sites.

16.2 An extended library scenario

The library scenario in section 14.3 assumed that the library operates at only one site. We now consider an extended scenario in which the service is provided through a number of branch libraries situated in towns and villages throughout a wider area. The term *global* is used to refer to the library as a whole; the term *local* refers to a branch library. For example, the *global* book stock is the total stock held by the library; the *local* book stock is the stock held by an individual branch. Each borrower is issued, on registration, with a plastic card bearing a bar-coded borrowerNo which is globally unique. Each copy is labelled with a bar-coded accessionNo which is globally unique.

Remember that a distinction was made in section 14.3 between a book (identified by ISBNX) and a copy (identified by accessionNo). There may be many copies of the same book.

Assume the following enterprise rules:

'A borrower registers at only one branch.'
'A borrower may borrow from any branch and reserve at any branch.'
'A borrower may reserve any book stocked by the library (globally).'
'A borrower may not have more than one reservation in force (globally) for the same book.'
'A loan must be collected from the branch that issues the loan.'
'A reservation must be collected from the branch where the reservation was made.'
'A loaned copy must be returned to the branch that issued the loan.'
'A branch loans only its own (local) copies and copies of (global) reservations made at that branch.'
'The loan limit applies globally, not per branch. The number of copies a borrower has on loan at any given time is calculated globally and compared with the global loan limit.'

A borrower will usually register at the branch that the borrower will use most frequently. This would typically be the branch nearest the borrower's home, nearest the place of work, or where the borrower usually shops. The book stock varies from branch to branch, though several (or all) branches may stock copies of the same books. From time to time, books are rotated between branches to vary the choice available to local borrowers. At any given time, the database shows which copies currently belong to which branch. Reservations are processed each morning before the branch opens to the public. For each reservation, the reservation system checks whether there is a copy of the reserved book on the shelves of the branch making the reservation. If so, that copy is reserved. Otherwise, the stock is searched globally for a shelved copy at another branch. If this search is successful, the system issues instructions for the copy to be sent to the reserving branch. Should all copies (globally) be on loan, the reservation system reserves the first copy to be returned from loan and issues instructions for that copy to be retained (if it is returned to the reserving branch) or to be sent to the reserving branch (if returned to another branch). Once the copy is available, the borrower is notified and collects from the reserving branch as though it is a normal loan. The copy is, in due course, returned by the borrower to the reserving branch which then (unless it is local stock) sends it back to the branch from whence it came.

Processing of loans and returns must be fast, otherwise queues of borrowers will build up. Processing of reservations may be slower. Reservations are handled at a separate desk and there are far fewer reservations than loans.

A first-level E-R model for the extended library scenario is shown in Fig. 16.1. There are several changes to the original E-R model in Fig. 14.2. A Branch entity type has been introduced. Reservation is now shown as an entity type to avoid a complex relationship associating borrowers, books and the branches making the reservations. The use of an entity type allows the otherwise complex relationship to be expressed more clearly as three distinct relationships between a Reservation entity type and the Borrower, Book and Branch entity types, respectively. The Registered relationship shows the branch at which each borrower has registered. The BranchStock relationship shows which copies are currently owned by which branches. The Stock relationship of Fig. 14.2 is re-labelled BookStock to distinguish its role more clearly from BranchStock. BookStock shows which Copies exist for which Book.

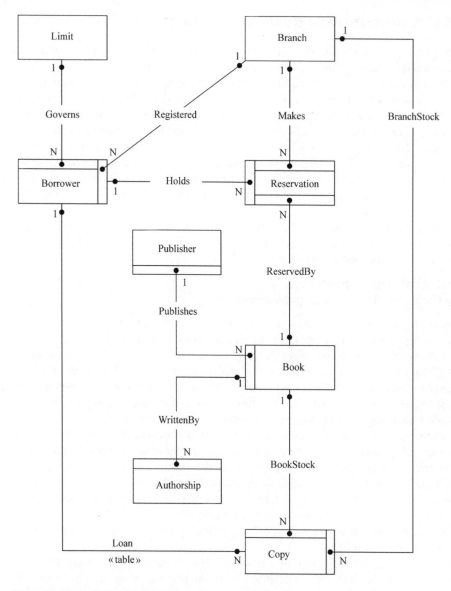

Branch (<u>branchNo</u>, branchName, branchAddress)
Borrower (<u>borrowerNo</u>, borrowerName, borrowerAddress, borrowerStatus, branchNo)
Copy (<u>accessionNo</u>, ISBNX, purchasePrice, branchNo)
Book (<u>ISBNX</u>, title, publicationDate, currentPrice)
Limit (<u>borrowerStatus</u>, loanLimit)
Authorship (<u>ISBNX, authorName</u>)
Publisher (<u>publisherCode</u>, publisherName)
Loan (<u>accessionNo</u>, borrowerNo, loanDate)
Reservation (<u>borrowerNo, ISBNX</u>, reservationDate, branchNo)

Fig. 16.1   First-level E-R model for extended library scenario

16.3   A distributed database design

Data may be distributed by *fragmentation* and *replication* of tables. Fragmentation may be horizontal (splitting by table rows) or vertical (splitting by table columns).

The Borrower table in Fig. 16.1 contains details of all borrowers registered with the library. It makes sense to fragment this table horizontally by branchNo. For each branch there will be one fragment containing just those rows relating to the borrowers who are registered at that branch. Most loans are made to locally registered borrowers, so access to the borrower information (borrowerNo and borrowerStatus) required in making a loan will be local and therefore fast. Failure of the communications network, or of the computer systems at other sites, will not affect the branch's ability to access information about most of the borrowers who visit the branch during the failure.

The Book table contains the attribute currentPrice. Suppose this information is normally required only by central administrative staff, not by branch staff. The Book table could be fragmented vertically into:

BookCost (ISBNX, currentPrice)
BookCatalogue (ISBNX, title, publicationDate)

Note that the identifier ISBNX must appear in both fragments in order to link corresponding rows. The BookCost fragment would be stored at the central administrative site. The BookCatalogue fragment contains the data needed by users and staff to search the catalogue of the global book stock. Where should this fragment be stored? It could be stored at, say, the branch site with the greatest number of users, but users at other sites may suffer a slow response to catalogue searches and would be vulnerable to failure of the network. All users would be vulnerable to failure of the site where the BookCatalogue fragment is stored. Also, that site would need sufficiently powerful hardware to cope with the demands of all users at peak times.

An alternative solution would be to *replicate* the BookCatalogue fragment at all sites, or perhaps just the busiest sites. Each site with a replica would enjoy fast access and immunity to network failure. Failure at a site affects only that site's users. The disadvantages are that replication requires more storage, and that any updates (insertions, amendments or deletions) affecting BookCatalogue must be propagated to all instances of the replica.

Reservations are made locally at individual branches, which suggests that the Reservation table should be fragmented horizontally by branchNo so that all reservations made by a branch are stored at that branch. However, according to the extended library scenario, if all copies (globally) of a reserved book are out on loan, then the first copy returned at any branch should be used to fulfil the reservation. Given this operational requirement, every return to every branch must be checked against the Reservation fragment at each branch, in case the returned copy is a copy of a reserved book that has been reserved at that branch. (There may be several reservations, globally or locally, for the same book, in which case assume that a reservation having the earliest reservationDate takes priority.) It would be much simpler and faster to process reservations if the whole Reservation table were stored at one site.

Similar considerations apply to the distribution of the rest of the database. Even for a small-scale E-R model, there is likely to be a large number of solutions. Finding an adequate, never mind optimal, solution is not easy and can be very sensitive to the exact nature of the user requirements. It is very probable that the distribution of data will need to be adjusted in the light of experience and changing usage.

Questions

1. Identify some advantages and disadvantages of implementing the library system as a single, centralised database as opposed to a distributed database. (3 min)

2. Assess the merits of a globally accessible database (whether distributed or centralised) compared with independent databases, one at each branch. Assume that each branch database holds only data about the borrowers, books, copies, loans, reservations etc. owned by that branch. (3 min)

3. Should the Branch table be fragmented or replicated in a distributed implementation? (2 min)

4. The Loan table could be fragmented so that all loans made by a branch are stored at that branch, but Loan does not contain branchNo, so how can the rows belonging to each fragment be specified? (2 min)

5. A borrower may take out loans from many branches but may not exceed the loan limit globally. Discuss the design of the distributed database and the method of processing loan transactions, with reference to enforcement of the global loan limit. (5 min)

6. It is not possible to update all replicas of a table simultaneously. How can a DDBMS ensure that users do not access inconsistent data? (1 min)

7. Suppose a table is replicated at every site. An application that updates the table must update every replica. If one or more sites has failed, the update cannot be completed, so the application may be unable to proceed until the site(s) come back on-line. How might this difficulty be avoided? Is there a disadvantage to your solution? (3 min)

16.4 Distributed data independence

In principle, users and applications should not need to know:

> how tables are fragmented (fragmentation transparency)
> how tables and fragments are replicated (replication transparency)
> how data is distributed among sites (location transparency).

Fragmentation, replication and location transparency are aspects of *distributed data independence*, the advantage of which is that the way the data is distributed can be changed as necessary without affecting existing programs. The idea of distributed data independence is an extension to the concept of data independence as introduced in Chapter 1.

The distributed database appears to users and applications as though it is a centralised database. It is the responsibility of the DDBMS to translate operations that refer to this centralised view into operations on the actual tables, fragments and replicas of the distributed database. The three-level architecture of Chapter 2, containing conceptual, external and internal schemas, needs to be supplemented by a distribution schema.

The DDBMS maintains a directory of information about tables, views, fragments, replicas, user access rights, etc. which it uses in interpreting queries and in compiling and executing application programs. Just as a distribution schema for the user data must be designed, so must a distribution schema for the DDBMS directory. If any user is to be able to query any data in the database, then the DDBMS query processor must have access to the full directory. Two possibilities are:

> Store the directory at a single site.
> Replicate the directory at every site.

Storing the directory at a single site destroys the ability of other sites to function independently (known as *site autonomy*) should the network or the directory site fail. Replication ensures that every site has fast and reliable access to the directory, but updates cannot be performed simultaneously, so replicas will sometimes be temporarily inconsistent.

Question

1. Why might a distribution schema be changed? (2 min)

16.5 Avoiding complications

A distributed database is potentially very complex to design and manage compared with a centralised database (whether accessed locally or remotely). The situation is much easier to manage if there are restrictions on updating the database. For example, it may be feasible to restrict users to retrieval operations during their working day, with updates being processed overnight. Alternatively, it may be possible to allow retrieval from any site, with updates being restricted to each user's local site.

We have assumed that the same DBMS is used at every site (a homogeneous system). In general, different sites could be running under different database management systems from a variety of vendors (a heterogeneous system) where each site is linked to the network through software known as a *gateway*. Heterogeneous systems typically occur where a company has grown by acquiring other companies and wants to link disparate systems. The standardisation of SQL (see Chapters 19 and 20) as a database language helps to make this feasible; even so, a heterogeneous system is unlikely to be successful unless the interaction between sites is carefully controlled in the design and operation of the system.

Answer pointers

Section 16.3

1. Accessing the central site gives every branch access to the whole database. Execution by the DBMS of a transaction about a borrower registered at another branch is no more complicated than the same query about a borrower registered at the querying branch, and similarly for transactions about books, copies, loans and reservations. It is easy to check the validity of a borrower's library card, easy to search

the whole book stock for titles of interest, and easy to handle loans and reservations, all regardless of which branch the borrower uses. In contrast, with a distributed database, the DDBMS may have to access data stored at various sites. This is likely to take longer and it may not be possible to complete a transaction because one or more sites, or network connections, has failed. Disadvantages include the vulnerability of a branch to failure of its network connection, vulnerability of all branches to failure of the central site, and relatively slow processing of transactions compared with access to local data. A DDBMS is more expensive and more resource hungry than a centralised DBMS. The implementation will be more difficult to debug and troubleshoot.

2.   The global database enables the library to offer an efficient service to borrowers, regardless of which branch they attend on any occasion. With separate databases, a borrower's library card would be valid only at the branch at which they registered. A borrower would have to register separately at each branch used, which would probably mean carrying a separate card for each branch. The loan limit could not be enforced globally. Reservations would be limited to the local book stock. Maintenance of the separate systems would be more difficult. For example, updates to the software would have to be rolled out separately to each branch.

3.   Each branch will need the addresses of other branches in order to handle reservations. It will probably be convenient to use the computer system to generate address labels. There is no point in fragmenting the Branch table; each branch needs the addresses of all the other branches and there is little to be gained by providing local access to just some of the addresses. As the Branch table is likely to be small and stable (addresses rarely change and it is unusual for new branches to be opened or existing branches to be closed down) it is a strong candidate for replication at all branches. There should not be any difficulty in maintaining the consistency of the replicas.

4.   The attribute accessionNo links the Loan and Copy tables, so the branchNo values can be found from the Copy table. In terms of relational algebra and SQL (see Chapters 17 and 19) the Loan and Copy tables can be joined on accessionNo. The appropriate columns and rows can then be extended to form the required fragments.

5.   Suppose the Loan table is fragmented according to branch, as in question 4, but that there is no replication. When a loan request is processed, each fragment would need to be checked to see how many copies the borrower already had on loan from each branch. This would make the issuing of loans very inefficient. It would be more efficient to store the whole Loan table at one site. Another solution would be to include (in Borrower) a loanCount attribute that is updated when copies are loaned or returned. The disadvantage would be that the value in loanCount might become inconsistent with that derivable from Loan. Yet another solution would be to replicate Loan at all sites. What would be the disadvantages?

6.   A DDBMS needs a mechanism for locking all replicas of a table, so that users cannot access the data until the DDBMS is certain that all replicas have been updated successfully. Issuing locks across a multitude of sites could seriously impact performance.

7.   Designate one replica as the primary copy. Provided that this copy is updated successfully, the application may proceed, leaving the DDBMS to update the remaining copies. The disadvantages are that the data in some replicas could become out of date, and that updating is dependent on the availability of the primary copy. It may not be necessary for updates to be propagated to sites immediately, as it is often sufficient for users to work with data that is correct as of the close of the previous working day, or working week. If so, performance during the working day can be improved by propagating updates from the primary copy overnight or at weekends.

Section 16.4

1. Slow response times to certain queries. Upgrades to software or hardware (including the network). New applications. Changing patterns of use. Addition or deletion of sites.

17

Relational algebra

17.1 Table-at-a-time processing

The outcome of the data modelling techniques described in Parts 2 and 3 of this book is a set of tables (i.e. relations) that provide a logical structure for the information of interest to the enterprise. In order to use this information (for example, to process borrower registration, loans, returns and reservations in the library example) some means of manipulating the data is needed.

Relational algebra is a data manipulation language that provides a set of operators, each of which processes a complete table, or tables, at a time. It is a higher-level language than those programming languages that process only a record, or a row of a table, at a time. In comparison with *record-at-a-time* languages, a *table-at-a-time* language offers more powerful, more concise commands that simplify data manipulation and are better suited to automatic optimisation.

Although relational algebra, as such, is not often used as an implemented language, the basic ideas appear in different guises in other, more user-friendly languages. In particular, the SQL data manipulation language (see Chapter 19) is based on the table manipulation concepts considered in the present chapter.

The tables that relational algebra operates upon must be normalised, as described in section 3.2, but they need not obey any higher normalisation conditions, such as the Boyce/Codd rule.

17.2 Relational algebra operations

The three most important operations in relational algebra are those for constructing a new table (a) by selecting rows from an existing table, (b) by selecting columns from an existing table, and (c) by linking together tables on the basis of values in specified columns of each. Examples of each of these operations are given below, based on the Employee, Room and Telephone tables shown in Fig. 17.1. The syntax used here is designed to be easy to remember; it is not rigorously defined, nor should it be assumed that an implementation exists. In each example, the result of the operation is placed in table TR.

17.2.1 Selection of rows

The *Rows* operation selects out those rows in a table which satisfy a given condition. The syntax is:

<result table name> = Rows of <table name> where <condition>.

Only attributes within <table name> may be referenced by the <condition>, but the latter may include the usual range of comparisons and logical operators, such as >, =, <, AND, OR, NOT.

Employee

employeeNo	employeeName	roomNo
E1	Baker	R2
E4	Smith	R4
E2	Moss	R2
E5	Smith	R3
E8	Smith	R4
E9	Wells	R4
E7	Smith	R6

Room

roomNo	capacity
R1	5
R2	4
R3	1
R4	3
R5	4
R6	1
R7	2

Telephone

roomNo	extensionNo
R2	217
R2	218
R2	219
R3	350
R4	451
R4	454
R5	910

Fig. 17.1   Tables used in relational algebra examples

Example 1

TR = Rows of Employee where employeeName = 'Smith'.

TR will contain just those rows from Employee for which the employeeName is Smith.

TR

employeeNo	employeeName	roomNo
E4	Smith	R4
E5	Smith	R3
E8	Smith	R4
E7	Smith	R6

Example 2

TR = Rows of Employee where roomNo = 'R4' and employeeName = 'Smith'.

TR

employeeNo	employeeName	roomNo
E4	Smith	R4
E8	Smith	R4

Example 3

TR = Rows of Room where capacity <4 and roomNo ≠ 'R7'.

TR

roomNo	capacity
R3	1
R4	3
R6	1

17.2.2 Selection of columns

The *Column(s)* operation selects out nominated column(s) from a table. The syntax is:

<result table name> = Column(s) of <table name> under <attribute list>.

Example 1

TR = Column of Employee under roomNo.

TR	roomNo
	R2
	R4
	R3
	R6

The seven rows in Employee have been reduced to four rows in TR because of the rule that duplicate rows are not allowed in a table (see section 3.2).

Example 2

TR = Columns of Employee under roomNo, employeeName.

TR	roomNo	employeeName
	R2	Baker
	R4	Smith
	R2	Moss
	R3	Smith
	R4	Wells
	R6	Smith

The order of attributes in the attribute list governs the order of columns in the result table. Notice that a duplicate row, R4 Smith, has been deleted. TR allows the number of employees with distinct names in a given room to be deduced, but not the total number of employees in the room. There are three employees in roomNo R4, but two of them have the same name.

17.2.3 Linking tables

The *Join* operation links tables together on the basis of specified columns in each. The syntax is:

<result table name> = Join of <table list> on <attribute list>.

In the examples below the <attribute list> consists of only one attribute, which is the commonest situation. The generalisation to several attributes is straightforward, as they may be regarded as being a single composite attribute.

Example 1

TR = Join of Employee, Room on roomNo.

TR

employeeNo	employeeName	roomNo	roomNo	capacity
E1	Baker	R2	R2	4
E4	Smith	R4	R4	3
E2	Moss	R2	R2	4
E5	Smith	R3	R3	1
E8	Smith	R4	R4	3
E9	Wells	R4	R4	3
E7	Smith	R6	R6	1

Notice that no row appears in the result table unless the same roomNo value is present in both the Employee and Room tables. Thus there are no rows in TR for the roomNo(s) R1, R5 or R7. As the contents of the roomNo columns in the result table are necessarily identical, it is possible to delete one of them without losing information. The result is then known as a *natural join* rather than the *equi-join* illustrated. Equi-joins are used in the examples in this section, as it is then easier to follow the derivation of the result. Normally, natural joins would be preferred.

Example 2

TR = Join of Employee, Telephone on roomNo.

TR

employeeNo	employeeName	roomNo	roomNo	extensionNo
E1	Baker	R2	R2	217
E1	Baker	R2	R2	218
E1	Baker	R2	R2	219
E4	Smith	R4	R4	451
E4	Smith	R4	R4	454
E2	Moss	R2	R2	217
E2	Moss	R2	R2	218
E2	Moss	R2	R2	219
E5	Smith	R3	R3	350
E8	Smith	R4	R4	451
E8	Smith	R4	R4	454
E9	Wells	R4	R4	451
E9	Wells	R4	R4	454

This is a more complicated example, because duplicate roomNo values occur within the Employee table and also within the Telephone table. The result table, TR, contains one row for each possible pair of rows in Employee and Telephone for which the roomNo values are the same. TR is constructed by taking each row of Employee in turn, and coupling it with all those rows in Telephone which have the same value of roomNo. The rows in TR have been split up into blocks to emphasise this process.

17.3 Sample queries

Since the result of a relational algebra operation is itself a table, there is no reason why that table should not itself be the subject of further relational algebra operations. Examples of queries that require a succession of operations are given below. In each case, the final result is placed in table TR. The join operations are assumed to be natural joins.

Example 1
Which rooms contain one or more employees called Smith?

      T1 = Rows of Employee where employeeName = 'Smith'.
      TR = Column of T1 under roomNo.

Example 2
What is the capacity of the room occupied by employee E9?

      T1 = Rows of Employee where employeeNo = 'E9'.
      T2 = Column of T1 under roomNo.
      T3 = Join of T2, Room on roomNo.
      TR = Column of T3 under capacity.

Several other sequences of operations could have been used. In particular, the second statement could have been omitted (provided that T2 were altered to T1 in the following statement), but superfluous data would then be carried through into the join operation.

Example 3
What is the employeeName, roomNo and extensionNo of each employee who occupies a room with a capacity of between two and four people inclusive?

      T1 = Rows of Room where capacity $\geq$ 2 and capacity $\leq$ 4.
      T2 = Join of T1, Employee on roomNo.
      T3 = Columns of T2 under employeeName, roomNo.
      TR = Join of T3, Telephone on roomNo.

Questions

These questions refer to the following tables:

Eats

animalName	food
camel	buns
zebra	hay
snake	people
camel	hay
snake	mice
lion	people

Keeper

keeperNo	keeperName
100	Morris
101	Dennis
102	Darwin
103	Morris

Supervision

keeperNo	animalName
100	camel
100	snake
100	lion
101	zebra
103	snake

1. Write down the table occurrences generated by each of the following:
(a)   TR = Column of Keeper under keeperName.
(b)   TR = Columns of Eats under food, animalName.
(c)   TR = Rows of Supervision where keeperNo = '101'.
(d)   TR = Rows of Eats where animalName = 'camel'.
(e)   TR = Rows of Eats where animalName = 'camel' and food = 'hay'.
(f)   T1 = Rows of Supervision where animalName = 'snake'.
       TR = Column of T1 under keeperNo.   (4 min)
2.   Write down relational algebra statements to derive the answer to each of the following queries. The result table should not contain any superfluous data. Write down the table occurrence generated by each statement.
(a)   What does a camel eat?
(b)   What does a kangaroo eat?
(c)   What are the keeperNo(s) of keepers called Morris?   (3 min)
3.   Write down the table occurrences generated by each of the following. Assume equi-joins throughout.
(a)   TR = Join of Supervision and Keeper on keeperNo.
(b)   T1 = Join of Eats and Supervision on animalName.
       TR = Columns of T1 under keeperNo, food.   (3 min)
4.   Write down relational algebra statements to derive the answer to each of the following queries. The result table should not contain any superfluous data. Write down the table occurrence generated by each statement. Use natural joins throughout.
(a)   What is supervised by a keeper called Morris?
(b)   What are the keeperNo(s) of the hay-eaters?
(c)   What are the name(s) of the keeper(s) who keep people-eaters?   (4 min)
5.   What difference, if any, is there between the results of the following statements:
       T1 = Join of Eats and Supervision on animalName.
       T2 = Join of Supervision and Eats on animalName.
What general rule does this example suggest?   (2 min)

17.4   Further join operations

The join operation is not restricted to tables which happen to have an attribute name in common. What matters is whether the columns controlling the join contain attribute values which can sensibly be compared. For example, it would be perfectly reasonable to join Employee and Room on roomNo even if roomNo in Employee had happened to be called officeNo. The syntax would need to be extended slightly; for example:

       T1 = Join of Employee, Room on officeNo = roomNo.

However, it would not normally be considered reasonable to perform the following join:

       T2 = Join of Room, Telephone on capacity = extensionNo.

The difference between these two examples may be expressed by saying that the values of the attributes officeNo and roomNo are taken from the same *domain*, whereas the values of capacity and extensionNo are not. A domain is a pool of values of a particular type. The values of a given attribute always come from one domain, but the same domain may be shared by many attributes. In the final analysis, the scope of a domain is whatever you decide to make it, but some choices are more reasonable than others.

The syntax used in the above examples suggests that the join operation could be extended to allow operators other than equals. The equi-join and natural join could be supplemented by the *greater-than-join, less-than-join, not-equal-to-join*, and so on, though there is unlikely to be much call for these kinds of operations in practice. If they are used, there will not be a redundant column to strike out, as in the natural join, so it may be necessary to qualify attribute names in the result table to avoid ambiguity. For example, the roomNo attributes in Employee, Room and Telephone (Fig. 17.1) could be renamed Employee.roomNo, Room.roomNo and Telephone.roomNo, respectively.

Questions

1. Would you regard the attributes orderDate and deliveryDate as being defined on the same domain? (2 min)

2. A table may be joined with itself. With reference to Fig. 12.12, what interpretation would you place on the result of:

T1 = Join of Structure on majorPartNo = minorPartNo.
TR = Column of T1 under majorPartNo. (3 min)

17.5 Union, intersection and difference

The *Union, Intersection* and *Difference* operations apply only to tables that have compatible layouts; that is, they must have the same number of columns, and the values in the corresponding columns of each table must be drawn from the same domain. For simplicity, we assume that the same attribute names are used in corresponding columns. The examples below are based on the tables in Fig. 17.2.

Current Employee

employeeNo	employeeName
E32	Wroe
E75	Blunt
E54	Mistry
E63	Morris
E41	Cox

RetiredEmployee

employeeNo	employeeName
E17	Morris
E41	Cox
E48	Page
E75	Blunt

Fig. 17.2   Tables used in relational algebra examples. Two of the retired employees are employed as part-time consultants, and consequently appear in both tables

17.5.1 Union

The *Union* operation merges tables into a result table which contains all the rows from the source tables, but with duplicate rows struck out. Each row in the result table appears in one or more of the source tables. The syntax is:

<result table name> = Union of <table list>.

Example

List employeeNo and employeeName for all current and retired employees.

TR = Union of CurrentEmployee, RetiredEmployee.

TR	employeeNo	employeeName
	E32	Wroe
	E75	Blunt
	E54	Mistry
	E63	Morris
	E41	Cox
	E17	Morris
	E48	Page

Employees E75 and E41 appear in both the source tables, but only once in the result table.

17.5.2   Intersection

The *Intersection* operation selects out those rows which appear in all the source tables. The syntax is:

<result table name> = Intersection of <table list>.

Example

Which retired employees are also currently employed (e.g. as part-time consultants)?

TR = Intersection of CurrentEmployee, RetiredEmployee.

TR	employeeNo	employeeName
	E75	Blunt
	E41	Cox

17.5.3   Difference

The *Difference* operation removes from the first table in a list those rows which also appear in the other tables in the list. The syntax is:

<result table name> = Difference of <table list>.

Example

Which retired employees are not also currently employed?

TR = Difference of RetiredEmployee, CurrentEmployee.

TR	employeeNo	employeeName
	E17	Morris
	E48	Page

The order of the table names is important. The result table contains all the rows in the first table, minus those rows which also appear in the second table.

Question

1. Write down the result table occurrence generated by:

> TR = Difference of CurrentEmployee, RetiredEmployee. (1 min)

17.6 Division

The *Division* operation selects out rows from one table under the control of a set of values in another table. The syntax is:

> <result table name> = Division of <table-1> by <table-2>.

<table-1> is called the dividend and <table-2> the divisor. Each attribute in the divisor must share the same domain as the corresponding attribute in the dividend.

Example
With reference to Fig. 17.3, suppose that a list is required of all projects to which those employees in the EmployeeGroup table are assigned. All the employees in EmployeeGroup must be assigned to a project for it to be included in the list. The required division statement is:

> TR = Division of Assignment by EmployeeGroup.

To see how the division operation works, the rows in Fig. 17.3a have been rearranged into groups in Fig. 17.3b. A group contains the same value of projectNo throughout, coupled where possible with the complete set of values which appear in the EmployeeGroup table. The result table, Fig. 17.3c, comprises the projectNo values from each of these complete groups.

The division operation can be applied in a similar way to tables with any number of columns, provided that the dividend has more columns than the divisor. The simplest way to view the process is to regard the divisor's attributes as a single composite attribute A2, and the dividend's attributes as two composite attributes A1, A2.

Question

1. The projectNo values P3, P5 are stored in an occurrence of table ProjectGroup. With reference to Fig. 17.3, write a relational algebra statement to answer the query:

> 'Which employees work on both projects P3 and P5?' (1 min)

Assignment

projectNo	employeeNo
P1	E4
P5	E1
P3	E2
P1	E1
P2	E5
P3	E4
P1	E2
P3	E5
P5	E2
P1	E8
P2	E2
P5	E4
P1	E5

(a)

EmployeeGroup

employeeNo
E2
E4
E5

projectNo	employeeNo	
P1	E2	} Complete group
P1	E4	
P1	E5	
P1	E1	
P1	E8	
P2	E2	
P2	E5	
P3	E2	} Complete group
P3	E4	
P3	E5	
P5	E1	
P5	E2	
P5	E4	

(b)

TR

projectNo
P1
P3

(c)

Fig. 17.3   Example of the division operation
(a)   The Assignment and EmployeeGroup tables
(b)   The Assignment table rearranged into groups according to the contents of EmployeeGroup
(c)   The result of dividing Assignment by EmployeeGroup is a list of those projects to which the complete group has been assigned

17.7   Extended Cartesian product

In an *Extended Cartesian Product*, the result table contains one row for each possible combination of rows from the source tables. All the attributes in the original tables appear in the result table. The syntax is:

TR = Product of <table list>.

Example

TR = Product of Doctor, Patient.

If there are five rows in Doctor, and eleven rows in Patient, there will be fifty-five rows in TR.

Question

1. The table types Doctor and Patient are defined as follows:

> Doctor (doctorNo, doctorName)
> Patient (patientNo, patientName, doctorNo)

Write down a sequence of Product, Rows, and Columns relational algebra statements which have the same effect as:

> TR = Join of Doctor, Patient on Doctor.doctorNo = Patient.doctorNo.

Assume a natural join. Note the qualification of doctorNo by table name to eliminate ambiguity over which doctorNo attribute is being referenced.   (2 min)

17.8   Update

In principle, the union and difference operations could be adapted to handle the insertion and deletion of rows.

Example 1
Insert the row P2 E8 into the Assignment table of Fig. 17.3.

> Assignment = Union of Assignment, {'P2', 'E8'}.

Example 2
Delete all rows where projectNo = 'P3' in the Assignment table of Fig. 17.3.

> Assignment = Difference of Assignment, {'P3', *}.

Question

1. What practical problem arises in amending only some of the attributes in a row, assuming that only difference and union operations are available?   (1 min)

17.9   Nested operations

The output of a relational algebra operation is a table, and the input is one or more tables. Consequently, it is logically possible to nest a series of operations rather than generating intermediate tables.

Example
With reference to Fig. 17.1, list the extensionNo(s) of rooms with a capacity of 1 person. An unnested solution is:

> T1 = Rows of Room where capacity = 1.
> T2 = Join of T1, Telephone on roomNo.
> TR = Column of T2 under extensionNo.

To obtain the nested version, work up from the last statement to the first.

Substituting for T2 in the last statement gives:

TR = Column of [Join of T1, Telephone on roomNo]$_{T2}$ under extensionNo.

Now substitute for T1:

TR = Column of [Join of {Rows of Room where capacity = 1}$_{T1}$, Telephone on roomNo]$_{T2}$ under extensionNo.

The square and curly brackets, and subscripts T1 and T2, have been inserted in order to make the correspondence between the nested and unnested versions clearer. Normally, the nested version would be written simply as:

TR = Column of (Join of (Rows of Room where capacity = 1), Telephone on roomNo) under extensionNo.

We will see in the following chapter that it is easier for a database management system to optimise its query processing performance if the query is expressed as a single statement.

Questions

1. Is it likely to be more efficient to do a join before selecting out the rows required, or to select rows before doing a join? (1 min)

2. (a) With reference to the Eats, Keeper and Supervision tables shown in the questions for section 17.3, write a sequence of unnested relational algebra operations to find the foods eaten by animals supervised by keepers called Morris.

(b) Write a single, nested relational algebra statement that answers the part (a) query.

Assignment

1. Prove that a table list in a relational algebra statement need never contain more than two tables.

Answer pointers

Section 17.3

1. (a) TR

keeperName
Morris
Dennis
Darwin

(b) Same as Eats, but with columns reversed.

(c) TR

keeperNo	animalName
101	zebra

(d) TR

animalName	food
camel	buns
camel	hay

(e) TR

animalName	food
camel	hay

(f) T1

keeperNo	animalName
100	snake
103	snake

TR

keeperNo
100
103

2. (a) T1 = Rows of Eats where animalName = 'camel'.
TR = Column of T1 under food.

T1

animalName	food
camel	buns
camel	hay

TR

food
buns
hay

(b) Similar to 2(a), but the table occurrences for T1 and TR will be null.

(c) T1 = Rows of Keeper where keeperName = 'Morris'.
TR = Column of T1 under keeperNo.

T1

keeperNo	keeperName
100	Morris
103	Morris

TR

keeperNo
100
103

3. (a) TR

keeperNo	animalName	keeperNo	keeperName
100	camel	100	Morris
100	snake	100	Morris
100	lion	100	Morris
101	zebra	101	Dennis
103	snake	103	Morris

(b) T1

animalName	food	keeperNo	animalName
camel	buns	100	camel
zebra	hay	101	zebra
snake	people	100	snake
snake	people	103	snake
camel	hay	100	camel
snake	mice	100	snake
snake	mice	103	snake
lion	people	100	lion

TR

keeperNo	food
100	buns
101	hay
100	people
103	people
100	hay
100	mice
103	mice

4. (a)   T1 = Rows of Keeper where keeperName = 'Morris'.
     T2 = Join of T1, Supervision on keeperNo.
     TR = Column of T2 under animalName.

T1

keeperNo	keeperName
100	Morris
103	Morris

T2

keeperNo	keeperName	animalName
100	Morris	camel
100	Morris	snake
100	Morris	lion
103	Morris	snake

TR

animalName
camel
snake
lion

(b)   T1 = Rows of Eats where food = 'hay'.
     T2 = Join of T1, Supervision on animalName.
     TR = Column of T2 under keeperNo.

T1

animalName	food
zebra	hay
camel	hay

T2

animalName	food	keeperNo
zebra	hay	101
camel	hay	100

TR

keeperNo
101
100

(c)   T1 = Rows of Eats where food = 'people'.
     T2 = Column of T1 under animalName.
     T3 = Join of T2, Supervision on animalName.
     T4 = Column of T3 under keeperNo.
     T5 = Join of T4, Keeper on keeperNo.
     TR = Column of T5 under keeperName.

T1

animalName	food
snake	people
lion	people

T2

animalName
snake
lion

T3

animalName	keeperNo
snake	100
snake	103
lion	100

T4

keeperNo
100
103

T5	keeperNo	keeperName
	100	Morris
	103	Morris

TR	keeperName
	Morris

This solution demonstrates the use of column operations to minimise the amount of data carried through into the joins.

5. The contents of T1 and T2 will be the same, but the order of rows may differ. (The order of rows in a table is immaterial, in that it conveys no information, though as a matter of convenience, a user would expect to be able to specify ordering of the output.) The general rule is that the sequence in which the table names are written in a join statement is not significant.

Section 17.4

1. They would probably both be regarded as being defined on the domain of all possible dates (this domain could have a cut-off point at the date the company started business). There would be a difference in their ranges if deliveryDate could be in the future, but orderDate could not. Even so, it would make sense to ask questions like, 'For which orders is the deliveryDate equal to the orderDate?' Incidentally, assuming that there is a table type Order (orderNo, orderDate, deliveryDate), this query could be answered by a Rows operation of the form:

TR = Rows of Order where orderDate = deliveryDate.

2. The result would be a list of all partNo(s) that are both major and minor parts. Final assemblies and components would be excluded from the list.

Section 17.5.3

1. TR

employeeNo	employeeName
E32	Wroe
E54	Mistry
E63	Morris

The result table represents all current employees who are not on the list of retired employees.

Section 17.6

1. TR = Division of Assignment by ProductGroup.

Section 17.7

1. T1 = Product of Doctor, Patient.
   T2 = Rows of T1 where Doctor.doctorNo = Patient.doctorNo.
   TR = Columns of T2 under Doctor.doctorNo, doctorName, patientNo, patientName.
The final statement (TR = . . .) could have referred to Patient.doctorNo instead of Doctor.doctorNo.

Section 17.8

1.   The problem is how to carry forward those attribute values which are not being amended. In practice, a relational algebra update operation would need to be defined.

Section 17.9

1.   It is normally more efficient to select rows first; this can substantially reduce the number of rows involved in the join operation.

2.   (a)   T1 = Rows of Keeper where keeperName = 'Morris'.
          T2 = Join of T1, Supervision on keeperNo.
          T3 = Join of T2, Eats on animalName.
          TR = Column of T3 under food.

   (b)   TR = Column of (Join of (Join of (Rows of Keeper where keeperName = 'Morris'), Supervision on keeperNo), Eats on animalName) under food.

18

Query optimisation

18.1   Query processing

The performance of a database is judged by measures such as the response time for interactive queries, the time to generate reports, and the time for batch processing (e.g. a monthly payroll run). In general, even if the program source code is not altered, the performance will change over time. Payroll may be calculated, orders invoiced and production scheduled just as they always were, using the same program source code, yet the performance may differ because of changes to volumes, frequencies and priorities.

There may be more (or fewer) employees on the payroll, changes in the relative demand for different products, and more (or fewer) levels of sub-assembly between final assemblies and components. There may also be requests for improved performance. Certain reports may prove to be particularly useful, so they are requested more often and users want them to be generated more quickly. Some applications may be given higher priority (e.g. Internet order processing over mail order processing). Applications may be upgraded with new or amended programs and entirely new applications implemented.

The database administrator can change the internal (storage) schema to optimise the overall performance as database usage evolves. Particular attention will be paid to those applications or functions where the response time is critical (e.g. issuing a loan in the library example) while endeavouring to maintain an acceptable response for less time-critical functions (e.g. deleting a borrower). However, it is usually neither desirable nor feasible to rewrite program code to adapt it to changes in the internal schema. Not only is rewriting and testing expensive, but the consequential cost if errors are introduced into the code could be severe. Provided that the database management system supports adequate data independence, there is no logical need to change the source code used in application and interactive queries; the code will still work correctly. The performance of the database is a different matter. In order to process queries (retrievals, updates and deletions) efficiently, the database management system must automatically tailor its access routines to suit the state of the database at the time the query is executed. For example, a table with 100 rows of moderate length could be read into main memory and processed there. Should that table grow to 100 000 rows, it may well be too large to process in this way.

Because most databases are subject to change, a crucial component of a database management system is the *query optimiser*. The query optimiser accepts a query command issued by an application program or interactive user and (at least in principle) works out the fastest way to process that query, taking into account the state of the database at that point in time. The state of the database includes factors, discussed later in this chapter, such as the physical storage structure used for each table, the existence of indexes that allow fast access to rows in a table, the number of rows in each table, and the distribution of attribute values within a table (e.g. how many values of the salary attribute in an Employee table fall in the ranges 0–9999, 10000–19999, etc.). For a distributed database management system, factors such as the location of data and the speed of the data communication links need to be considered.

A query optimiser is usually designed to operate on just one relational command at a time but, as noted in section 17.9, that command may very well comprise many relational operations (e.g. row, column, join) so there is plenty of scope for optimisation. The language most commonly used to access relational databases is SQL (see Chapter 19). The optimiser breaks down the SQL command to its equivalent relational algebra operations and then constructs an efficient *query plan* to carry out the command.

18.2   Query plans

In practice, there are often very many ways of processing a query. The time taken for a query optimiser to evaluate all possible query plans may not be justifiable, because the response time seen by an interactive user is the sum of (a) the time taken to choose a query plan and (b) the time taken to execute that query plan. Queries by interactive users are normally compiled (or interpreted) at the time they are issued, though it may be possible to save frequently used queries in compiled form. A query optimiser should contain rules that tell it when it is no longer worth prolonging the search for a better plan than it has so far found.

The situation is different for an application that is pre-compiled, in that the time taken to choose a query plan does not affect the response time seen by an end-user. It is therefore worthwhile for the query optimiser to spend longer searching for a very efficient plan. A disadvantage of pre-compilation is that the query plan may have become invalid by the time the application is run. For example, the plan may use an index (see section 18.3.4) to access a table, but that index may no longer exist. One solution is for the database management system to re-compile every query plan affected by a change at the time the change is made. Alternatively, the database management system could simply flag each affected query plan as invalid and then compile a new plan only when the affected application is next invoked.

Questions

1.   Suggest some simple rules to determine when a query optimiser should stop searching for a better plan.   (2 min)

2.   For pre-compiled query plans, what are the relative merits of dealing with a change to the internal schema by (a) re-compiling every affected query plan at the time a change is made, and (b) compiling a new plan only when an affected application is next invoked?   (3 min)

18.3 Storage structures

A query optimiser needs to know the storage structures used for tables. Some of the commonly used storage structures are outlined here. We assume that tables are stored on direct access devices such as disk drives. The discussion refers to the Student table shown in Fig. 18.1. As this sample table contains only a few rows and columns, it could

Student

studentNo	studentName
103	Desai
218	Wong
920	Jones
100	Miller
357	Davis
108	Miller
305	King

Student (studentNo, studentName)

Fig. 18.1   Sample table of students

be held entirely in main memory and searched by a simple linear scan of the rows. It is used here to illustrate techniques that are used to access the much larger tables likely to be encountered in reality. It is worth bearing in mind, though, that one of the most effective ways of improving performance is to increase main memory capacity, as the optimiser can then construct query plans that make greater use of the very much faster speed of main memory compared to disk.

The description of the storage structures is simplified by assuming that the unit of storage and access is the table row. (Lines are drawn between rows in the Figures to emphasise that these are physically stored rows, not rows in a conceptual or external model.) In practice, data is stored and accessed in *pages* (blocks) of data, where the page size could be several kilobytes and contain multiple rows.

18.3.1 Unordered structure

This is the simplest, often the default, structure for a table. The rows are in no particular order, as in Fig. 18.1. New rows can be inserted at the end of the table, or in space left free by the deletion of rows, or indeed in any free space within the storage allocated to the table.

Questions

1. If the unordered Student table in Fig. 18.1 is searched by a linear scan through the rows, how many rows on average will have to be read to find:
   (a)   those rows with a given studentName;
   (b)   those rows with a given studentNo?   (2 min)

2. An unordered table contains 1000 rows, each 200 bytes long. A query needs to search the whole table. How many pages must be read if the page size is (a) 200 bytes, (b) 8 Kbytes?   (1 min)

18.3.2   Ordered structure

Rows could be ordered on one or more attributes. For example, the Student table could be ordered on studentNo, as in Fig. 18.2. In terms of the conceptual schema, the order

Student

studentNo	studentName
100	Miller
103	Desai
108	Miller
218	Wong
305	King
357	Davis
920	Jones

Fig. 18.2   Ordered storage structure. Student table ordered on studentNo

of rows in a relational model is immaterial (see Chapter 3) in that it conveys no information, such as whether one student enrolled before or after another, but that does not prevent the internal schema from specifying that the rows are physically stored in an order that facilitates access. There is an overhead in maintaining an ordered table. For example, insertion of a row '241 Baker' into the student table would necessitate physical reorganisation of the rows.

Question

1. Suggest how, as new rows are inserted into an ordered structure, the ordering of rows could be maintained without physically sorting the whole stored table for each insertion. Assume that more than the minimum storage space needed for the table is available and that several rows can be stored in a single page.   (3 min)

18.3.3   Hashed structure

In a hashed structure, a mathematical calculation (the *hash function*) is applied to an attribute value (the *hash key*) to obtain a storage address. Some form of a division/remainder algorithm is commonly used as the hash function. For example, it is likely that the Student table will need to be accessed frequently by studentNo. There are 7 rows in the Student table. To calculate the storage address of a row, divide the studentNo by 7 and take the remainder as the address. Taking studentNo '103' as an example, $103/7 = 14$ remainder 5, so the row for this studentNo should be stored at address 5 within the table's storage structure (Fig. 18.3).

Student

Home address	Storage address	studentNo	studentName	
0	0	357	Davis	
1	1	218	Wong	
2	2	100	Miller	
3	3	920	Jones	
3	4	108	Miller	← Overflow from home address 3
5	5	103	Desai	
4	6	305	King	← Overflow from home address 4

Fig. 18.3 Hashed storage structure. Student table hashed on studentNo

Note that the Student table requires enough storage for 7 rows, and that taking the remainder after division of a studentNo by 7 *guarantees* that the address falls within that range (i.e. the address must be within the range 0–6 inclusive). Whatever the range of attribute values (say, 100–999 in this example) the calculated storage address will always be within the range 0–6.

Different values of studentNo may hash to the same *home address*. For instance, studentNo(s) '108' and '920' both hash to address 3. This is an example of a *collision*. Both rows cannot be stored at the same address, so there must be some means of handling the *overflow*. A very simple solution is to store an overflow row at the next free address. The hashed version of Student would then be as shown in Fig. 18.3, assuming that the rows are inserted into the hashed structure by processing them in the order in which they appear in Fig. 18.1, so '103 Desai' is inserted first, '218 Wong' second, '920 Jones' third, and so on. The next two rows, '100 Miller' and '357 Davis' are also stored at their home addresses. Row '108 Miller' hashes to a home address of 3, but that location is already occupied by '920 Jones', so '108 Miller' overflows into the next free location, namely address 4. Finally, row '305 King' hashes to a home address of 4, but both addresses 4 and 5 are by now occupied, so '305 King' goes into the next free location, namely address 6.

In the interests of fast access, it is desirable that most rows should be stored at their home addresses, so it is usual to allow a larger address space than the minimum required. Fig. 18.4 shows the effect of allowing space for 11 rows. The hash function divisor is now 11, with possible remainders ranging over addresses 0–10. There is now one overflow row in this example.

Questions

1. How could a division/remainder hash function be applied to non-numeric attribute values? (1 min)

2. Why is it not possible, for the hashed structure described in this section, to use two different hash keys for the same table? (1 min)

3. Outline the steps a database management system would take to retrieve a row, for a given studentNo value, for the hashed structure and overflow mechanism described in this section. (3 min)

Student

Home address	Storage address	studentNo	studentName
	0		
1	1	100	Miller
	2		
	3		
4	4	103	Desai
5	5	357	Davis
	6		
7	7	920	Jones
8	8	305	King
9	9	218	Wong
9	10	108	Miller	← Overflow from home address 9

Fig. 18.4   Hashed storage structure with extra space allowed to reduce the number of collisions

18.3.4.   Indexed structure

Hashing offers fast access on the hash key, but cannot be applied to more than one (possibly composite) attribute in a table. Nor is hashing any help if sequential access is required, for example access to Student rows in studentNo order or studentName order. Indexed structures are free from these constraints.

Fig. 18.5 illustrates two indexes for the Student table. SNoInd indexes the table in ascending order of studentNo; SNameInd indexes the table in ascending order of studentName. Each index is organised into a hierarchy of index blocks, both indexes in this example are two-level hierarchies. Each entry in a top level index block contains the address of a lower level index block; it also contains the highest indexed value in that block. Entries within an index block are sorted into order (ascending in this example).

To find the rows where studentName = 'Miller', the database management system will perform the following steps. Search the SNameInd top level index block from its first entry until an entry is found that is greater than or equal to 'Miller'. Follow the address pointer in that entry to the lower level index block. Search the lower level block for occurrences of 'Miller'. Follow the address pointers for these entries to the table rows of Student. There might be further top level index entries for 'Miller', if so the search procedure would be repeated to retrieve the further row(s) of Student with this name.

There are no duplicate values of studentNo in the Student table, so there are no duplicate values in any given level of the SNoInd index. Assuming that the top level index block of SNoInd is held in main memory at run time but the lower level index blocks are stored on disk, any row in Student can be accessed with 1 read of an index block and 1 read of a table row. Given an index block size of 3 entries, 9 rows can be indexed with a two-level index, as in Fig. 18.5. Given an index block size of 100 entries, 10 000 rows can be indexed with a two-level index, i.e. one top level index block with 100

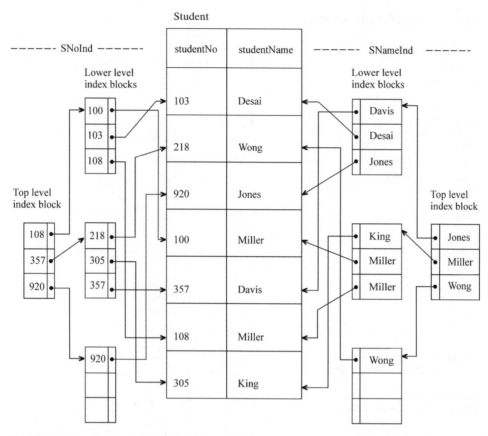

Fig. 18.5   Indexed storage structure. Student table indexed on studentNo and studentName

entries, each of which points to a lower level index block with 100 entries, each entry of which indexes one row in the table.

Questions

1.   How many rows can be indexed with an index block size of 100 entries and a three-level index hierarchy?   (1 min)
2.   Indexing speeds up retrievals. What is the effect on insertions of new rows?

                                                                                                                                  (1 min)
3.   State an advantage of indexing pages rather than rows.   (1 min)

18.3.5   Summary

If only a low proportion of rows in a table need to be accessed (a low *hit rate*), hashed or indexed structures are efficient. A hashed structure allows direct access on the hash key. An index allows direct and sequential access. If a high proportion of rows in a table need to be accessed (a high hit rate) it may be more efficient to scan the table from beginning to end rather than access individual rows by a hash key or index.

18.4   Optimisation

Fig. 18.6 shows some sample data for Student and Option tables that record which modules each student is studying at a college. Suppose there are 500 rows in Student and 4000 rows in Option.

Student

studentNo	studentName
103	Desai
218	Wong
920	Jones
100	Miller
357	Davis
108	Miller
305	King
etc......	etc......

Option

studentNo	moduleName
461	History
103	Engineering
854	Japanese
256	Computing
605	Japanese
103	Biophysics
357	Swedish
218	History
932	Geology
357	Computing
920	Spanish
357	Chemistry
103	Japanese
100	Geology
100	Biophysics
357	Spanish
305	Mathematics
etc......	etc......

Student (studentNo, studentName)
Option (studentNo, moduleName)

Number of Student rows =   500
Number of Option rows   = 4000

Fig. 18.6   Unordered storage structures for the Student and Option tables

The optimiser accepts a query language command (typically an SQL command, see Chapter 19) and breaks it down into an equivalent set of relational algebra operations. It needs to find an efficient sequence of operations, taking advantage of its knowledge of the database storage structures and other properties of the data.

Query optimisation is a specialist subject. We will look at only a few of the options available. In order to compare different query plans, the optimiser assigns a cost to each plan. The cost is usually a measure of how long each plan will take to execute and is typically based on an estimate of the number of disk input and output (I/O) operations required. An approximate cost is sufficient, as the optimiser only needs to eliminate poor plans and find a sufficiently efficient, though preferably optimal or near-optimal, plan. For simplicity, in the examples below, the cost is estimated in terms of the number of *row* I/Os. In practice, as data is transferred in blocks or pages (where the page size could be several kilobytes and contain multiple rows) the actual number of I/Os may be far fewer.

Several query plans and their cost estimates are considered below for the query:

'What are the studentNo(s) and studentName(s) of the students who study Japanese?'

Query Plan 1

T1 = Join of Student, Option on studentNo.
T2 = Rows of T1 where moduleName = 'Japanese'.
TR = Columns of T2 under studentNo, studentName.

Suppose Student and Option are stored as unordered structures. The join operation can be performed as follows. Read each row of Student in turn and, for each of these rows, search the Option table by a linear scan from start to finish to find those rows that match on studentNo. Write the joined rows to disk. Read the joined rows from disk and extract the columns under studentNo and studentName for those rows where moduleName = 'Japanese'.

The cost estimate is shown in Fig. 18.7. In step 3, the optimiser has calculated the number of rows to be output as 4000. It can only do this if it knows that studentNo in Option is a (non-null) posted identifier (foreign key) that references the identifier

	Step		Cost (estimated number of row I/Os)
	1.	Read 500 rows of Student, and . . .	500
Join operation	2.	. . . for each of these rows, read every row of Option, checking for matching studentNo(s), and . . .	$500 \times 4000 = 2\,000\,000$
	3.	. . . for each match write the joined rows to disk.	4000
	4.	Read the joined rows from step 3, . . .	4000
Row and column operations	5.	. . . for those rows for which moduleName = 'Japanese', extract the studentNo and studentName values.	(Store in main memory) 0
		Total cost =	2\,008\,500

Fig. 18.7   Cost estimate for Query Plan 1

(primary key) of Student. In other words, for every row in Option there must be precisely one row in Student with a matching studentNo value, so the number of rows in the join must equal the number of rows in Option. In general, a join of M rows of one table with N rows of another could generate $M \times N$ joined rows (i.e. where every row in the tables contains the same value of the join attribute). With 500 rows in one table and 4000 in the other, there would be 2\,000\,000 rows in the join. This example demonstrates that sensible cost estimates can only be made if the optimiser has sufficient information available and is designed to use it effectively.

In step 5, the optimiser has recognised that the Row and Column operations can both be applied in the same pass through the joined rows that are read in step 4. The cost of step 5 has been estimated as zero. The reason for this is that an efficient optimiser has access to statistics on the frequency of occurrence of attribute values. For example, the statistics could record the number of moduleName values starting with each letter of the alphabet. We will assume that there are, say, 10 moduleName values starting with the letter 'J', so that there are at most 10 occurrences of 'Japanese' in the Option table. The optimiser could decide that the output of step 5 can be held in main memory, so there is no need to write the output to disk. In any case, the cost of step 5 (and also steps 1, 3 and 4) is negligible compared with step 2.

Query Plan 1 could be marginally improved if the optimiser could recognise that steps 3 and 4 are unnecessary (step 5 can be combined with step 2) but the main cost remains the expensive join operation in step 2.

Query Plan 2
The Student and Option tables are unordered, but there is no reason why the optimiser could not choose to sort each of them on the join attribute studentNo. Once the tables are sorted (Fig. 18.8) the join can be performed by merging matching rows. In this example (a 1:many relationship) the merge would involve reading each row once, giving a total of $500 + 4000 = 4500$ rows read. This technique is known as a sort-merge join.

Student

studentNo	studentName
100	Miller
103	Desai
108	Miller
218	Wong
305	King
357	Davis
920	Jones
etc.....	etc.....

Option

studentNo	moduleName
100	Geology
100	Biophysics
103	Engineering
103	Biophysics
103	Japanese
218	History
256	Computing
305	Mathematics
357	Swedish
357	Computing
357	Chemistry
357	Spanish
461	History
605	Japanese
854	Japanese
920	Spanish
932	Geology
etc.....	etc.....

Student (studentNo, studentName)
Option (studentNo, moduleName)

Number of Student rows = 500
Number of Option rows = 4000

Fig. 18.8 Student and Option tables ordered on studentNo

Sorting and merging can be performed very efficiently. If the tables are not too large, they can be sorted and merged entirely within main memory, but even large tables can be sorted and merged in just a few passes through the rows. In general, a sort-merge join is efficient for a high hit rate.

It should be evident that Query Plan 2 would be a major improvement on Query Plan 1. We will not attempt a detailed cost estimate, as Query Plan 3 (below) is clearly better still.

Query Plan 3
As join operations are expensive, it is sensible to try to minimise the number of rows involved. It would be more efficient to pick out the rows of Option (Fig. 18.6) where moduleName = 'Japanese' first, and then join those rows with Student. The sequence of relational algebra operations is:

T1 = Rows of Option where moduleName = 'Japanese'.
T2 = Join of T1, Student on studentNo.
TR = Columns of T2 under studentNo, studentName.

The cost estimate is shown in Fig. 18.9. In step 3 the query optimiser recognises that only half the Student table need be searched on average, as there must be just one matching row in Student (see the answer pointer for question 1, section 18.3.1). The simple strategy of restricting the number of rows involved in the join makes Query Plan 3 a dramatic improvement on Query Plan 1.

	Step		Cost (estimated number of row I/Os)
Row operation	1.	Read 4 000 rows of Option	4 000
	2.	... selecting those rows for which moduleName = 'Japanese' (a maximum of 10 rows).	(Store in main memory) 0
Join operation	3.	For each row from step 2, search Student for a matching row, and ...	10 (max.) × 250 = 2 500
Column operation	4.	... extract the studentNo and studentName values.	(Store in main memory) 0
		Total cost =	6 500

Fig. 18.9   Cost estimate for Query Plan 3

Query Plan 4
Although Query Plan 3 improved substantially on previous attempts, the response time for the query might still not be fast enough to satisfy the end-users, so the database administrator may decide to amend the internal schema. Suppose that the database administrator indexes the Option table on moduleName and hashes the Student table on studentNo. The previous query plans are still applicable, but the optimiser can now devise a query plan that takes advantage of these new storage structures. The cost estimate is shown in Fig. 18.10. For an index block size of, say, 100 entries, with each block 80% full on average, there will be a two-level index for moduleName with 50 index blocks at the lower level (50 blocks × 80 entries per block = 4000 rows indexed). The statistics show that there are, at most, 10 rows in Option where the moduleName = 'Japanese'. If the top level index can be held in main memory, at most 2 (lower level) index blocks will need to be accessed (step 1) to locate the entries for the 'Japanese'

	Step		Cost (estimated number of row or index block I/Os)
Row operation	1.	Read index on Option table to find 'Japanese' entries, and ...	Maximum = 2
	2.	... for each of these entries, read the Option row addressed by the entry, and ...	Maximum = 10
Join operation	3.	... for each of these rows, hash the studentNo value and read the matching Student row.	10×1.2 = 12
Column operation	4.	Extract the studentNo and studentName values.	(Store in main memory) 0
		Total cost =	24

Fig. 18.10   Cost estimate for Query Plan 4

rows. A maximum of 10 rows of Option will then be read (step 2). For each of these rows, the studentNo value is hashed (step 3) to find the matching row in Student. Most matching rows will be found with 1 read, with overflow rows taking more. Allow an average of 1.2 reads per row accessed. No rows are written to disk, because intermediate results can be held in main memory.

The total cost estimate for Query Plan 4 is 24 I/Os. This may be an overestimate, as the number of enrolments for 'Japanese' might be fewer than 10; some of these students may be studying joinery or journalism. More detailed statistics would improve the estimate, but the main point is that the estimate is sufficient to show that Query Plan 4 is far more efficient than the previous query plans. In this example, Query Plan 4 would not have been possible without the intervention of the database administrator, who recognised the advantages of using indexed and hashed structures. A database management system could incorporate internal schema optimisation software to make such changes automatically (see question 4, below).

Questions

1.   For Query Plan 1, the Student and Option tables were joined by taking each Student row in turn and scanning the Option table for matching studentNo values. The scan of Option formed an inner loop within an outer loop that scanned Student. Would there be any performance advantage if Student were scanned as an inner loop within an outer loop that scanned Option?   (3 min)
2.   Query Plan 2 uses a sort-merge join. Fig. 18.8 shows the Student and Option tables sorted into ascending order of studentNo. Satisfy yourself that the sorted tables can be joined by reading each row only once. Cover the rows in Student with one piece of paper and the rows in Option with another. To read a row, slide a card down. Write down each joined row, assuming a natural join.   (3 min)
3.   Repeat the procedure in question 2 for the unordered tables in Fig. 18.6. Satisfy yourself that repeated scans of a table are necessary.   (2 min)
4.   Identify some issues in automatic internal schema optimisation.   (10 min)

18.5 Distributed database optimisation

For a distributed database management system, optimisation is even more critical. Suppose, in the context of the extended library scenario, that staff at the Oakby branch want to find which of the other branches stock copies of a book with a given ISBNX. The Branch and Copy tables for the first-level E-R model are:

Branch (<u>branchNo</u>, branchName, branchAddress)
Copy (<u>accessionNo</u>, ISBNX, purchasePrice, branchNo)

Assume that the Copy table is horizontally fragmented by branchNo. Each branch stores the fragment containing just those rows relating to the copies stocked at that branch. There is no replication of Copy or fragments of Copy. There is an average of 10000 copies at each of 50 branches. The copy fragments are indexed by ISBNX. The Branch table is replicated at every site.

Distributed Query Plan 1
Transmit the Copy fragments from the other 49 branches to Oakby.
Search each fragment for a row with the given ISBNX (on average 5000 rows need to be searched per fragment).
For each fragment with a matching row, use branchNo to find the name and address of the branch from the Branch replica at Oakby.

Distributed Query Plan 2
Transmit the ISBNX to each of the other 49 branches.
At each branch use the index on the Copy fragment to find whether there is a copy at that branch; if so transmit the branchNo back to Oakby.
Use branchNo to find the name and address of the branch from the Branch replica at Oakby.

It should be obvious that Query Plan 2 is more efficient. This is because:
- far less data is transmitted over the relatively slow communications network;
- the Copy fragments are searched efficiently using the index;
- searching of the Copy fragments is shared between the computers at all the sites.

An efficient query plan is normally one that minimises data transmission, or reduces it to near the minimum. Other factors, such as storage structures, statistics and available computer power at different sites, may be significant in determining an optimal, or near optimal, plan.

18.6 Summary

In spite of the simplifications made, in particular that the unit of I/O is the row not the page, the above examples have demonstrated that different query plans can have very different costs. The discussion was not aimed at making accurate estimates of cost, but indicated the potential complexity of a query optimiser, the type of information that it could use, and the importance of an efficient optimiser to end-user satisfaction and the commercial success of a database management system.

Answer pointers

Section 18.2

1. If the best plan so far takes less than 0.1 seconds to execute, stop the search. If the best plan so far takes less time to execute than twice the search time so far, stop the search.
2. (a) Re-compiling a query plan will have been unnecessary if there is a subsequent amendment before the plan is used. (b) Compiling a new plan when an application is next invoked will affect the application's performance for that first invocation.

Section 18.3.1

1. (a) All the rows (i.e. 7). Duplicate values are allowed for studentName, so every row must be checked for a match. (b) As studentNo is the identifier of Student, there are no duplicate values. The search can stop as soon as a match is found. Assuming that all the studentNo values in the table are equally likely to be the subject of a query, and that only values that exist in the table are used, on average half the table will need to be searched. More precisely, if there are N rows, then $(N+1)/2$ rows will be searched on average. If N is much greater than 1, $(N+1)/2$ approximates to $N/2$.
2. (a) 1000. (b) Number of rows per page = 8000/200 = 40. Number of pages = 1000/40 = 25.

Section 18.3.2

1. Each page could be partially filled. There would then be room to insert a new row, and only the rows in the page affected by the insertion need be sorted. When a page becomes full, a new page could be allocated and the rows shared between the old and new pages. The pages could be stored in a linked list, so that the physical order of pages need not be the same as the logical order of the rows.

Section 18.3.3

1. Each value is a bit string which can be treated as a binary numeric value.
2. Each hash key will determine a different set of physical addresses for the rows. The same row cannot be in two places at once.
3. Hash the given studentNo value (the hash key) to obtain the home address. Retrieve the row at that address. Compare the studentNo value in the row with the hash key; if equal, the row has been found. If not equal, search successive locations for a matching key. If the whole stored table has been searched (for this purpose, the first row is regarded as following the last row) without finding a match, there is no row with the given key.

Note that missing keys would yield a slow response for a large table. There are better overflow mechanisms, e.g. the creation of a linked list of address pointers from a home address through all the overflow rows belonging to that home address. An unsuccessful search would terminate when an end-of-list indicator was found.

Section 18.3.4

1. $100 \times 100 \times 100 = 1000000$.
2. All indexes for that table must be updated. A penalty for faster retrievals is slower insertions. Updates and deletions of rows will also be affected.

3. The index will be smaller, so it can be searched more quickly. For high hit rate operations (see section 18.3.5) one input operation may transfer many of the required rows.

Section 18.4

1. If Student has M rows and Option has N rows, the number of rows read when the scan of Student is the outer loop is $M + M \times N$. The number of rows read when the scan of Option is the outer loop would be $N + N \times M$, if every row of option needed to be read. However, studentNo is the identifier of Student, so once a matching value is found there is no need to scan further. See also section 18.3.1, question 1 and its answer pointer.

4. It would often not be worth changing internal schema storage structure(s) because it would take too long; it could be quicker to process a query some other way, using the existing storage structures. The internal schema optimiser might make changes to suit queries that are never, or rarely, encountered again. It might be wasteful of resources, optimising for speed only without regard for storage requirements. It might be unaware of the business environment, for example that the demand for toys and ice-cream has seasonal peaks and troughs; in trying not to react too quickly it might react too slowly. A distinction could be made between temporary and more permanent changes to the internal schema, where a temporary change would persist only for the duration of the execution of a program or application. An internal schema optimiser could work as an expert adviser to a database administrator.

19

The SQL language

19.1 Introduction

The kind of operations needed in a table-at-a-time language were introduced in the form of relational algebra in Chapter 17. For tutorial purposes, relational algebra has the advantages that fundamental operations such as selecting rows, selecting columns and joining tables are expressed explicitly as separate statements. Relational algebra also complies with the requirements of the relational model. In practice, the table-at-a-time language provided with almost all relational database management systems is the SQL (pronounced ess-cue-ell) language, which combines row, column and join operations into a single statement and which deviates in some respects from the principles of the relational model.

SQL is an evolving language, both in terms of actual implementations and the standardisation process. This chapter is based upon the ISO SQL92 standard, but its aim is to convey the flavour of SQL rather than give an exhaustive description of a particular implementation or standard. Consequently, certain facilities are omitted or only touched upon lightly. Some SQL99 developments are outlined in Chapter 20.

The main features are illustrated in terms of the room, telephone and employee tables shown in Fig. 19.1. In SQL, attributes are referred to as *columns*. Names, such as table and column names, are case insensitive, for instance roomNo, roomno, RoomNo and ROOMNO all refer to the same column name. We will use lower case letters and underscores, as in room_no, rather than capitalisation for such user-defined names. SQL keywords, such as CREATE, SELECT, DELETE, are also case insensitive. We will write these in upper case. Character literal values are case sensitive and enclosed in quote marks, so 'Smith', 'SMITH', and 'sMiTh' are three distinct values. A null is usually displayed as space(s), but we will represent it by <null> to distinguish it from a character literal of space(s).

The rows in Fig. 19.1 are in room_no order so as to make it easier to compare the contents of the tables and follow the SQL examples. As required by the relational model, SQL makes no assumption about the order of the rows.

We will omit terminators from SQL statements; the usual terminator is a semicolon.

19.2 Table creation

The structure of the room, telephone and employee tables is defined in SQL as shown in Fig. 19.2. CREATE TABLE sets up a named table that persists in the database until it is explicitly dropped. It is also possible to set up temporary tables.

room	room_no	capacity
	R1	5
	R2	4
	R3	1
	R4	3
	R5	4
	R6	1
	R7	2
	R8	<null>

telephone	room_no	extension
	R2	217
	R2	218
	R2	219
	R3	350
	R4	451
	R4	454
	R5	910

employee	emp_no	emp_name	room_no	sup_no
	E1	Baker	R2	E5
	E2	Moss	R2	E9
	E5	Smith	R3	E4
	E4	Smith	R4	<null>
	E9	Wells	R4	E4
	E8	Smith	R4	E9
	E7	Smith	R6	E5

Fig. 19.1   Tables used in the SQL examples. In the room table, capacity represents the maximum number of people who can be allocated to a room. In the telephone table, extension represents the telephone extension number. In the employee table, emp_no represents the employee number, emp_name the employee name, and sup_no the employee number of the employee's supervisor

The CREATE TABLE statement sets up a *base table*. It is convenient to think of a base table as physically existing in the internal schema, although there is no requirement that it be stored in this form. For example, it could be stored physically split into several tables or as records linked by pointers.

We now consider various aspects of Fig. 19.2 and associated SQL features.

```
CREATE TABLE room
        (room_no CHAR(2),
        capacity NUMERIC(2),
        PRIMARY KEY (room_no))

CREATE TABLE telephone
        (room_no CHAR(2),
        extension CHAR(3),
        PRIMARY KEY (extension),
        FOREIGN KEY (room_no) REFERENCES room)

CREATE TABLE employee
        (emp_no CHAR(2),
        emp_name VARCHAR(15) NOT NULL,
        room_no CHAR(2),
        sup_no CHAR(2),
        PRIMARY KEY (emp_no),
        FOREIGN KEY (room_no) REFERENCES room,
        FOREIGN KEY (sup_no) REFERENCES employee)
```

Fig. 19.2   Table declarations

19.2.1   Data types

CHAR(2) and CHAR(3) specify columns that contain fixed length character strings of 2 and 3 characters, respectively. VARCHAR(15) specifies a variable length character string with up to 15 characters. NUMERIC(2) specifies a 2 digit (signed) decimal number with no decimal places.

There is a fixed set of data types available in SQL92. The character, bit and numeric data types are shown in Fig. 19.3. There are also three kinds of *datetime* data type, known as DATE, TIME and TIMESTAMP.

DATE is used for calendar dates and comprises YEAR, MONTH and DAY components. TIME is used for times and comprises HOUR, MINUTE and SECOND

Data type	Keyword	Meaning	Sample declaration(s)	Sample value(s)
Character string	CHARACTER or CHAR	Fixed length character string (padded with spaces, if necessary).	CHAR(4)	'AbCd' 'Ab ' (Ab followed by two spaces)
	CHARACTER VARYING or VARCHAR	Variable length character string.	VARCHAR(4)	'AbCd' 'Ab'
Bit string	BIT BIT VARYING	Fixed length bit string. Variable length bit string.	BIT(4) BIT VARYING (4)	'1010' '1010' '10'
Exact numeric	NUMERIC	Decimal number.	NUMERIC(5) NUMERIC(5,2)	12345 123.45
	DECIMAL or DEC	As for NUMERIC, except that the number could be stored with a higher (implementation-defined) precision, e.g. DEC(4) could hold a 5 digit number.		
	INTEGER or INT	Whole number. The precision is implementation-defined (e.g. a 4 byte integer).	INTEGER	12345678
	SMALLINT	Whole number. The precision is implementation-defined (e.g. a 2 byte integer) but must not exceed that for INTEGER.	SMALLINT	1234
Approximate numeric	FLOAT	Floating point number of at least the stated precision.	FLOAT(4)	0.1234E+05
	REAL	Floating point number with implementation-defined precision.	REAL	
	DOUBLE PRECISION	Floating point number of a higher precision than REAL.	DOUBLE PRECISION	

Numeric data types represent signed (+ or –) numbers.

Fig. 19.3   Character, bit and numeric data types

components. TIMESTAMP is used for dates with times and comprises YEAR, MONTH, DAY, HOUR, MINUTE and SECOND components. Examples of datetime data type definitions are:

loan_date DATE
admission_time TIME
lap_time TIME(3)
internet_sale TIMESTAMP
share_transaction TIMESTAMP(3)

TIME(3) and TIMESTAMP(3) specify that the SECOND component is stored with a fractional precision of 3 decimal places. The default fractional precision is 0 for TIME, and 6 for TIMESTAMP. Consequently, values of admission_time can be stored to a second, internet_sale to a microsecond, and lap_time and share_transaction to a millisecond.

The INTERVAL data type (which is not itself classified as a datetime data type) represents a (signed) period of time. Examples are:

period_of_study INTERVAL YEAR(1)
   period of study may be up to 9 years.
planetary_orbit INTERVAL DAY(3) TO SECOND(3)
   planetary_orbit is measured in days, hours, minutes and (to 3 decimal places) seconds.
   The maximum stored value is 999 days, 23 hours, 59 minutes and 59.999 seconds.
reaction_time INTERVAL SECOND(4,2)
   reaction_time may be up to 9999.99 seconds.

A WITH TIME ZONE clause can optionally be used with TIME and TIMESTAMP. At any given instant, people in different time zones around the world will have different local times. WITH TIME ZONE specifies that a time is to be regarded as comprising two elements, the Co-ordinated Universal Time (known as UTC time) and a time zone displacement. This format makes it easy to calculate, say, the flight time of an aircraft whose departure time and arrival time have been logged in different time zones.

Question

1. What is the maximum value that could be stored with a data type of:
(a) INTERVAL SECOND (4,2)
(b) NUMERIC (4,2)?   (2 min)

19.2.2   Constraints

Several kinds of integrity constraint can be specified.

The emp_name column of the employee table in Fig. 19.2 is specified as NOT NULL. This clause ensures that any attempt to insert null into this column will fail.

The PRIMARY KEY clause ensures that the database management system will not allow the table identifier to be null or duplicated. One effect of declaring a PRIMARY KEY is therefore to enforce what is known as the *entity integrity* rule of the relational model, namely that a primary key (i.e. a table identifier) may not be null.

The FOREIGN KEY clause is used to indicate which column(s) (i.e. attributes) are posted identifiers. FOREIGN KEY declarations are significant because they enable the database management system to enforce the *referential integrity* rule of the relational model, namely that a foreign key value must either occur also as a value of a candidate key (usually the primary key) of the associated table or else be null. For example, if an employee is assigned to a room, then the value of room_no in the employee table must match a value of room_no in the room table. If an employee is *not* assigned to a room, then room_no in employee is set to null. If every employee *must* be assigned to a room, then a NOT NULL clause should be included in the declaration of room_no in employee.

In the employee table, the foreign key sup_no (the employee number of the employee's supervisor) references the employee table itself.

A FOREIGN KEY can only reference column(s) declared either as the PRIMARY KEY or as (see below) UNIQUE.

Constraints can be named, as in:

emp_name CHAR(2) CONSTRAINT emp_con_1 NOT NULL
CONSTRAINT room_pk PRIMARY KEY (room_no)

where the names chosen for the constraints are emp_con_1 and room_pk. The advantage of naming a constraint is that the name can be inserted in diagnostic messages that are generated when the constraint is violated.

Other constraints include UNIQUE, CHECK and ASSERTION.

UNIQUE specifies that no duplicate values are allowed in certain column(s). It would be used for an *alternate key*, i.e. a candidate key that is not chosen as the primary key. As UNIQUE permits one null entry, the appropriate specification for an alternate key is UNIQUE NOT NULL.

CHECK is a versatile constraint that allows a wide range of rules to be specified, including range checks and presence in a list of values, as in:

room_no CHAR(2) CHECK(room_no >= 'R1' AND room_no <= 'R9')
room_no CHAR(2) CHECK(room_no BETWEEN 'R1' AND 'R9')
room_no CHAR(2) CHECK(room_no IN ('R1', 'R2', 'R3', 'R4', 'R5', 'R6', 'R7', 'R8', 'R9'))

or:

capacity NUMERIC(2) CHECK(capacity >= 1 AND capacity <= 10)
capacity NUMERIC(2) CHECK(capacity BETWEEN 1 AND 10)

Note that the constraint condition in:
CHECK(capacity BETWEEN 10 AND 1)
would never evaluate to true, because it is equivalent to:
CHECK(capacity >= 10 AND capacity <= 1)

The SQL comparison operators are: =, <, >, <= (less than or equal to), >= (greater than or equal to), <> (not equal to). The logical operators are AND, OR, NOT.

A CHECK clause can be applied to a column or to a table. When applied to a column, only that column name may be referenced in the constraint definition. A CHECK clause applied to one table can refer to other table(s). For example, suppose telephone extensions are fitted in staff rooms but not rooms such as storerooms. The telephone table could contain a CHECK clause to ensure that a row could not be inserted if the room's capacity (as recorded in the room table) were zero or null. Amendments to room_no values in the telephone table would also be checked, as would updates to the room table.

So far, each constraint has been written as part of a column or table declaration. In contrast, an ASSERTION is a standalone constraint in the sense that it is written separately, not as part of a table declaration. An ASSERTION usually refers to more than one table and is normally preferred to CHECK clause(s) where there is no particular reason for attaching the constraint to one table rather than another.

Questions

1. Suppose the only integrity constraint on the capacity column in the room table is: CHECK(capacity >= 1). Would you expect a null capacity to be valid?   (1 min)
2. There is no NOT NULL clause on emp_no in the employee table. Can this column contain null?   (1 min)
3. The syntax for declaring PRIMARY KEY and FOREIGN KEY is designed to cope with composite keys, e.g. PRIMARY KEY (A, B, C). Suggest a simpler syntax for a CREATE TABLE declaration where the primary key and foreign key(s) are each single columns.   (2 min)

19.2.3   Domains

A domain is the set of legal values from which the values in a column can be chosen. A data type declaration is one way of limiting the domain for a column. For instance:

room_no CHAR(2)   This limits the domain of room_no to a two-character string.
capacity NUMERIC(2)   This limits the domain of capacity to a two-digit, signed integer.

The addition of a CHECK clause limits the domain's values further, as in:

room_no CHAR(2) CHECK(room_no BETWEEN 'R1' AND 'R9')

Columns in different tables will often share the same domain. In particular, a foreign key would be expected to share the same domain as the primary key of the table(s) it references. By creating a specific, named domain, we can ensure that exactly the same domain specification is used in each of the three tables, room, telephone and employee. The following statement declares a domain named room_type:

CREATE DOMAIN room_type CHAR(2)
    CHECK(VALUE IN ('R1', 'R2', 'R3', 'R4', 'R5', 'R6', 'R7', 'R8', 'R9'))

The domain name room_type can then be used in each of the CREATE TABLE declarations, as in:

CREATE TABLE room
    (room_no room_type,
    capacity NUMERIC(2),
    PRIMARY KEY (room_no))

and similarly for tables telephone and employee. There is actually no need to use the same name, room_no, in all three tables. For example, the room_no column in the employee table could have been called office_no and declared as:

office_no room_type

The FOREIGN KEY, room_no, in the employee table would also need to be changed to office_no.

SQL92 provides a weak form of domain which only partially implements the relational model's concept of domain. A stronger version would restrict operations such as join to columns that share the same domain.

Question

1. Why might different domains be declared for telephone.room_no and room.room_no?   (2 min)

19.2.4   Defaults

A default can be defined for a column or a domain. For example:

capacity NUMERIC(2) DEFAULT 1

specifies that, if a value of capacity is not explicitly supplied when a row is inserted into room, then the default value 1 is to be used. DEFAULT NULL may also be specified.

Questions

1. What do you suggest should happen if a default value is declared for a domain and also for a column defined on that domain, assuming that the default values differ?

(2 min)

2. The referential integrity rule has implications for the updating (insertion, deletion or amendment) of rows. By considering the relationship between employee and room, describe the actions which you might want the database management system to enforce in each of the following cases.
(a)   Insertion of a new row in the employee table.
(b)   Amendment of a room_no value in a row of employee.
(c)   Deletion of a row from the room table.
(d)   Amendment of a room_no value in a row of room.   (10 min)

19.3   Retrieving data

19.3.1   Selection of rows

Example 1
SELECT *
FROM employee
WHERE emp_name = 'Smith'

Those rows of employee for which emp_name is 'Smith' are retrieved. The asterisk (*)

indicates that all the columns of employee are to be retrieved (in the order in which they appear in the CREATE statement). The asterisk notation should be used with some caution; tables can be altered by the addition or deletion of columns, so the effect of SELECT * may change.

emp_no	emp_name	room_no	sup_no
E5	Smith	R3	E4
E4	Smith	R4	<null>
E8	Smith	R4	E9
E7	Smith	R6	E5

Example 2
SELECT *
FROM employee
WHERE room_no = 'R4' AND emp_name = 'Smith'

emp_no	emp_name	room_no	sup_no
E4	Smith	R4	<null>
E8	Smith	R4	E9

Example 3
SELECT *
FROM room
WHERE capacity < 4 AND room_no <> 'R7'

room_no	capacity
R3	1
R4	3
R6	1

Note that any row of room for which the WHERE clause evaluates to either *false* or *unknown* is excluded. In particular, the row for room_no 'R8' is excluded because its capacity is NULL and so the outcome of the condition, capacity < 4, is *unknown*. (One might say that it is known to be *unknown*.)

19.3.2   Selection of columns

Example 1
SELECT room_no
FROM employee

room_no
R2
R2
R3
R4
R4
R4
R6

Although the relational model prohibits them, SQL does not automatically eliminate duplicate rows from a table. Elimination of duplicates must be requested explicitly by using the keyword DISTINCT.

SELECT DISTINCT room_no
FROM employee

room_no
R2
R3
R4
R6

Example 2
SELECT room_no AS office_no, emp_name
FROM employee

office_no	emp_name
R2	Baker
R2	Moss
R3	Smith
R4	Smith
R4	Wells
R4	Smith
R6	Smith

The order of columns in the column list governs the order of columns in the result table. The room_no column has been renamed office_no. In this context the keyword AS is a *noiseword*; it improves readability but could be omitted. A SELECT DISTINCT statement would have eliminated one of the duplicate rows for 'R4 Smith'.

19.3.3   Sample queries

The equivalent of relational algebra Row and Column operations can be combined into a single SELECT statement.

Example 1
Which rooms contain one or more employees called 'Smith'?

SELECT room_no
FROM employee
WHERE emp_name = 'Smith'

room_no
R3
R4
R4
R6

Example 2
How many filing cabinets are there in room 'R5'? Assume that the number of filing cabinets per room is twice the capacity of the room in people. This example shows how to include a calculation and name the result.

SELECT room_no, 2 * capacity AS filing_cabinets
FROM room
WHERE room_no = 'R5'

room_no	filing_cabinets
R5	8

Question

1. Suppose the employee table contains the rows:
      F4   Harris   \<null\>   E9
      F7   Harris   \<null\>   E2
There are two different employees, both called 'Harris', neither of whom has been allocated to a room. Give arguments for and against treating:
      Harris   \<null\>
      Harris   \<null\>
as duplicate rows in the execution of the statement:
         SELECT DISTINCT emp_name, room_no FROM employee   (4 min)

19.3.4   Selection of NULL/NOT NULL

Example 1
SELECT *
FROM room
WHERE capacity IS NULL

room_no	capacity
R8	\<null\>

Those rooms for which the capacity is unknown or not defined (e.g. storerooms) are retrieved. Note that it is incorrect to write:
         capacity = NULL

NULL is not a particular value (strictly speaking, it is not a value at all) so it is illogical to ask whether capacity is *equal* to NULL.
   Those rooms that *do* have an actual capacity recorded in the database can be retrieved by:

SELECT * FROM room
 WHERE capacity IS NOT NULL

19.3.5   Selection using a list

SELECT room_no FROM room
WHERE capacity IN (2, 4, 6)

The WHERE clause is simply a shorter way of specifying:
   WHERE capacity = 2 OR capacity = 4 OR capacity = 6

The converse of IN is NOT IN.

19.3.6   Ordering rows

SELECT * FROM room
WHERE room_no >= 'R3'
ORDER BY capacity

room_no	capacity
R3	1
R6	1
R7	2
R4	3
R5	4
R8	<null>

For the purposes of the ORDER BY clause, nulls are considered to be *either* less than *or* greater than all non-nulls; the choice is implementation-defined. The first two rows in the result could have been in either order. To ensure that they appear as shown, the ORDER BY clause should be:

   ORDER BY capacity, room_no

The result is then sorted into room_no within capacity order.
   Ascending order is assumed by default. Ascending or descending order can be specified by the keywords ASC and DESC, as in:

   ORDER BY capacity ASC, room_no DESC

ORDER BY does not, of course, affect the order of the rows in the base table (for which no inherent order should be assumed) but is used to determine the order in which the rows appear in the result table.

19.3.7   Aggregate functions

There are five aggregate functions, each of which returns a single value.

COUNT	counts the number of values in a column.
SUM	sums the values in a column.
AVG	calculates the average of the values in a column.
MIN	finds the smallest value in a column.
MAX	finds the largest value in a column.

COUNT(*) is a special version of COUNT that counts all the rows in a table, regardless of whether there are nulls present. Otherwise, each function ignores nulls. The keyword DISTINCT is used if duplicate values are to be eliminated before the function is applied. SUM and AVERAGE may be used only on numeric data.

If an aggregate function is applied to an empty set of values, then COUNT returns zero and the other aggregate functions return null.

Example 1
SELECT COUNT (*)
FROM employee
WHERE emp_name = 'Smith'

COUNT (*)
4

This statement counts the number of rows in the employee table for which emp_name = 'Smith'.

Example 2
SELECT COUNT (room_no)
FROM telephone

COUNT(room_no)
7

This statement counts the number of room_no value(s), including duplicates. Any nulls would be ignored.

Example 3
SELECT COUNT (DISTINCT room_no)
FROM telephone

COUNT(DISTINCT room_no)
4

This statement counts the number of different room_no value(s). Any nulls would be ignored.

Example 4
SELECT SUM (capacity)
FROM room
WHERE capacity = 4

SUM(capacity)
8

This statement calculates the total capacity of those rooms able to hold 4 people. Any rooms with a null capacity are ignored.

Example 5
SELECT AVG (capacity)
FROM room
WHERE room_no IN ('R1', 'R3', 'R4')

AVG(capacity)
3

Example 6
SELECT MIN (extension), MAX (extension)
FROM telephone

MIN(extension)	MAX(extension)
217	910

Question

1. Would you expect the following statements to yield different results?
        SELECT MIN (capacity) FROM room
        SELECT DISTINCT MIN (capacity) FROM room   (1 min)

19.3.8   Grouping results

Example 1
SELECT room_no, COUNT (*) FROM telephone
GROUP BY (room_no)
ORDER BY (room_no)

room_no	COUNT(*)
R2	3
R3	1
R4	2
R5	1

Conceptually, the query is processed by first grouping the rows by room_no.

room_no	extension
R2	217
R2	218
R2	219
R3	350
R4	451
R4	454
R5	910

Then, for each group, a single row is extracted comprising room_no and the count of the number of rows in that group.

Example 2
A HAVING clause allows a condition to be applied to each group as a whole.

SELECT room_no, COUNT (*) FROM telephone
GROUP BY (room_no)
HAVING COUNT (*) > 1

room_no	COUNT(*)
R2	3
R4	2

Two of the rows in the *Example 1* result are eliminated by the HAVING clause.

19.3.9 Nested subqueries

SELECT statements may be nested.

Example 1
Which employees are in rooms with a capacity of 4 people?

SELECT emp_no, emp_name
FROM employee
WHERE room_no IN
        (SELECT room_no FROM room
        WHERE capacity = 4)

Conceptually, the inner SELECT is processed first, giving an intermediate table of room_no(s) with a capacity of 4 people. The outer SELECT is then processed by applying the condition that only those rows of employee are considered for which the room_no is present in the intermediate table.

The keywords EXISTS, NOT EXISTS, ANY (or SOME) can be applied to a subquery. EXISTS checks whether there is at least one row in the result table returned by the subquery. ANY (or SOME) may be used when a subquery returns a single result column; it checks whether at least one of the values satisfies some given condition.

19.3.10 Joining tables

Example 1
SELECT emp_no, emp_name, employee.room_no, sup_no, capacity
FROM employee, room
WHERE employee.room_no = room.room_no

emp_no	emp_name	room_no	sup_no	capacity
E1	Baker	R2	E5	4
E2	Moss	R2	E9	4
E5	Smith	R3	E4	1
E4	Smith	R4	<null>	3
E9	Wells	R4	E4	3
E8	Smith	R4	E9	3
E7	Smith	R6	E5	1

The result is a join on room_no of the employee and room tables. Notice that the FROM clause of the SELECT statement lists all the tables that must be accessed to process the query. As room_no appears in both tables, it is qualified with a table name (employee. room_no, room.room_no) to show which room_no column is being referenced. A row appears in the result for every combination of rows from the two tables that have matching values of room_no. Although 'R1', 'R5', 'R7' and 'R8' appear in room.room_no, they do not appear in the join because there are no matching values in employee.room_no.

If there had been a row, such as 'E6', 'Jones', <null>, 'E4', in employee, it would not appear in the resulting join because a null does not match an actual value. Nor does a null match a null.

Example 2
SELECT emp_no, emp_name, sup_no, telephone.room_no, extension
FROM employee, telephone
WHERE employee. room_no = telephone.room_no

emp_no	emp_name	sup_no	room_no	extension
E1	Baker	E5	R2	217
E1	Baker	E5	R2	218
E1	Baker	E5	R2	219
E2	Moss	E9	R2	217
E2	Moss	E9	R2	218
E2	Moss	E9	R2	219
E5	Smith	E4	R3	350
E4	Smith	<null>	R4	451
E4	Smith	<null>	R4	454
E9	Wells	E4	R4	451
E9	Wells	E4	R4	454
E8	Smith	E9	R4	451
E8	Smith	E9	R4	454

This is a slightly more complicated join, as both the employee and telephone tables contain duplicate values of room_no. Just as for the previous example, a row appears in the result for every combination of rows from the two tables that have matching values of room_no.

Example 3
SELECT emp_no, emp_name, sup_no, t.room_no, extension
FROM employee AS e, telephone AS t
WHERE e. room_no = t.room_no

This is an alternative form of *Example 2*. The FROM clause specifies *aliases* e for employee and t for telephone, which are used as a convenient shorthand for the table names in e.room_no and t.room_no. In this context the keyword AS is a noiseword; it improves readability but could be omitted.

19.3.11   Sample queries

The equivalent of relational algebra Row, Column and Join operations can be combined into a single SELECT statement.

Example 1
What is the capacity of the room occupied by employee 'E9'?

SELECT capacity
FROM room, employee
WHERE emp_no = 'E9'
AND room.room_no = employee.room_no

capacity
3

Example 2
What is the employee name, room number and extension of each employee who occupies a room with a capacity of between one and three people inclusive? This example involves the joining of all three tables.

SELECT emp_name, room.room_no, extension
FROM employee, room, telephone
WHERE capacity BETWEEN 1 AND 3
AND employee.room_no = room.room_no
AND room.room_no = telephone.room_no

emp_name	room_no	extension
Smith	R3	350
Smith	R4	451
Smith	R4	454
Wells	R4	451
Wells	R4	454
Smith	R4	451
Smith	R4	454

Example 3
To find, say, the name of the supervisor of employee 'E2' we need to join the employee table to itself (a self-join). This can be done by defining aliases for the table. We will call these e (for employee) and s (for supervisor). The required statement is:

SELECT s.emp_name
FROM employee AS e, employee AS s
WHERE e.emp_no = 'E2'
AND e.sup_no = s.emp_no

emp_name
Wells

Conceptually, it is helpful to imagine that there are two identical copies of the employee table, called e and s. These are joined and the WHERE clause applied in the usual way.

The table's actual name, employee, could have been used in place of one of the aliases.

Questions

1. Could the join condition employee.room_no = telephone.room_no have been substituted for one of the join conditions in *Example 2*?   (2 min)

2. Write a SELECT statement that returns the names of employees supervised by employee(s) called 'Smith'.   (2 min)

19.3.12 More JOINs

There are several other ways of specifying a join, as shown below.

Example 1
SELECT emp_no, emp_name, telephone.room_no, extension
FROM employee JOIN telephone
ON employee.room_no = telephone.room_no

The JOIN itself includes employee.room_no and telephone.room_no columns (which will have identical values). In this example, the SELECT clause eliminates the employee.room_no column.

Example 2
SELECT emp_no, emp_name, room_no, extension
FROM employee JOIN telephone
USING (room_no)

The column(s) specified in the USING clause must appear in both the tables being joined. One column from each of these matching pairs of column names is eliminated from the result of the JOIN part of the statement. As this column could come from either table (the values being identical) it is incorrect to write either USING (employee. room_no) or USING (telephone.room_no) because USING is not referring to a room_no column in a particular table, but to a column name that is shared by both tables. Similarly, room_no must not be qualified with a table name in the SELECT clause.

Example 3
SELECT emp_no, emp_name, room_no, extension
FROM employee NATURAL JOIN telephone

A NATURAL JOIN works the same way as a JOIN . . . USING, except that all column(s) with the same name in both tables are used (just room_no in this example).

The above examples are all *inner* joins, that is no unmatched rows appear in the result. The row with value 'R6' for employee.room_no does not match any of the values in telephone.room_no, therefore that row from the employee table does not appear in the resulting join. Similarly, the row with value 'R5' for telephone.room_no does not match any of the values in employee.room_no, therefore that row from the telephone table does not appear in the resulting join either.

In contrast, an *outer* join preserves unmatched rows from either the left, right or both tables, where the left table is the first table referenced and the right table is the second table referenced.

Example 4
SELECT employee.*, telephone.*
FROM employee LEFT JOIN telephone
ON employee.room_no = telephone.room_no
WHERE emp_name = 'Smith'

emp_no	emp_name	room_no	sup_no	room_no	extension
E5	Smith	R3	E4	R3	350
E4	Smith	R4	<null>	R4	451
E4	Smith	R4	<null>	R4	454
E8	Smith	R4	E9	R4	451
E8	Smith	R4	E9	R4	454
E7	Smith	R6	E5	<null>	<null>

All the rows from employee (where emp_name = 'Smith', in this example) are preserved in the result. Nulls are inserted where there are no matching row(s) in the right hand table, as is the case for room_no 'R6' which does not have a telephone extension.

Similarly, a RIGHT JOIN preserves all rows from the right table. A FULL JOIN preserves all rows from both tables.

The keywords INNER and OUTER can optionally be used to distinguish clearly between inner and outer joins, as in INNER JOIN, RIGHT OUTER JOIN, etc.

All our examples of joins have been equi-joins (e.g. employee.room_no = room. room_no) as it is unusual to need anything other than an equi-join. However, it is perfectly legal to use other comparison operators (e.g. employee.room_no > room.room_no).

Example 5
SELECT employee.*, telephone.*
FROM employee, telephone

This statement (note the omission of a WHERE clause) generates the Extended Cartesian Product of the tables. Although this is not often needed, it is worth remembering that accidental omission of a WHERE clause for a multi-table select could generate a huge table. For example, the Extended Cartesian Product of three tables, each having one thousand rows, will have one thousand million rows.

Example 6
SELECT employee.*, telephone.*
FROM employee CROSS JOIN telephone

This is an alternative way of specifying an Extended Cartesian Product.

19.3.13   Combining result tables

The UNION, INTERSECT and EXCEPT operators are used to combine the results of two or more queries into one result table. They are similar to the relational algebra operations Union, Intersect and Difference.

Example 1
SELECT room_no FROM employee
UNION
SELECT room_no FROM telephone

R2
R3
R4
R5
R6

Duplicate rows are omitted unless UNION ALL is specified. (This contrasts with SELECT, for which duplicate rows are retained unless SELECT DISTINCT is specified.) The column name is not shown in the final result because, in general, the names of the contributing columns could have been different and there is no reason to prefer one over the other.

A UNION may involve one or more columns from each contributing table; there must be the same number of columns from each and corresponding columns must have compatible data types. For example, all numeric data types are compatible with each other. Similarly all character types are compatible with each other (with certain exceptions, such as the use of multiple character sets).

Example 2
SELECT room_no FROM employee
INTERSECT
SELECT room_no FROM telephone

R2
R3
R4

The result is the room_no values that the employee and telephone tables have in common.

Example 3
SELECT room_no FROM employee
EXCEPT
SELECT room_no FROM telephone

R6

The result is the room_no values in employee that do not also occur in telephone.

19.4   Updating data

Data may be updated by inserting new rows (INSERT), amending existing rows (UPDATE) and deleting existing rows (DELETE). Note that 'update' (in lower case) generally means insert, amend or delete, whereas UPDATE (in upper case) is the SQL command to amend a row.

19.4.1   Inserting data

Example 1
INSERT INTO employee VALUES ('E6', 'Patel', 'R3', 'E4')

This inserts a new row into the employee table. The values are inserted into the columns of employee in the order in which those columns appear in the CREATE TABLE statement.

Example 2
INSERT INTO employee (emp_no, emp_name, sup_no) VALUES ('E3', 'Jones', 'E9')

This inserts the given values into the named columns. In general, any value that is not specified will be set to its default value. If no default value is specified, it will be set to NULL, so in this example the room_no value will be set to NULL.

Example 3
INSERT INTO room_4_employee
(SELECT emp_no, emp_name
FROM employee
WHERE room_no = 'R4')

We assume that a table called room_4_employee has been created with columns emp_no and emp_name. The INSERT command copies into room_4_employee the values of emp_no and emp_name from all the rows of employee for which room_no = 'R4'.

Questions

1.   A PRIMARY KEY has been declared for a base table. What are the performance implications for the insertion of a row?   (2 min)
2.   Can rows be inserted into the employee table (Fig. 19.2) in the sequence in which they appear in Fig. 19.1? If not, how can the table be populated with this data?   (2 min)

19.4.2   Amending data

Example 1
UPDATE room
SET capacity = capacity + 1

The capacity is incremented by 1 in every row of the table.

Example 2
UPDATE employee
SET emp_name = 'Morris', room_no = 'R7'
WHERE emp_no = 'E8'

The name of employee 'E8' is changed to 'Morris' and the employee's room_no to 'R7'.

19.4.3   Deleting data

Example 1
DELETE FROM employee

All the rows in the employee table are deleted, leaving an empty table.

Example 2
DELETE FROM telephone
WHERE room_no = 'R4'

All the rows for which room_no = 'R4' are deleted.

Questions

Questions 1–6 relate to the following tables. For question 1, assume that the tables do not yet exist. For question 2, assume that the tables exist but have not yet been populated with any data. Otherwise, assume that the tables have been populated with the data values shown.

animal

animal_name
camel
zebra
snake
lion

keeper

keeper_no	keeper_name
100	Morris
101	Dennis
102	Darwin
103	Morris

supervision

keeper_no	animal_name
100	camel
100	snake
100	lion
101	zebra
103	snake

eats

animal_name	food
camel	buns
zebra	hay
snake	people
camel	hay
snake	mice
lion	people

1. Write CREATE statements for the animal, keeper, supervision and eats tables. Choose suitable data type declarations for the columns.   (2 min)
2. Write INSERT statements to put the first two rows into the animal table.   (1 min)
3. Write down the table occurrences generated by each of the following:

(a) SELECT keeper_name FROM keeper
(b) SELECT DISTINCT food FROM eats
(c) SELECT animal_name FROM eats WHERE food = 'hay' OR food = 'people'
(d) SELECT animal_name, keeper_no FROM supervision WHERE keeper_no
     > '100'   (4 min)
4.   Write SQL statements to derive the answers to the following queries. Each result
table should not contain any superfluous data.
(a) What does a camel eat?
(b) What are the keeper_no(s) of the keepers called Morris?   (1 min)
5.   Write down the table occurrences generated by each of the following queries.
(a) SELECT * FROM eats JOIN supervision USING (animal_name)
(b) SELECT food FROM eats, supervision
     WHERE eats.animal_name = supervision.animal_name
     AND keeper_no = '100'   (3 min)
6.   Write down SQL statements to derive the answers to the following queries. Each
result table should not contain any superfluous data.
(a) What is supervised by a keeper called Morris?
(b) What are the keeper_no(s) of the hay eaters?
(c) What are the keeper_no(s) and name(s) of the keepers who keep people-eaters?
                                                                    (3 min)
7.   A base table has been created for car (make, colour) to record all cars passing a
census point. As there may be duplicate rows, neither PRIMARY KEY nor UNIQUE
has been used in the table declaration. What will be the consequences of the following
updates?
(a) A sighting of a blue Ford was incorrect and needs to be changed to a black Ford.
(b) A sighting of a gold Toyota needs to be deleted as it was a truck not a car.
                                                                    (2 min)

19.5   Views

The SQL equivalent of an external schema is provided by the ability to declare *views*.
Suppose a user needs information only about the names and employee numbers of
employees in room_no 'R4'. A view could be defined which picks out just the required
data.

CREATE VIEW roomR4staff
AS   SELECT emp_name, emp_no
     FROM employee
     WHERE room_no = 'R4'

roomR4staff	emp_name	emp_no
	Smith	E4
	Wells	E9
	Smith	E8

The view definition's FROM clause may refer to base table(s) and/or view(s), so it is
possible to have, for example, a view of a view. A view does not physically exist as stored

data. Use of a view simplifies data manipulation and improves security. For example, the query on the base table:

SELECT emp_name, emp_no
FROM employee
WHERE room_no = 'R4' AND emp_name = 'Smith'

is simplified when querying the view to:

SELECT emp_name, emp_no
FROM roomR4staff
WHERE emp_name = 'Smith'

or

SELECT * FROM roomR4staff WHERE emp_name = 'Smith'

The database management system translates the query on the view into an equivalent query on the base table.

Column(s) may be given different names in a view to those used in the base table(s). For example, in a view of the telephone table, room_no and extension could be renamed office_no and tel_no, respectively:

CREATE VIEW phone_location (office_no, tel_no)
AS   SELECT room_no, extension
        FROM telephone

Questions

1.   With reference to Fig. 19.2, write a statement which creates a view called ert that consists of the join on room_no of the employee, room and telephone tables (excluding duplicated columns). Compare the query on the base tables with the query on the view needed to find the name, room capacity and telephone extension(s) for employee 'E4'.

(4 min)

2.   From the standpoint of data independence, is it better to query views or base tables?   (1 min)

19.5.1   View updating

A view may be updated (using INSERT, UPDATE, DELETE) but there are important restrictions, some of which are outlined here. For an INSERT operation, the DEFAULT value will be inserted in any base table column not included in the view; where there is no DEFAULT value, NULL will be used.

To update a view, it must at least be theoretically possible to update the base table(s) on which the view is defined. Remember that a view does not physically exist as stored data, whereas a base table can at least be thought of as existing as stored data. Consider the view:

CREATE VIEW tot_space (total_capacity)
AS SELECT SUM (capacity) FROM room

Suppose total_capacity is to be increased by 5, and the room table contains the rows shown in Fig. 19.1. The update to the view could not be reflected as an update of room because there is no logical way of deciding which row(s) should be amended. Similarly, a view whose specification involves a join is often not updatable.

SQL imposes several restrictions on view updating. These are more severe than theoretically necessary, but they do eliminate the overhead from the database management system of having to determine whether a view is or is not updatable, which may depend not only on the definition of the view but also on what data it contains at the time and which data is to be updated. The restrictions are:

- DISTINCT is not allowed in the query that defines the view.
- The SELECT list that defines the query must contain only column name(s) (or the * shorthand) each of which can appear only once. Consequently, constants, expressions and aggregate functions are excluded.
- The FROM clause specifies only one table; consequently a view involving a join is not updatable. If the table specified is a view, then that view must itself be updatable.
- The WHERE clause does not involve any subquery that references the same table as is referenced in the main FROM clause.
- There is no GROUP BY or HAVING clause in the query that defines the view.

Clearly, an update will be rejected if it violates any integrity constraint. For example, if a PRIMARY KEY column is outside the view, and does not have a non-NULL default, then an INSERT operation on the view will fail because the PRIMARY KEY may not contain NULL.

Question

1. Consider the base tables A, B and the view AJB which is a join of A and B on column c. Give examples of operations on view AJB to insert a row, amend a row and delete a row, that cannot be implemented as base table updates. (3 min)

A

a	c
a_1	c_1
a_2	c_1

B

b	c
b_1	c_1
b_2	c_1

AJB

a	b	c
a_1	b_1	c_1
a_1	b_2	c_1
a_2	b_1	c_1
a_2	b_2	c_1

19.5.2 WITH CHECK OPTION

When a view is updated, row(s) may be generated that do not belong to that view. Suppose a view is defined as:

```
CREATE VIEW roomR2phones
AS   SELECT room_no, extension
     FROM telephone
     WHERE room_no = 'R2'
```

room_no	extension
R2	217
R2	218
R2	219

Suppose extension 218 is re-assigned to room 'R4' by updating the view:

UPDATE roomR2phones
SET room_no = 'R4'
WHERE extension = '218'

The effect of the update is to disqualify the updated row from the view, since the condition that defines the view is that room_no = 'R2'. Consequently, the row would be updated in the base table but would vanish from the view.

A WITH CHECK OPTION clause, which prevents such behaviour, can be appended to the view definition:

CREATE VIEW roomR2phones
AS   SELECT room_no, extension
        FROM telephone
        WHERE room_no = 'R2'
        WITH CHECK OPTION

19.6   DROP

A base table can be dropped, that is it will no longer exist in the database.

Example 1
DROP TABLE employee RESTRICT

There may be knock-on effects from such a DROP statement. For instance, any view defined on employee would become invalid if the base table were dropped. The RESTRICT option ensures that the DROP statement will fail in such a situation. The alternative to RESTRICT is CASCADE, which states that dropping the base table should be cascaded through to dropping any views defined on that base table (and any views defined on those views, and so on).

Other database components, such as views, domains and integrity constraints can be dropped; each component being subject to various knock-on effects (see, for example, Question 1 below).

Question

1.   A domain called room_type has been declared. It has been used to specify the data type and integrity constraints for several base table columns. What would you expect the effect to be on these columns of:
DROP DOMAIN room_type CASCADE?   (2 min)

19.7   ALTER

An ALTER TABLE statement allows a new column to be added to a base table, or an existing column to be dropped from a base table. Similarly, a CONSTRAINT can be added or dropped, and a DEFAULT can be set or dropped.

Example 1
ALTER TABLE employee ADD COLUMN salary NUMERIC(8,2) DEFAULT 10000

An ALTER DOMAIN statement allows a domain declaration to be changed.

19.8 Granting and revoking privileges

The GRANT statement is used to give users permission to access various database components, for example to query specific base tables or views. The following privileges may be controlled for each user:

SELECT   -   retrieval from any column(s) in a named table.
UPDATE   -   amendment of value(s) in any, or named, column(s).
DELETE   -   deletion of rows from a named table.
INSERT   -   insertion of value(s) into any, or named, column(s) of a named table.
REFERENCES   -   reference to any, or named, column(s) of a named table in an integrity constraint (not just a referential constraint for a foreign key).
USAGE   -   use of a named domain.

In this context, a table may, in general, be a base table or a view. For UPDATE, INSERT and REFERENCES, the GRANT statement may list the column(s) for which access is being granted, otherwise access is granted to all column(s) in the table. USAGE controls the privilege to use character sets, collations and translations (see the Bibliography for information on these facilities).

A user who creates a database component, such as a base table, view or domain, automatically receives all the privileges needed to access that component.

Example 1
GRANT ALL PRIVILEGES
ON employee
TO user_1
WITH GRANT OPTION

All privileges are granted, with respect to the employee table, to the user identified by user_1. The WITH GRANT OPTION clause means that the user identified as user_1 can pass on any, or all, of the privileges to other users.

Example 2
GRANT SELECT, DELETE, UPDATE (emp_name, room_no)
ON employee
TO user_1, user_3

The users identified as user_1 and user_3 can access the employee table with SELECT and DELETE statements, and can UPDATE only the emp_name and room_no columns of employee.

Example 3
GRANT SELECT
ON employee
TO PUBLIC

The SELECT privilege is granted to all users.

The REVOKE statement is used to withdraw some, or all, privileges from a user, as in:

Example 4
REVOKE DELETE
ON employee
FROM user_3

Questions

1. Granting a SELECT privilege permits retrieval from any column(s) in a table. How would you restrict retrievals to certain column(s), e.g. to just the emp_no and emp_name columns in the employee table?   (2 min)

2. Suppose user_1 has granted privileges to user_2 (WITH GRANT OPTION) and user_2 then grants these privileges to user_3. What might the consequences be to user_3 if user_1 then revokes the privileges that he or she granted to user_2? How could the knock-on effects of revoking privileges be managed?   (3 min)

19.9   Embedded SQL

SQL can be used interactively or by embedding SQL statements within a host programming language such as C, COBOL or Fortran. The advantage of embedding is that the host language's capability for detailed data manipulation is combined with the powerful, concise, relational facilities of SQL.

Embedding is often necessary because SQL92 does not provide statements to control program flow, such as IF, LOOP, WHILE, CALL and RETURN, although such facilities are often available with commercial implementations of SQL and do feature in SQL99.

Here, we will mention just one important aspect of embedding, namely *cursors*. As we have seen, SQL is a table-at-a-time (a set oriented) language. Operations, such as SELECT, UPDATE and DELETE, refer to a complete table (or table(s), for SELECT) and typically involve many rows in a single execution of the operation. In contrast, languages such as C, COBOL and Fortran are record-at-a-time languages that are designed to process only one record, equivalent to a table row, at a time. There is therefore a fundamental mismatch between SQL and such host languages.

Embedded UPDATE and DELETE operations do not pose the same problem, because it is the relational database management system, rather than the host language, that handles the multiple rows. However, SELECT does pose a problem as it will, in general, deliver multiple rows to the host program. The solution adopted by SQL is to use a device called a *cursor*. A cursor acts like a bookmark, in this case keeping track of which row the program is currently processing within the multiple rows returned by a query.

A DECLARE CURSOR statement associates a cursor name with a query. An OPEN statement then positions the cursor in front of the first row of the query result table. A FETCH statement then retrieves the next row of the query and advances the cursor by one row. Successive executions of a FETCH statement (usually the same FETCH statement within a program loop) therefore retrieve the first, second, third, etc. rows from the query result table. When a FETCH statement advances the cursor beyond the last row, a special variable (SQLSTATE) is set to indicate NOT FOUND.

A cursor is not necessary if a SELECT statement returns only one (or zero) rows. Conversely, a cursor may be used for UPDATE and DELETE operations in order to show that they apply only to the current row indicated by the cursor.

19.10 Some SQL issues

This chapter has outlined some of the main features of SQL92 to show how a data model may be manipulated by a relationally oriented, commercially significant language. (Other important features, such as transactions and the Call-Level Interface, are outside the scope of this book.)

Almost all relational database management systems are supplied with an SQL interface but, in spite of its popularity, SQL has been subjected to various criticisms (some of which relate to alleged deficiencies in the relational model itself) including:

- SQL has become unnecessarily complex, with many ways to perform the same operation.
- SQL does not adhere strictly to the principles of the relational model (e.g. duplicate rows are allowed; the implementation of domains is weak).
- SQL is inconsistent (e.g. the treatment of duplicate rows in SELECT and UNION; the side-effects of DROP TABLE compared with DROP DOMAIN).
- The relational model, and hence SQL, is limited in its ability to represent real-world entities. (See Chapter 20 for SQL99 features.)
- It is debatable whether the relational model should permit nulls. The inclusion of nulls in SQL complicates the definition, implementation and use of the language.

Answer pointers

Section 19.2.1

1. (a) 9999.99   (b) 99.99

Section 19.2.2

1. In SQL, an integrity constraint is violated only if it evaluates to *false*. The result of applying the constraint, capacity >= 1, to null is *unknown*, so the constraint is not violated. Nulls involve a three-valued logic, *true, false* and *unknown*. In contrast, Boolean logic is two-valued, having just *true* and *false* values.
2. No. Since emp_no is declared as the PRIMARY KEY, it cannot be null.

3. SQL permits a CREATE TABLE statement, such as:
  CREATE TABLE employee
  (emp_no CHAR(2) PRIMARY KEY,
  emp_name VARCHAR(15) NOT NULL,
  room_no CHAR(2) REFERENCES room,
  sup_no CHAR(2) REFERENCES employee)
As the REFERENCES clauses reference table names, there must be a PRIMARY KEY declaration in each of the referenced tables. It is then assumed that it is the PRIMARY KEY column(s) that the foreign key is referencing. If there is no such PRIMARY KEY declaration, the column(s) being referenced must be named, as in:
  room_no CHAR(2) REFERENCES room (room_no)
and: sup_no CHAR(2) REFERENCES employee (emp_no)
  The same requirement applies to the FOREIGN KEY declaration format used in Fig. 19.2.

Section 19.2.3

1. There might be types of room, for instance rest rooms or storerooms, that are never equipped with telephone extensions, so the domain of telephone.room_no is a subset of the room.room_no domain.

Section 19.2.4

1. In SQL92, the column default takes precedence.
2. (a) Reject insertion if room_no in the new employee row is not null and does not match a value of room_no in the room table.
(b) Reject amendment if room_no in employee is not updated to either null or a value that already exists for room_no in the room table.
(c)(i)   Reject deletion if any reference to the room_no value being deleted occurs in the room_no column of the employee table. That is, do not delete a room if any employee is still assigned to that room.
or (ii)   Delete the row from room and also all rows from employee which reference that room_no value. That is, delete information about the employees associated with that room.
or (iii)   Set to null those values of room_no in employee which match the room_no value in the row being deleted. That is, retain information about the employees formerly associated with that room, but disassociate them from the room table.
or (iv)   Set to a default value those values of room_no in employee which match the room_no value in the row being deleted. That is, transfer all employees who were in that room to a default room. The default value is declared in the usual way as a column or domain default. A matching default value must be present in room.room_no, unless the default is null.
  In SQL92 the choice of option from c(i)–c(iv) is specified as part of the FOREIGN KEY clause. For c(ii):

FOREIGN KEY (room_no) REFERENCES room ON DELETE CASCADE

ON DELETE CASCADE specifies that referential integrity is to be maintained by automatically deleting any rows of employee that reference the deleted row in room.

Other options are:

(c)(i) ON DELETE NO ACTION

(This has the same effect as omitting the ON DELETE clause. Note that NO ACTION means 'reject a deletion that would violate referential integrity if nothing were done to maintain referential integrity'.)

(c)(iii) ON DELETE SET NULL

(The delete will fail if there is a NOT NULL constraint on the foreign key column(s).)

(c)(iv) ON DELETE SET DEFAULT

(The foreign key column(s) must have a default value defined. The delete will fail if the default value(s) are not already present in the column(s) referenced, except where a default value is null.)

The same set of options may be used with an ON UPDATE clause.

(d) Similar considerations apply.

Section 19.3.3

1. SQL92 treats these as duplicate rows. Some arguments for and against are:
(a) If null means *unknown*, one *unknown* is not equal to another (the result of the comparison is *unknown*) so the rows *are not* duplicates. (b) Both rows have the same value of emp_name and both room_no components are in the same null state, so the rows *are* duplicates. (c) The nulls might have different meanings. One null might mean 'applicable, but unknown at present', the other might mean 'not applicable' (perhaps the employee works at home) so the rows *are not necessarily* duplicates. (d) Nulls should be ignored in this situation and the comparison made on the non-null values, so the rows *are* duplicates (but what if there are no non-null values. . . .?).

Section 19.3.7

1. No. MIN returns a single value (or null) so DISTINCT, although legal, has no effect here. The same is true for MAX.

Section 19.3.11

1. Yes. In general, A = B = C can be expressed as either A = B and B = C, or as A = B and C = A, or as B = C and C = A.
2. SELECT subordinate.emp_name
   FROM employee, employee AS subordinate
   WHERE employee.emp_name = 'Smith'
   AND employee.emp_no = subordinate.sup_no

Section 19.4.1

1. The database management system must check that no part of the primary key is null and that no duplicates of the new row's primary key value exist in the table. The null check is easily done by inspection of the new row. The speed with which the existence of duplicate primary key values can be checked depends on the size of the table and its storage structure. Duplicates can be detected quickly if there is, for example, an index on the primary key, because the index will be maintained in key sequence and can be

accessed directly by key value. Similarly, a hash structure can be checked quickly. In the worst case, the whole table will have to be searched. The database management system could be designed to impose automatically a suitable storage structure for validation of primary key uniqueness.

2.   No. The referential integrity check on sup_no will fail unless the value of sup_no is already present as an emp_no value in the table, or else sup_no is null. Consequently, the rows shown should be inserted in a sequence (we use the primary key, emp_no, in the following list to identify the rows) such as: 'E4', 'E5', 'E9', 'E1', 'E7', 'E2', 'E8'.

Section 19.4.3

1.   CREATE TABLE animal
(animal_name VARCHAR(8),
PRIMARY KEY (animal_name))

CREATE TABLE keeper
(keeper_no CHAR(3),
keeper_name VARCHAR(12),
PRIMARY KEY (keeper_no))

CREATE TABLE supervision
(keeper_no CHAR(3) DEFAULT '102',
animal_name VARCHAR(8),
PRIMARY KEY (keeper_no, animal_name),
FOREIGN KEY (keeper_no) REFERENCES keeper
    ON DELETE CASCADE
    ON UPDATE CASCADE,
FOREIGN KEY (animal_name) REFERENCES animal
    ON DELETE CASCADE
    ON UPDATE CASCADE)

CREATE TABLE eats
(animal_name VARCHAR(8),
food VARCHAR(8),
PRIMARY KEY (animal_name, food),
FOREIGN KEY (animal_name) REFERENCES animal
    ON DELETE CASCADE
    ON UPDATE CASCADE)

The inclusion of the animal table allows the referential integrity of the supervision and eats tables to be checked against the animal table. It is not possible to make animal_name in eats a foreign key of supervision (nor animal_name in supervision a foreign key of eats) because animal_name may have duplicate values in the referenced table, so it cannot be declared as either the PRIMARY KEY or UNIQUE in the referenced table. (You may wish to consider the relative merits of a less satisfactory solution in which the animal table is omitted and a CHECK . . . EXISTS . . . column constraint is declared between the eats and supervision tables.)

2.   INSERT INTO animal VALUES ('camel')
INSERT INTO animal VALUES ('zebra')

3. (a)

keeper_name
Morris
Dennis
Darwin
Morris

(b)

food
buns
hay
people
mice

(c)

animal_name
zebra
snake
camel
lion

(d)

animal_name	keeper_no
zebra	101
snake	103

4. (a) SELECT food FROM eats WHERE animal_name = 'camel'
(b) SELECT keeper_no FROM keeper WHERE keeper_name = 'Morris'

5. (a)

animal_name	food	keeper_no
camel	buns	100
zebra	hay	101
snake	people	100
snake	people	103
camel	hay	100
snake	mice	100
snake	mice	103
lion	people	100

(b)

food
buns
people
hay
mice
people

6. (a) SELECT DISTINCT animal_name FROM keeper, supervision
        WHERE keeper_name = 'Morris'
        AND keeper.keeper_no = supervision.keeper_no
(b) SELECT DISTINCT keeper_no FROM supervision, eats
        WHERE food = 'hay'
        AND eats.animal_name = supervision.animal_name
(c) SELECT keeper.keeper_no, keeper_name FROM keeper, supervision, eats
        WHERE food = 'people'
        AND eats.animal_name = supervision.animal_name
        AND supervision.keeper_no = keeper.keeper_no
Other forms of the join operation could have been used.

7.   It is, of course, very bad practice to create a table that does not have a primary key. This question illustrates one of the reasons why this is so. There may be many duplicate rows, for example many 'blue Ford' rows. It is not possible with a relational language to address an individual row among a set of duplicates. In part (a) *all* 'blue Ford' rows will be amended to 'black Ford' rows. In part (b) *all* sightings of gold Toyotas will be deleted (DELETE FROM car WHERE make = 'Toyota' AND colour = 'gold').

Section 19.5

1.   CREATE VIEW ert AS
        SELECT emp_no, emp_name, employee.room_no, sup_no, capacity, extension
        FROM employee, room, telephone
        WHERE employee.room_no = room.room_no
        AND room.room_no = telephone.room_no

Refer to the next answer pointer concerning the avoidance of SELECT * in the definition of a view.

Query on base tables:
    SELECT emp_name, capacity, extension
        FROM employee, room, telephone
        WHERE employee.room_no = room.room_no
        AND room.room_no = telephone.room_no
        AND emp_no = 'E4'

Query on view ert:
    SELECT emp_name, capacity, extension
        FROM ert
        WHERE emp_no = 'E4'

2.   It is better to query views, as base tables can then be changed (e.g. by adding new columns) without affecting SELECT * queries. (Note that the use of SELECT * in the CREATE VIEW statement itself should be avoided because its meaning may be misunderstood if the base table definition(s) are changed; the * would refer to the base table column(s) at the time the view was created, not as they are at the time the view is invoked.)

Section 19.5.1

1.   Insert the row 'a_3, b_1, c_1'. Amend the row 'a_1, b_1, c_1' to 'a_3, b_1, c_1'. Delete the row 'a_1, b_1, c_1'. Note that these updates would be theoretically possible (though not valid in SQL92) if table B contained only the first row 'b_1, c_1'.

Section 19.6

1.   Either the integrity constraints would be dropped when the domain is dropped, or the integrity constraints would become column constraints on the base table(s). SQL92 does the latter.

Section 19.8

1.   Create a view of employee containing only the emp_no and emp_name columns. Grant the SELECT privilege on this view. Do not also grant the SELECT privilege on the base table employee.

2.   One would expect user_3 to lose the privileges. Note that user_3 would lose only the privileges granted by user_2. If user_1 had granted the same privileges to user_4 (WITH GRANT OPTION) who had then granted them to user_3, then user_3 would be able to use those privileges. In SQL92, knock-on effects can be managed with RESTRICT and CASCADE options.

20

Object-orientation

20.1   Introduction

The relational model, the entity-relationship model and the SQL92 implementation of a relational-style language, provide effective ways of modelling and manipulating database designs for many applications. However, the demand for more complex information systems, for faster system development and more reliable systems has created pressure for extensions to modelling and data manipulation facilities.

This chapter reviews some basic concepts drawn from what is known as the *object-oriented* model. We then look at how some of these concepts can be incorporated into a relational database management system.

20.2   Overview of object-orientation

20.2.1   Objects

The basic concept in object-oriented modelling is that of the *object*. An object is similar to an entity occurrence in that it has attribute values, but with the fundamental difference that an object is represented by its attributes *plus* the operations that are defined for that object. An object also has an object identifier (*object-id*), sometimes known as an object reference, which is not normally visible to the user but can be used in creating links between objects.

20.2.2   Encapsulation

In non-object-oriented systems, an application is built from program code that acts upon the database, but which is written and stored independently of the data. In an object-oriented system, an application is built from objects which pass messages to each other. A message passed to an object requests the execution of an operation that is part of the definition of that object. The operations and attributes defined for an object are said to be *encapsulated* in the object. This means that, at least in principle, it is not possible to access the object's data except by executing one or other of that object's operations. This situation contrasts with conventional systems where any procedure could access any of the data in the database (subject to the appropriate access privileges).

20.2.3   Classes

In entity-relationship modelling it is convenient to work with entity types, rather than simply entity occurrences. In much the same way, object-oriented modelling uses the concept of an *object class* (or *class* for short) to represent all occurrences (or *instances*) of an object that have the same definition (attributes + operations). (Some authors distinguish between an *object type*, which is an implementation-free concept, and an *object class*, which is an implementation construct.)

20.2.4   Data structures

Object-oriented modelling also differs from the basic relational model in that the former favours the use of more complex data structures if these are seen as modelling the real-world more accurately. For example, data need not be normalised and relationships between objects can be implemented by pointers rather than solely by foreign keys. Proponents of the object-oriented model argue that a model should have sufficiently complex features to enable it to mirror the real-world. Proponents of the fundamental relational model argue that the simplicity of the relational model, and its formal basis in set theory, makes it possible to prove how a relational database, and associated facilities such as query optimisers, will behave.

20.2.5   Methods

The implementation of an operation is called a *method*. Suppose the operation calculateDiscount is defined for a Product class. This operation will be implemented in program code as a method. Encapsulation means that the actual implementation is invisible outside the class definition. Consequently, a method can be changed with few, if any, side-effects. For example, a method cannot alter data used by the methods of other classes, except by the well-defined process of passing messages to those classes. Reasons for changing a method are, firstly, to make the implementation of an operation more efficient and, secondly, because the operation itself may need to work differently, for example the business rules for calculating a discounted price may have changed, so the calculateDiscount method must be changed to suit.

20.2.6   Polymorphism

Because operations are encapsulated within classes, the same operation may have a different effect on different classes. For example, a calculateDiscount operation could have quite different effects when applied to an InsurancePolicy class rather than a Product class. Similarly, many classes may have an operation such as printDetails, but the method implementing this operation would differ from one class to the next. This feature, whereby the implementation of an operation may take many forms, is known as *polymorphism*.

20.3   Class diagrams

Object-oriented models are represented by class diagrams, showing the attributes and operations for each class and also the relationships between the classes. Other forms of diagram are also used to describe object-oriented models but these are beyond the scope of this book. Class diagrams are often drawn using the Unified Modelling Language (UML) notation. Figure 20.1 shows a UML class diagram for an amended version of the library scenario that was originally described in section 14.3.

A class is represented by a rectangular box which is divided horizontally into three sections, the top section for the class name, the middle section for the attributes, and the bottom section for the operations. Figure 20.1 includes a sample of the operations required by the library. Conventionally, class names start with an uppercase letter; attribute and operation names start with a lowercase letter. Subsequent words in a name usually start with an uppercase letter.

The large open arrowhead below Borrower shows that the Adult and Junior classes are *subclasses* of the *superclass* Borrower. This means that a Borrower may be either an Adult borrower or a Junior borrower. The Adult and Junior subclasses both *inherit* all the attributes and operations of the superclass Borrower. Only the Adult class has the attribute *interest* (from time to time the Library notifies adult borrowers of books that match their interests). Only the Junior class has the attributes *guardianName* and *guardianAddress* (the name and address of a parent or legal guardian). The mechanism whereby a subclass inherits the properties of a superclass is known as *inheritance*. A subclass is said to be a *specialisation* of a superclass; a superclass is said to be a *generalisation* of a subclass. A subclass could, itself, be subclassed, in which case it would be the superclass of its own subclass(es).

The superclass, Borrower, is described in the class diagram as an *abstract* class, which means that, in this example, there will be no actual instances of Borrower. A borrower is either an adult or a junior borrower, so there will be instances only of the Adult and Junior classes.

A relationship between classes is usually referred to as an *association*. The degree of an association is commonly shown by the multiplicity notation (see section 9.4). In Fig. 20.1, the association *reserves* represents the relationship between borrowers and the books they reserve. The reservation_date is an attribute of the reserves association. This attribute, and the operations on it are contained in the *association class*, Reservation. An association class is attached to its association by a dashed line. Similarly, Loan is an association class of the *borrows* association.

Some of the attributes (author, interest) are repeating groups, denoted by an asterisk [*]. Both author and interest could each have been represented as a class, but it is assumed here that operations involving them are essentially operations on Book and Borrower objects, respectively, rather than on Author and Interest objects. Consequently, it has been deemed more natural to view them as attributes of the Book and Borrower classes. It can be seen that object-oriented modelling is more intuitive and less prescriptive than relational modelling, particularly where the latter uses fully normalised relations. In practice, normalisation rules may be used in an object-oriented design as an aid to identifying suitable classes. The design may then be denormalised by relaxing the rules so that the design matches the real-world situation more closely.

Question

1. Suppose that *interest* is not required as an attribute in the library class diagram (Fig. 20.1). (a) Would the class Adult be necessary? (b) Would the class Adult be useful?

(5 min)

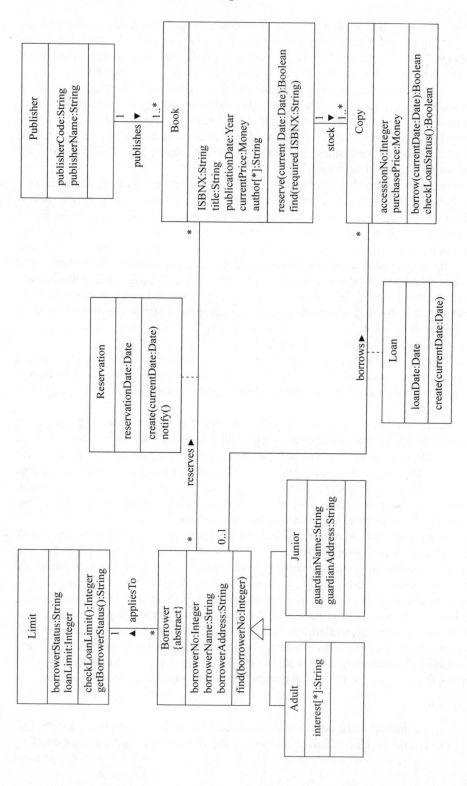

Fig. 20.1   Class diagram for library scenario

20.4   Object-oriented developments

Object-oriented developments in database management systems fall into two main categories.

The purely object-oriented database management systems (*OODBMS*) abandon the principles of the relational model as being too restrictive. They use the same data structures for the data stored in the database (the *persistent* data) as they do for the possibly complex data structures of an object-oriented programming language, such as C++ or Java, used to manipulate that data. Ideally there is no difference between the structure used for *persistent* data on backing storage and for its representation as *transient* data in main memory.

The object-relational approach prefers to retain at least some of the proven advantages of the relational approach, while incorporating some object-oriented features. Given the massive investment in relational database management systems (*RDBMS*), there is a demand for object-relational database management systems (*ORDBMS*) that are compatible with the many SQL-based RDBMS in use today.

Consideration of OODBMS would take us too far afield for the scope of this book. We will consider instead some of the ORDBMS features associated with SQL. Most of the features described are part of the ISO SQL99 standard.

20.5   Further data types

SQL99 extends the range of built-in data types. These additional data types have been available in some other languages for many years, in some shape or form. They are object-relational features in that an ORDBMS would be expected to have a wider selection of data types for modelling applications than SQL92 provides.

20.5.1   Boolean data type

The Boolean data type takes the values TRUE or FALSE. It may also, somewhat controversially, represent *unknown* by NULL. The following section includes an example of a Boolean data type.

20.5.2   Large object (LOB) data types

There are two kinds of LOB, the CLOB and the BLOB. These data types are provided to support multimedia applications. The length of a LOB is expressed in bytes (the default value), kilobytes (K), megabytes (M) or gigabytes (G).

A CLOB is a *character large object*. It is used for large text items such as pages, documents or books. CLOBs can be compared with one another (using comparison operators such as <, =, >) and consequently can be sorted using ORDER BY. They can also be operated on by SQL string functions, for example to search for a specified text substring or to concatenate CLOBs into a larger CLOB.

A BLOB is a *binary large object*. It is used for large binary items such as those found in graphics, audio and video. It is possible to test whether one BLOB is equal to another or not (using the comparison operators = and <>). However, BLOBs are not sortable as, for example, it makes little sense to ask whether one audio recording is greater than another (at least in terms of a sort order). SQL string functions and operators may be used with BLOBs, for example to search for a given substring within a BLOB or to concatenate BLOBs together into a larger BLOB.

The following example illustrates the use of LOB and Boolean data types in the declaration of an employee table for a personnel department. The table is used to store the signature, picture and curriculum vitae of each employee. The probationer attribute takes the value TRUE if the employee is working a probationary period, otherwise it is FALSE.

```
CREATE TABLE employee
     (emp_no CHAR(6),
     emp_name VARCHAR(25),
     signature BLOB(100K),
     picture BLOB(15M),
     curriculum_vitae CLOB(20K),
     probationer BOOLEAN)
```

Question

1. Suggest some ways in which CLOBs and BLOBs might be useful in a library's database.   (2 min)

20.5.3   Row type

It is sometimes convenient to treat associated data items as a named group of fields. This can be done in SQL99 by using a *row data type*, as in:

```
CREATE TABLE customer
     (cust_no CHAR(4),
     cust_name VARCHAR(25),
     cust_address ROW
             (
             street VARCHAR(25),
             town VARCHAR(25),
             postcode VARCHAR(8)
             )
     )
```

This is an example of an *unnamed* row type. The name cust_address is the name of a *column* in the table; that column is of unnamed data type ROW, and that row comprises the fields named street, town and postcode. Because cust_address has an internal structure accessible by the SQL99 query language, the table is unnormalised, since a normalised table has only a single value at a row/column intersection. Having a group name, cust_address, makes it simpler to pass a complete row to or from a procedure. On the other hand, the unnormalised structure complicates the query language. Inserting data into the table will require a more complex notation, for example:

INSERT INTO customer VALUES
('C456', 'Cashdown', ('18 Greenback Road', 'Burton', 'LP12 4DE'))

Named row types can be created, as in:

CREATE ROW TYPE address
(street VARCHAR(25),
town VARCHAR(25),
postcode VARCHAR(8))

This statement does not create a table, it simply defines a row type named *address* which can then be used as a data type in creating tables. For example:

CREATE TABLE customer
(cust_no CHAR(4),
cust_name VARCHAR(25),
invoice_address address,
delivery_address address)

Just as cust_no is of data type CHAR(4) and cust_name is of data type VARCHAR(25), so invoice_address and delivery_address are both of data type address.

Questions

1. Use unnamed row types to create a customer table containing columns cust_no, cust_name and cust_address, where cust_address comprises street, town and postcode fields, and postcode consists of the subfields area_code and locality_code. (2 min)
2. State an advantage of using a named row type, rather than an unnamed row type, for an address attribute. (1 min)
3. What issues arise in comparing and sorting row type attributes? (4 min)

20.5.4 Reference type

The reference type (REF) implements the idea of a pointer. Reference types can be used to create more complex structures and to improve performance. For example, table rows can be linked directly rather than by joining tables.

20.5.5 Array data type

An array data type is a one dimensional array with a maximum number of elements. Suppose an employee may have up to three qualifications recorded. The employee table could be declared, without using an array, as:

CREATE TABLE employee
(emp_no CHAR(6),
emp_name VARCHAR(25),
qual1 VARCHAR(6),
qual2 VARCHAR(6),
qual3 VARCHAR(6))

Searching for all employees with at least one BSc qualification is quite cumbersome:

SELECT emp_no, emp_name FROM employee
WHERE qual1 = 'BSc' OR qual2 = 'BSc' OR qual3 = 'BSc'

Using an array allows a more concise declaration:

CREATE TABLE employee
    (emp_no CHAR(6),
    emp_name VARCHAR(25),
    qual VARCHAR(6) ARRAY(3))

This table could be searched in much the same way as before:

SELECT emp_no, emp_name FROM employee
WHERE qual(1) = 'BSc' OR qual(2) = 'BSc' OR qual(3) = 'BSc'

However, the use of an array permits a more concise statement:

SELECT emp_no, emp_name FROM employee
WHERE ANY qual = 'BSc'

The array data type is an example of an SQL *collection type*.

Questions

1. How would employee numbers, names and qualifications be represented in a fully normalised table structure? Comment on the merits of the fully-normalised solution compared with the use of an array.   (5 min)
2. In everyday spoken English, does the word *any* have the same meaning in the following sentences?

> 'I am taller than any of you.'
> 'Am I taller than any of you?'   (2 min)

20.5.6   Further collection types

Other collection types have been proposed for inclusion in a future SQL standard. A SET is an unordered collection that has no duplicates. A MULTISET is an unordered collection that may have duplicates. A LIST is an ordered collection that may have duplicates.

20.6   SQL99 inheritance

The idea of inheritance was introduced in section 20.3. We will now look more closely at the advantages of inheritance and see how tables and data types can be inherited. Suppose an employee entity table is defined as:

Employee (emp_no, emp_name, date_of_birth, salary)

Some employees are salespersons. Each salesperson has an individual sales target and a percentage bonus that is paid if the sales target is achieved. The entity table can be extended to include these attributes:

Employee (emp_no, emp_name, date_of_birth, salary, sales_target, bonus_percent)

Some employees are managers. Each manager has an individual stock option entitling him or her to purchase shares in the company at a favourable discount. The entity table can be extended to include the stock_option:

Employee (emp_no, emp_name, date_of_birth, salary, sales_target, bonus_percent, stock_option)

Is this table an accurate representation of the real-world situation, where there are salespersons, managers and also employees who are neither salespersons nor managers? For most employees, sales_target, bonus_percent and/or stock_option will be null, so there is a poor match between the real-world entities and their tabular representation. An alternative design would be to have a table for each type of employee:

Employee (emp_no, emp_name, date_of_birth, salary)
Salesperson (emp_no, emp_name, date_of_birth, salary, sales_target, bonus_percent)
Manager (emp_no, emp_name, date_of_birth, salary, stock_option)

Each of these tables represents a real-world entity type, but there is nothing explicit in this structure to show that all three represent types of employee. More particularly, there is no guarantee that each of the common attributes will be defined in the same way in each of the tables. For example, emp_name might be declared as 15 characters in one table, 18 characters in another and 25 characters in a third.

The inheritance mechanism represents the association between the Employee, Salesperson and Manager tables in a more controlled fashion. The tables could be declared as:

```
CREATE TABLE employee
    (emp_no CHAR(6),
    emp_name VARCHAR(25),
    date_of_birth DATE,
    salary NUMERIC(7,2))

CREATE TABLE salesperson UNDER employee
    (sales_target NUMERIC(6),
    bonus_percent NUMERIC(2))

CREATE TABLE manager UNDER employee
    (stock_option NUMERIC(6))
```

The keyword UNDER is used to specify that the salesperson and manager tables are *subtables* of the *supertable* employee. This means that the salesperson and manager tables each inherit the attributes of the employee table, that is they possess all the attributes of employee as well as their own subtable attributes.

Questions

1. New entity types need to be incorporated into a relational database design as business needs evolve. Summarise the advantages of inheritance in accommodating such changes. (2 min)

2. The manager of the Sales Department is both a manager and a salesperson. How could data about this manager be represented?   (3 min)
3. With reference to the library scenario and Fig. 20.1, write table declarations for Borrower, Adult and Junior. Use plausible data type declarations.   (3 min)

20.7   User defined types (UDTs)

A language such as SQL99 provides a variety of built-in data types, such as CHAR, NUMERIC, REAL, BOOLEAN, BLOB, CLOB, DATE, and TIME. Although built-in data types may continue to be added to the language, it is not feasible to provide a complete set of data types to cover the myriad applications for which databases are now used. SQL99 therefore allows users to define their own data types, or user defined types (UDTs) as they are known. There are two types of UDT; the simple *distinct* UDT (considered later) and the more sophisticated *structured* UDT. Libraries of structured UDTs can be developed for specialised application areas.

A UDT is created with a CREATE TYPE declaration. A structured UDT can inherit properties from another type, that is supertypes and subtypes can be declared. Suppose a manufacturer stores data about lighting equipment. There are various kinds of lamp, such as electric and gas lamps. Electric lamps may be filament lamps or fluorescent lamps. Gas lamps may be fuelled by natural gas, town gas or biogas. Filament and fluorescent lamps have different attributes; gas lamps all have the same attributes. The inheritance diagram is shown in Fig. 20.2 and the data structure of the UDTs in Fig. 20.3. We follow our convention of using lower case letters and underscores for user-defined names in SQL.

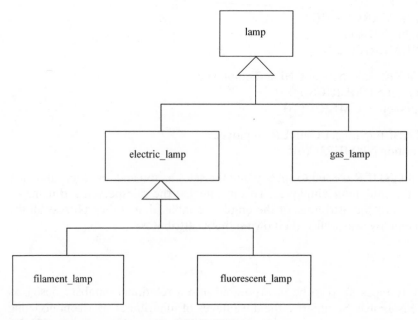

Fig. 20.2   Inheritance diagram for SQL99 UDT data structure

```
CREATE TYPE lamp AS
        (product_no CHAR(5),
        luminosity NUMERIC(4),
        energy_consumption NUMERIC(4))
        NOT INSTANTIABLE
        NOT FINAL

CREATE TYPE electric_lamp UNDER lamp AS
        (voltage NUMERIC(4),
        fitting CHAR(5))
        NOT INSTANTIABLE
        NOT FINAL

CREATE TYPE gas_lamp UNDER lamp AS
        (fuel VARCHAR(12),
        burner_code CHAR(2))
        INSTANTIABLE
        FINAL

CREATE TYPE filament_lamp UNDER electric_lamp AS
        (bulb_code CHAR(5))
        INSTANTIABLE
        FINAL

CREATE TYPE fluorescent_lamp UNDER electric_lamp AS
        (tube_length NUMERIC(4))
        INSTANTIABLE
        FINAL
```

Fig. 20.3   UDT data structure

In this example we assume that there will be no actual instances of type lamp. There are no lamps that are simply lamps; they are all either electric or gas lamps. Similarly, there are no instances of electric_lamp, as such; they are all either filament or fluorescent lamps. Consequently, lamp and electric_lamp are described in Fig. 20.3 as NOT INSTANTIABLE, whereas gas_lamp, filament_lamp and fluorescent_lamp are described as INSTANTIABLE. The term NOT INSTANTIABLE has a similar meaning to *abstract* in object-oriented terminology.

Also, in Fig. 20.3, both lamp and electric_lamp have subtypes, so they are described as NOT FINAL. In contrast, gas_lamp, filament_lamp and fluorescent_lamp do not have subtypes and are described as FINAL.

As well as the data structure, the operations on a structured UDT must be defined. These may include comparison operators (which would allow equality of instances, and the effect of ORDER BY, to be determined) as well as other operations relevant to the application area for which the UDT is designed. The SQL99 standard includes facilities for writing functions and procedures for UDTs.

A structured UDT can be used to type a column or a complete table. For example:

```
CREATE TABLE lamp_table
    (lamp_data lamp,
    PRIMARY KEY product_no)
```

where lamp_data is the name of a column of type lamp, or

```
CREATE TABLE lamp_table OF lamp
    (PRIMARY KEY product_no)
```

where lamp_table is the name of a table of type lamp.

A structured UDT can inherit the properties of more than one supertype (this is known as *multiple* inheritance, as contrasted with *single* inheritance). Conflicts may occur in multiple inheritance. For example, a subtype may inherit different attributes that happen to have the same name. SQL99 has precise rules governing such situations.

A *distinct* UDT is a much simpler type than a structured UDT. It is essentially a renamed version of a built-in data type. For example, suppose goods are sold in UK currency (pounds, pence) and also in US currency (dollars, cents). The columns uk_price and us_price could be declared as:

```
uk_price NUMERIC(6,2)
us_price  NUMERIC(6,2)
```

The disadvantage of these declarations is that expressions such as (uk_price < us_price) or (uk_price − us_price) would be syntactically valid, but normally logically meaningless as different currencies are involved. The solution is to create distinct types, uk_money and us_money:

```
CREATE DISTINCT TYPE uk_money NUMERIC(6,2)
CREATE DISTINCT TYPE us_money NUMERIC(6,2)
```

Columns can then be declared as:

```
uk_price uk_money
us_price us_money
```

Now the columns cannot be directly compared (without generating an error) as they are defined on different data types. A comparison could be made, say, by explicitly converting one distinct data type into the other via the basic data type NUMERIC(6,2), taking into account the appropriate currency conversion factor. SQL provides a CAST function that converts one data type to another.

Questions

1. The lighting equipment manufacturer intends to make a range of electric battery operated torches. What questions would you need to ask in order to include torches in the inheritance structure? How should the inheritance diagram be amended? Make any plausible assumptions necessary.   (4 min)
2. With reference to question 1 and Fig. 20.3, what changes would be needed in the UDT declarations?   (2 min)

Answer pointers

Section 20.3

(a) No. All Adult objects could be instances of the Borrower class, which would no longer be an abstract class. (b) Without the Adult class, all adults would be objects in the

Borrower class. The structure then gives the impression that juniors are special cases of adults. Perhaps they are, but you may prefer to continue to think of both adults and juniors as special cases of borrowers, as represented by Fig. 20.1. Furthermore, the original diagram makes it easier to add new attributes and new operations that apply only to the Adult class.

Section 20.5.2

1. The library could add facilities to an on-line catalogue. It could make the catalogue and items in its collection accessible through the Internet. The CLOB data type could be used for book reviews, or even complete books. The BLOB data type could be used for audio recordings, thumbnail images of items in an art collection, or complete works of art.

Section 20.5.3

1. CREATE TABLE customer
        (cust_no CHAR(4),
        cust_name VARCHAR(25),
        cust_address ROW
                (street VARCHAR(25),
                town VARCHAR(25),
                postcode ROW
                        (area_code VARCHAR(4),
                        locality code VARCHAR(3)
)
)
)

2. Using a named row type ensures that wherever an address is declared, whether in the same or different tables, it will have the same description.

3. In a comparison, such as A < B, does every field in A have to be less than the corresponding field in B, or are the fields compared in major to minor order? For example, is (4, 7, 5) less than or greater than (5, 6, 4)? What happens if A and B have different numbers of fields? What happens if a field is NULL?

Section 20.5.5

1. Employee (empNo, empName)
        EmployeeQualification (empNo, qualification)
With this structure, the number of qualifications per employee is not limited to three. The structure is simpler to manipulate, in that no additional syntax is required to access array elements. Unlike an array, no order of precedence of qualifications or chronological order can be implied. With an array, qual(1) could be the most prestigious or earliest qualification, and so on for qual(2) and qual(3). Of course, implying rather than explicitly showing information is very bad practice. The single table/array solution in section 20.5.5 may model employees more directly, in that qualifications are seen as attributes of Employee. In terms of performance, finding the qualifications of a given employee should be faster using the single table/array structure (in effect, the join operation is already done) but finding all employees (e.g. numbers and names) who have a given qualification may take longer.

2. Probably not. 'I am taller than any of you' implies that I am the tallest person in the group. 'Am I taller than any of you?' asks whether there is at least one person shorter than me. In SQL 'ANY' means 'at least one of'.

Section 20.6

1. Any new subtables of an existing supertable will automatically inherit from the supertable the same column names and data type declarations as the existing subtables. If the inheritance structure models the business structure well, it should be possible to accommodate business evolution (though not necessarily business revolution) through straightforward changes to the inheritance structure.

2. A sales manager could be represented as an occurrence of salesperson plus an occurrence of manager. This would not be altogether satisfactory, as it may give the impression that there are two people, not one. A more accurate model would be to define *salesmanager* as a subtable which has both salesperson and manager as supertables (*multiple inheritance* rather than *single inheritance*).

3. Assuming that an *address* row type has been declared:

```
CREATE TABLE borrower
    (borrower_no INTEGER,
    borrower_name VARCHAR(20),
    borrower_address address)

CREATE TABLE adult UNDER borrower
    (interest VARCHAR(20) ARRAY(5))

CREATE TABLE junior UNDER borrower
    (guardian_name VARCHAR(25),
    guardian_address address)
```

Section 20.7

1. Is a torch a kind of filament lamp or a kind of fluorescent lamp, or could it be either? What attributes (e.g. *battery_type*) does a torch have that are not attributes of lamp, electric_lamp, filament_lamp (and/or fluorescent_lamp)? Assuming that a torch is a kind of filament lamp, torch would be a subtype of filament_lamp. Other possibilities would need to be investigated. Is a torch a lamp at all, or is a torch a complete assembly whereas a lamp is just the bit that lights up?

2. Assuming that torch is a subtype of filament_lamp, the latter would still be INSTANTIABLE but would now be NOT FINAL. A torch UDT would be required:

```
CREATE TYPE torch UNDER filament_lamp AS
    (battery_type VARCHAR(4))
    INSTANTIABLE
    FINAL
```

Appendix A

The Codasyl (network) model

The Codasyl (network) model provides a contrast to the relational model. The appendix is divided into three parts:

A1: Basics of the Codasyl (network) model
A2: Further Codasyl schema facilities
A3: Further Codasyl DML facilities

Acknowledgements to CODASYL

A product of CODASYL is not the property of any individual, company, or organisation or of any group of individuals, companies or organisations.

No warranty, expressed or implied, is made by any contributor or by any CODASYL committee as to the accuracy and functioning of any system developed as a result of this product.

Moreover, no responsibility is assumed by any contributor or by any committee in connection therewith.

This product neither states the opinion of, nor implies concurrence of, the sponsoring institutions.

A1

Basics of the Codasyl (network) model

A1.1 Introduction

The Codasyl approach to a database management system architecture stemmed from the work of a number of committees set up under the auspices of the Conference on Data Systems Languages (Codasyl) organisation, a body composed of volunteer representatives of computer manufacturers and users. The Codasyl architecture is an example of a *network* model, in that it allows a general network of relationships between entity types to be represented. Some earlier architectures were restricted to hierarchical relationships only.

Although the Codasyl model has been superseded in commercial database applications by the relational model and, to some extent by object-relational and object-oriented developments, Codasyl implementations still provide efficient support for many legacy applications. More importantly for our purposes, the Codasyl model offers an instructive contrast to the relational model. The treatment here is based on the 1981 Codasyl Data Description Language Committee Journal of Development (or 1981 Codasyl DDLC JOD, for short).

The architecture of a Codasyl system comprises a *schema, subschema(s)* and a *storage schema*, which correspond to the concepts of conceptual, external and internal schemas respectively. (To minimise confusion between schema as a generic term, and schema in its narrower Codasyl sense, we will refer to the latter as a conceptual schema unless the meaning is clear from the context.) For each type of schema there is a corresponding *description language*. Application programs interface to the database via *data manipulation language* (DML) commands embedded in a high-level programming language such as COBOL, which is the language that we will use in examples of application program code. The DBMS handles exceptions by placing a numeric code in a special register, DB-STATUS, as the last step in executing a DML command. A zero value in DB-STATUS means that the command has been executed normally. An application program can test the value in DB-STATUS and act accordingly.

Although it is plainly an important aspect of application programming, we will omit exception handling code from our examples for the sake of clarity. Furthermore, the examples in part A1 of this Appendix assume that the conceptual schema and subschema content is essentially the same.

A1.2   Record types

A conceptual schema is seen by Codasyl as a collection of associated *record types*. Figure A1.1 is an example of a very simple schema which describes a single record type EMPLOYEE. (The 1981 Codasyl DDLC JOD substituted the underscore for the previously used hyphen as an allowable character in a word. We will continue to use hyphens, to simplify compatibility with COBOL.)

```
SCHEMA NAME IS EMPDATABASE.                              1

RECORD NAME IS EMPLOYEE;                                 2
   KEY EMP-NO-KEY IS EMP-NO                              3
          DUPLICATES ARE NOT ALLOWED;                    4
   KEY EMP-NAME-KEY IS EMP-NAME                          5
          DUPLICATES ARE LAST.                           6
      EMP-NO; TYPE CHARACTER 6.                          7
      EMP-NAME; TYPE CHARACTER 25.                       8
      EMP-SALARY; TYPE FIXED 7,2.                        9
```

Fig. A1.1   Record type declaration

In Fig. A1.1 line 1 names the conceptual schema, and line 2 names a record type within the schema. Lines 3–4 declare EMP-NO to be a record key for EMPLOYEE, which means that the DBMS must provide direct access via this record key. The syntax requires the declaration of a key-name (EMP-NO-KEY in line 3) so that a single name can be used to reference the key even if it is composite. Lines 5–6 define an alternative record key, EMP-NAME-KEY. The data items (lines 7–9) may optionally be prefixed by level numbers. The semicolons (lines 2, 4, 7–9) are optional clause separators, but the periods (lines 1, 6, 7–9) are mandatory. Indentation of statements is purely for clarity. The TYPE declaration for EMP-SALARY (line 9) means that (at least) seven significant decimal digits will be maintained for values of this data item, with an assumed decimal point two places in from the right.

The PROCEDURE DIVISION code to store a new record in the database is of the form:

```
MOVE INPUT-EMP-NO TO EMP-NO.
MOVE INPUT-EMP-NAME TO EMP-NAME.
STORE EMPLOYEE.
```

The MOVE statements place data in the EMPLOYEE record area. The STORE statement places the record in the database.

In what follows, examples of application program code are simplified by writing comments within square brackets in place of actual code and by using arrows to indicate iteration.

The code for direct access, for example to retrieve the name of employee "E4", is of the form:

```
MOVE "E4" TO EMP-NO.
FIND ANY EMPLOYEE USING EMP-NO.
GET EMPLOYEE.
```

```
MOVE EMP-NAME TO [data item in output record].
[Display output record].
```

The MOVE statement primes the EMPLOYEE record area with a value of EMP-NO, which is then used by the FIND statement to locate the position of the record, but no data is transferred at this stage. It is the GET statement that delivers the EMPLOYEE record to the application program's record area. The reference to ANY EMPLOYEE is slightly misleading, particularly in the context of this example where the schema ensures that there can be, at most, only one EMPLOYEE record with the given value of EMP-NO. A *notfound* exception would be indicated by the placing of the value 0502400 in DB-STATUS.

Skip-sequential processing, for example to list the employee numbers of all employees called "JOHN", would take the form:

```
MOVE "JOHN" TO EMP-NAME.
FIND ANY EMPLOYEE USING EMP-NAME.
GET EMPLOYEE.
MOVE EMP-NO TO [data item in output record].
[Display output record].
FIND DUPLICATE EMPLOYEE USING EMP-NAME.
```

Each EMPLOYEE record with an EMP-NAME of "JOHN" will be retrieved exactly once. The value 0502100 will be placed in DB-STATUS when no further duplicate record can be found.

Question

1.   What use are level numbers in a record type declaration?   (1 min)

A1.3   Codasyl sets

The most characteristic feature of the Codasyl approach is the use of *Codasyl sets* to represent relationships.

A Codasyl set represents a 1:many relationship between record types. Figure A1.2a is an E-R type diagram of a 1:many Ward/Patient relationship. The Codasyl view of this structure is shown in the Codasyl type diagram of Fig. A1.2b. The differences between the two diagrams may appear trivial, but the change of notation serves to emphasise that the entity types and relationship type in Fig. A1.2a are being represented as Codasyl record types associated by a Codasyl set type in Fig. A1.2b. The arrow shows the 1:many direction of the relationship; it does not represent a determinancy. The record type (WARD) at the '1' end of the relationship is said to be the *owner* of the set type; the record type (PATIENT) at the 'many' end is said to be a *member* of the set type.

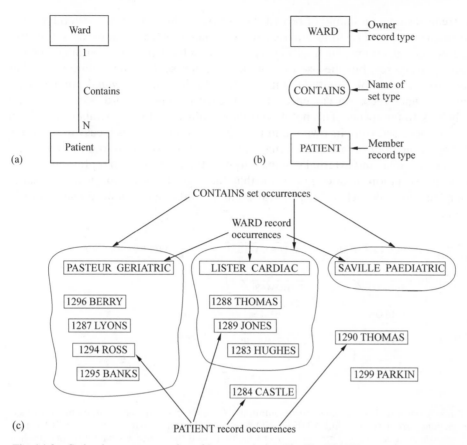

Fig. A1.2   Codasyl set representation of 1:many relationship. The WARD record type comprises the data items WARD-NAME and WARD-TYPE; the PATIENT record type comprises the data items PATIENT-NO and PATIENT-NAME
(a)   E-R diagram
(b)   Codasyl type diagram
(c)   Codasyl bubble occurrence diagram

The *Codasyl bubble occurrence diagram* in Fig. A1.2c illustrates some further features of the Codasyl view. Each bubble represents an occurrence of the CONTAINS set type. A set occurrence always contains exactly one occurrence of the owner record type (WARD), and may contain any number of occurrences (including zero and one) of the member record type (PATIENT). In general, member record occurrences (as exemplified by the records with PATIENT-NO(s) 1284, 1290 and 1299) may exist outside any occurrence of the set although, as we shall see, constraints on the independent existence of members may be specified in the schema. Notice that posted identifiers (foreign keys) are unnecessary, as the set occurrences represent the relationships between records.

Some new terms have been introduced in this discussion of the Codasyl view, but there are really no fundamentally new concepts as compared with the E-R view discussed in Chapter 9. The main difference is the emphasis on the idea of a set occurrence as being a family of records belonging to the same relationship type and associated via a fan of relationship occurrences emanating from a single owner record.

Occurrence diagrams, such as Fig. A1.2c, are helpful in understanding Codasyl database structures, but the use of 'bubbles' to represent set occurrences is rather cumbersome. A simpler method (Fig. A1.3) is to draw a *conceptual pointer chain* from the owner record occurrence, through each member record occurrence, and finally back to the owner. This notation serves to illustrate that a member record can always be accessed from its owner and *vice versa*, and also makes it easy to show any ordering of member records which may exist. It is, however, important to recognise that for conceptual and external schema purposes the pointer chain represents merely a logical association; it does not mean that the logical association will necessarily be implemented as a chain of physical pointers, although it quite possibly will in practice.

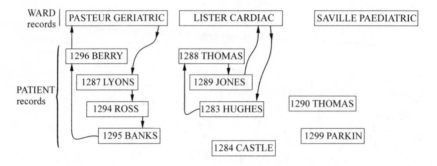

Fig. A1.3   Conceptual pointer chain representation of Codasyl set occurrences. The members of each set occurrence are accessible in PATIENT-NO sequence. Pointers leaving owner records have an extra arrowhead so as to avoid ambiguity over which record is the owner when a set occurrence has only one member

One way in which an application program could access a set occurrence would be to find a WARD record via a record key, as described in section A1.2. PATIENT records within this set occurrence could then be found by using commands such as:

```
        FIND NEXT PATIENT WITHIN CONTAINS.
or      FIND PATIENT WITHIN CONTAINS CURRENT USING PATIENT-NAME.
```

The first FIND command locates the PATIENT record which comes next in whatever order has been declared for the members in the set. An attempt to FIND a record beyond the last member in the set occurrence will generate an *end-of-set* exception. The second FIND command locates the first member record whose PATIENT-NAME value is equal to the record area's present value for PATIENT-NAME. The keyword 'CURRENT' ensures that the DBMS will continue to operate on the same set occurrence. Otherwise the target set occurrence would be determined by the set selection criterion (see section A1.5). Further records having the same value of PATIENT-NAME within the set occurrence can be found by repeated use of the command:

```
FIND DUPLICATE WITHIN CONTAINS USING PATIENT-NAME.
```

Similarly, having found a PATIENT record by some means, the WARD record which owns it can be found by the command:

```
FIND OWNER WITHIN CONTAINS.
```

A1.4 The conceptual schema data description language

The conceptual schema for the Ward/Patient model must start with a statement to name the schema, and must include declarations of the record and set types:

```
SCHEMA NAME IS HOSPITAL.

RECORD NAME IS WARD;
  KEY WARD-KEY IS WARD-NAME
        DUPLICATES ARE NOT ALLOWED.
    WARD-NAME; TYPE CHARACTER 7.
    WARD-TYPE; TYPE CHARACTER 10.

RECORD NAME IS PATIENT;
  KEY PATIENT-KEY IS PATIENT-NO
        DUPLICATES ARE NOT ALLOWED.
    PATIENT-NO; TYPE FIXED 4.
    PATIENT-NAME; TYPE CHARACTER 6.

SET NAME IS CONTAINS;
  OWNER IS WARD;
  MEMBER IS PATIENT.
```

The set declaration in the above schema is incomplete as it lacks clauses covering the ordering of member records, their membership class, and the way in which the correct set occurrences will be selected for certain operations on member records. These extensions are described below.

A1.4.1 Ordering of member records

The fact that member records are to be accessible in a particular key sequence within each set occurrence may be declared as follows:

```
SET NAME IS CONTAINS;
  OWNER IS WARD;
  ORDER IS SORTED BY DEFINED KEYS.
  MEMBER IS PATIENT;
    KEY IS ASCENDING PATIENT-NO
      DUPLICATES ARE NOT ALLOWED
      NULL IS NOT ALLOWED.
```

Notice that the existence of key sequence ordering is stated in the ORDER clause, but the actual sequence is declared separately in the KEY clause.

Questions

1. Suppose you know that the above declaration describes the only set in a schema, but that you do not know the record type declarations. Under what circumstances

would it be possible to store a PATIENT record having the same value of PATIENT-NO as an existing PATIENT record?   (2 min)
2.   Suggest five ways of ordering member records within a set occurrence other than in key sequence, and propose a suitable syntax. (*Hint:* start by considering how a chronological sequence could be maintained.)   (3 min)
3.   What options other than NOT ALLOWED would you expect to be available for a DUPLICATES clause?   (2 min)

A1.4.2   Membership class

Codasyl refines the basic ideas of obligatory and non-obligatory participation by distinguishing what happens when a member record is stored (the *insertion class*) from what happens when it is removed (the *retention class*). The insertion class may be AUTOMATIC or MANUAL; the retention class may be FIXED, MANDATORY or OPTIONAL. There are therefore six possible combinations of insertion and retention class from which to choose.

   The following examples assume that each in-patient must be assigned to a ward, and that an out-patient is not assigned to a ward.

AUTOMATIC insertion
Suppose the HOSPITAL database should contain details of in-patients only. The declaration INSERTION IS AUTOMATIC ensures that a PATIENT record cannot be stored in the database unless it also becomes a member of a CONTAINS set occurrence. Consequently, the PATIENT record will automatically be associated with a WARD record. The question of how the DBMS knows exactly which set occurrence to select is discussed in the next section.

MANUAL insertion
If the HOSPITAL database may contain details of both in-patients and out-patients, the appropriate declaration is INSERTION IS MANUAL. When a PATIENT record is stored, it should be inserted in an occurrence of CONTAINS only if it represents an in-patient, otherwise it should be stored independently of CONTAINS, as exemplified by the records with PATIENT-NO values 1284, 1290 and 1299 in Fig. A1.3. It is up to the application program to insert each in-patient record into its correct CONTAINS occurrence.

FIXED retention
Suppose the hospital has an enterprise rule that whenever an in-patient is discharged from a ward, that patient's record must be deleted. In this context a patient is considered to be discharged as a result of becoming an out-patient, or even as a consequence of being moved to another ward. In this situation the appropriate declaration is RETENTION IS FIXED. With FIXED retention a record occurrence, once it has become a member of a set occurrence, must remain a member of that particular occurrence until the record is deleted from the database. It cannot be moved to another occurrence of the set, nor can it be taken out of the set occurrence to exist independently. In other words, if an in-patient is moved to another ward,

or if an in-patient becomes an out-patient, that patient's record must be deleted; the only way of retaining the information in the database would be to store the record afresh.

MANDATORY retention
If RETENTION IS MANDATORY is specified, a PATIENT record could be moved from one CONTAINS set occurrence to another, to reflect the movement of an in-patient between wards; but once the record has become a member of an occurrence of the set, it must continue to belong to one or other of the set's occurrences until the record is deleted. In particular, if an in-patient becomes an out-patient, that patient's record must be deleted.

OPTIONAL retention
When RETENTION IS OPTIONAL is specified there are no constraints on the removal of a member record. A PATIENT record could be moved to another occurrence of the CONTAINS set, to reflect a change of ward, or it could be moved outside any occurrence of the CONTAINS set, to reflect a change from in-patient to out-patient status, or it could be deleted from the database altogether.

The syntax of the membership class declarations is shown in the following example, where it is assumed that PATIENT records may be stored for both in-patients and out-patients, and that the records may be retained in the database even after a patient is discharged.

```
SET NAME IS CONTAINS;
   OWNER IS WARD;
   ORDER IS ... .
   MEMBER IS PATIENT;
      INSERTION IS MANUAL
      RETENTION IS OPTIONAL;
      KEY ... .
```

Appropriate clauses should be substituted for the ellipses (...).

Questions

1. With reference to the HOSPITAL schema, choose appropriate insertion and retention classes for each of the following sets of enterprise rules.
(a) Patients are taken into the hospital's care only as in-patients, but they may continue to be treated as out-patients after discharge.
(b) Patients may be taken into the hospital's care as either in-patients or out-patients. In-patients may be transferred between wards. On discharge, an in-patient is referred to a family doctor and is no longer the hospital's responsibility.
(c) The hospital keeps records for in-patients only. Owing to demarcation disputes between consultants, it has been agreed that no patient can be transferred between wards except by being discharged and re-admitted as a new patient.   (4 min)
2. The member records in a given set type have FIXED retention. Could an occurrence of the member record type ever exist outside an occurrence of that set type?   (2 min)
3. What facilities in SQL would you identify as being in some sense analogous to the Codasyl membership class conditions?   (2 min)

A1.5 Set selection

Suppose the PATIENT record type has AUTOMATIC insertion in the CONTAINS set type. The DML command to store a PATIENT record in the database is:

```
STORE PATIENT
```

However, there may be many occurrences of CONTAINS. In which occurrence should the PATIENT record be placed? There are three main ways in which the DBMS can answer this question:

(a) By assuming that it should use whichever set occurrence happens to be current for this set type. (Normally this will be the most recently accessed occurrence; see section A3.4.)

(b) By assuming that the application program will have nominated the set occurrence by supplying the value of the owner record's key.

(c) By assuming that the member record itself will have nominated the set occurrence by supplying the value of the owner record's key.

A *set selection* clause in each set declaration tells the DBMS which method to use.

(a) Set selection via current set

A set occurrence can be made current by accessing (via a FIND or STORE command, for instance) either its owner or one of its member records. The general form of the schema syntax for this option is:

```
SET SELECTION IS THRU <set-name> IDENTIFIED BY APPLICATION
```

Using this option, the declaration for the CONTAINS set in the HOSPITAL schema would become:

```
SET NAME IS CONTAINS;
  OWNER IS WARD;
  ORDER IS ... .
  MEMBER IS PATIENT;
    INSERTION IS ...
    RETENTION IS ... ;
    KEY ... ;
  SET SELECTION IS THRU CONTAINS IDENTIFIED BY APPLICATION.
```

(b) Set selection via program's nomination of owner record

The syntax for this option is of the form:

```
SET SELECTION IS THRU <set-name> OWNER
      IDENTIFIED BY KEY <key-name>
```

The DBMS will expect the application program to have placed into the record area the value of <key-name> which identifies the owner of the set occurrence.

For the CONTAINS set declaration in the HOSPITAL schema, the set selection clause would be:

```
SET SELECTION IS THRU CONTAINS OWNER
      IDENTIFIED BY KEY WARD-KEY
```

Assuming that INSERTION IS AUTOMATIC for PATIENT records, a new PATIENT record could be stored as a member of the LISTER ward by the statements:

```
MOVE INPUT-PATIENT-NO TO PATIENT-NO.
MOVE INPUT-PATIENT-NAME TO PATIENT-NAME.
MOVE "LISTER" TO WARD-NAME.
STORE PATIENT.
```

The first two MOVE statements set up a record in the PATIENT record area. The third MOVE statement nominates the owner of the set occurrence in which the PATIENT record is to be stored. On executing the STORE command, the DBMS will use the value "LISTER" to select the appropriate CONTAINS occurrence. (The set selection clause refers to the record key WARD-KEY, rather than the data item WARD-NAME, because in general the record key could be composite. The association between WARD-KEY and WARD-NAME was stated in the declaration of the WARD record type (section A1.4).)

(c) Set selection via member record's nomination of owner record

The syntax for this option is of the form:

```
SET SELECTION IS THRU CONTAINS OWNER IDENTIFIED BY KEY WARD-KEY
               WARD-NAME OF WARD EQUAL TO WARD-NAME OF PATIENT
```

In this example, the DBMS will expect the member record itself to contain the value of the owner's record key.

In order to use this set selection option for the CONTAINS set in the HOSPITAL schema, the PATIENT record type would need to include a data item to hold a ward-name value. For example:

```
SCHEMA NAME IS HOSPITAL.

RECORD NAME IS WARD;
   KEY WARD-KEY IS WARD-NAME
         DUPLICATES ARE NOT ALLOWED.
   WARD-NAME; TYPE CHARACTER 7.
   WARD-TYPE; TYPE CHARACTER 10.

RECORD NAME IS PATIENT;
   KEY PATIENT-KEY IS PATIENT-NO
         DUPLICATES ARE NOT ALLOWED.
   PATIENT-NO; TYPE FIXED 4.
   PATIENT-NAME; TYPE CHARACTER 6.
   WARD-NAME; TYPE CHARACTER 7.

SET NAME IS CONTAINS;
   OWNER IS WARD;
   ORDER IS SORTED BY DEFINED KEYS.
   MEMBER IS PATIENT;
     INSERTION IS MANUAL
```

```
    RETENTION IS OPTIONAL;
    KEY IS ASCENDING PATIENT-NO
          DUPLICATES ARE NOT ALLOWED
          NULL IS NOT ALLOWED;
  SET SELECTION IS THRU CONTAINS OWNER IDENTIFIED
          BY KEY WARD-KEY WARD-NAME OF WARD EQUAL TO WARD-NAME OF PATIENT.
```

In fact, this option is even more general than the example implies, since the WARD-NAME value to be used in set selection could come from somewhere other than the member record.

Question

1. What duplicates constraint, if any, must apply to the record key of the owner record type for each of the set selection options?   (2 min)

A1.6   Singular sets

Suppose the PATIENT records in Fig. A1.3 need to be accessed in PATIENT-NO sequence, regardless of ward (i.e. in the sequence 1283, 1284, 1287, 1288, 1289, 1290, 1294, 1295, 1296, 1299). Sequential access can be achieved by declaring a set type having only one set occurrence which includes all the PATIENT records as members. The conceptual pointer chain will start from the owner record and run through all the PATIENT records in the required sequence before returning to the owner. In this situation the owner record is merely a device which permits the set type to be declared. It would be tiresome to have to declare the owner record type explicitly, and a nuisance to have to ensure that multiple occurrences of the set are not accidentally created. A special record type called SYSTEM is therefore provided. SYSTEM is not declared explicitly as a record type in the schema, but appears only within a set declaration; consequently it cannot contain any data items. Set types with owner SYSTEM are known as *singular sets*.

   The clause SET SELECTION IS THRU <set-name> IDENTIFIED BY SYSTEM is used to instruct the DBMS to select the singular set occurrence which exists for a SYSTEM-owned set type. A singular set to provide access to PATIENT records in ascending PATIENT-NO sequence would be declared as:

```
SET NAME IS SYS-PATIENT;
  OWNER IS SYSTEM;
  ORDER IS SORTED BY DEFINED KEYS.
  MEMBER IS PATIENT;
    INSERTION IS AUTOMATIC
    RETENTION IS FIXED;
    KEY IS ASCENDING PATIENT-NO
          DUPLICATES ARE NOT ALLOWED
          NULL IS NOT ALLOWED;
  SET SELECTION IS THRU SYS-PATIENT IDENTIFIED BY SYSTEM.
```

Question

1. Write a declaration for a singular set which provides access to all PATIENT records in descending order of PATIENT-NAME. Records with duplicate values of

PATIENT-NAME should be accessible in the chronological order in which they were
stored.   (2 min)

A1.7 Mapping an E-R model into a Codasyl conceptual schema

A record type may be the owner of several set types and/or a member in several set
types, so set types can be used to build up a network of relationships. The basic
technique for mapping an E-R model into a Codasyl conceptual schema is:

(a)   Decompose each many:many relationship into 1:many relationships.
(b)   Represent each entity type by a record type.
(c)   Represent each relationship (1:many or 1:1) by a set type.

    If it is known that a Codasyl-style DBMS will be used for implementation,
the design rules described in Chapter 12 may be modified to take account of the
fact that relationships will usually be represented by Codasyl sets rather than
posted identifiers or relationship tables. Alternatively, adaptation to a Codasyl
implementation may be deferred until completion of the first- or second-level design.
Either way, the record types defined in step (b) will not normally include posted
identifiers unless set selection is being handled this way (see section A1.5(c)). The
simplest way of dealing with any 1:many or 1:1 relationship tables will be to forbid
them in the first place. In other words, entity types with non-obligatory participation
will be treated in the same way as those with obligatory participation, which in fact is
what was done in the HOSPITAL example where, although the Patient entity type is
illustrated in Fig. A1.2c as having non-obligatory participation in the Contains
relationship, there is nothing in the schema equivalent to a Contains relationship
table as such. In particular, an attribute of the relationship, such as DATE-OF-
ADMISSION, would be held in the PATIENT record type. A variation on this solution
is to declare separate IN-PATIENT and OUT-PATIENT record types (see question 7,
below).
    There is, of course, nothing to prevent a relationship table being represented as a
record type which itself has relationships (implemented by set types or posted
identifiers) with other record types. This is effectively what happens with many:many
relationships anyway.
    The following points should be kept in mind when designing a Codasyl conceptual
schema:

(a)   A record type which is a member in more than one set type may be described
      differently in each set declaration. For example, the insertion class might be
      AUTOMATIC in some sets, but MANUAL in others.
(b)   The fact that a record type is a member in a set type does not mean that
      all occurrences of the record type must belong to occurrences of the set
      type, as witness the availability of MANUAL insertion and OPTIONAL
      retention.

(c)   A record occurrence can have, at most, one owner occurrence in each set type of which it is a member. It may, of course, have different owner occurrences in different set types, or even the same owner occurrence in different set types.
(d)   A record type may own itself; that is, it may be declared as both owner and member in the same set type in order to represent a recursive relationship.
(e)   A set type must have exactly one owner record type, but may have more than one member record type, although in most cases a single member record type will suffice.

Questions

For questions 1–4 inclusive:

(a)   Map the E-R type diagram into a Codasyl type diagram.
(b)   Draw a conceptual pointer chain diagram for the data supplied.
(c)   Write a Codasyl conceptual schema description.

(*Hint:* It is easier to do part (b) if the value of each record identifier is initially included in the diagram. Any values made redundant by the drawing of the pointer chain may subsequently be deleted. Distinguish occurrences of different set types by using different colours for the pointer chains.)

1.   The E-R diagram below shows a many:many relationship, Team, between the entity types Project and Employee. The identifiers of Project and Employee are projectNo and employeeNo, respectively. Project P1 OILSHALE is staffed by employees E1 HANSON, E2 WELLS, E4 ADAIR, and E5 DIGBY; project P2 SUNSHINE is staffed by employees E2 WELLS, E5 DIGBY, and E9 RAY.
(12 min)

2.   The E-R diagram below shows the relationships between entity types SalesArea, Warehouse and Product, whose identifiers are areaNo, warehouseNo and productNo, respectively.

The data to be stored is:

Sales Area

areaNo	areaName
A1	North
A2	South

Warehouse

warehouseNo	location
W2	Derby
W3	Bolton
W6	London
W7	Derby

Product

productNo	description
P3	pin
P5	bolt
P8	screw

Stocks

warehouseNo	productNo	stockLevel
W2	P3	25
W2	P5	17
W3	P5	40
W6	P5	62
W6	P8	25
W7	P8	84

Location

areaNo	warehouseNo
A1	W2
A1	W3
A2	W6
A2	W7

One of the Derby warehouses is in the northern sales-area, the other is in the southern sales-area. (15 min)

3. Map the supervisor/subordinate model of Fig. 12.10 into a Codasyl representation using a recursive set type. Include employeeName as an attribute of Employee. Employee E2 BEST supervises employees E4 GOOD and E9 TRYER; E4 supervises E1 MEEK, E5 GLUM and E6 SWEET; E5 supervises E3 LOW and E7 SMART. (10 min)

4. Map the parts' structure model of Fig. 12.12 into a Codasyl representation. Use the data given in the figure. (15 min)

5. With reference to the HOSPITAL model, assume that WARD, PATIENT and also CONTAINS are declared as record types. The relationship between WARD and CONTAINS is 1:many, and that between PATIENT and CONTAINS is 1:1. Sketch out a Codasyl conceptual schema description where each relationship is represented by a set type. (3 min)

6. Suggest a syntax for declaring multiple record types as members of the same set type. (1 min)

7. (a) With reference to the HOSPITAL model, state one advantage and one disadvantage of declaring IN-PATIENT and OUT-PATIENT as separate record types.

(b) How could the conceptual schema then provide access to all patient records in alphabetical order of PATIENT-NAME? (2 min)

8. Application programs will need to access EMPLOYEE records within DEPT in both EMPLOYEE-NO and EMPLOYEE-NAME sequence. Sketch out a suitable conceptual schema description. (2 min)

9. Identify a possible ambiguity in interpreting a SET SELECTION clause for a recursive set type. (2 min)

10. With reference to question 1, sketch out the DML commands to list the names of all employees on a given project. (3 min)

Assignments

1. Derive a Codasyl conceptual schema description for the first-level E-R library model of Fig. 14.2.

2. Derive a Codasyl conceptual schema description for the second-level E-R model of Fig. 15.2.

3. Discuss the proposition that the Codasyl set construct serves no useful purpose at the conceptual schema level, but merely serves to confuse.

Answer pointers

Section A1.2

1. To define group data items.

Section A1.4.1

1. The DUPLICATES clause in a record type declaration applies to all occurrences of the record type, whereas the DUPLICATES clause in the member sub-entry of a set declaration applies only to the member occurrences within a set occurrence. Consequently, the PATIENT record could be stored if (a) the record type declaration for PATIENT does not forbid duplicates for PATIENT-NO, and (b) the new record is connected into an occurrence of CONTAINS which does not already possess a duplicate value of PATIENT-NO (that is, the duplicate PATIENT-NO values must be associated with different WARD records).

2. FIRST, LAST, NEXT, PRIOR, DEFAULT. FIRST means immediately following the owner record on the conceptual pointer chain, i.e. reverse chronological order. LAST means immediately preceding the owner record, i.e. chronological order. NEXT, PRIOR refer to positions on the conceptual pointer chain relative to the most recently selected record in the set. DEFAULT means that records are to be maintained in the order most convenient to the DBMS. An example of the syntax for these options is: ORDER IS FIRST. The KEY clause is, of course, omitted from the set declaration if FIRST, LAST, NEXT, PRIOR, or DEFAULT is used.

3. Codasyl also allows duplicates to be declared as FIRST, LAST, or DEFAULT.

Section A1.4.2

1. (a) AUTOMATIC/OPTIONAL. (b) MANUAL/MANDATORY. (c) AUTO-MATIC/FIXED. (Incidentally, FIXED does allow a record to be moved within a set occurrence, so it would be possible to move patient records around to reflect, say, the movement of patients between beds in the same ward.)

2. If the insertion class is MANUAL a member record will necessarily exist independently until it is connected into a set occurrence.

3. The FOREIGN KEY and NOT NULL clauses in the CREATE TABLE statement.

Section A1.5

1. None if "THRU . . . APPLICATION". DUPLICATES NOT ALLOWED if "THRU . . . OWNER".

Section A1.6

1. Apart from a possible change of set name, the only difference from the SYS-PATIENT example (see also question 3, section A1.4.1) would be:

```
KEY IS DESCENDING PATIENT-NAME
     DUPLICATES ARE LAST
```

Section A1.7

1.   (a)

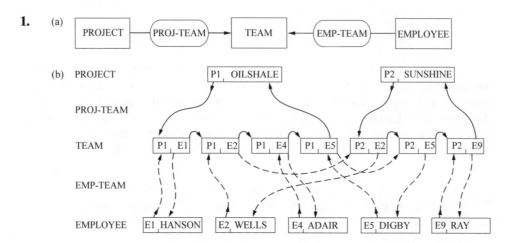

(b)   PROJECT

Solid lines and dashes are used to distinguish between the two set types: they have no
other significance. The projectNo/employeeNo values which identify the TEAM
records are shown for clarity, but should be deleted unless the schema is altered to
include these data items. Each PROJECT record owns, via PROJ-TEAM, all the
TEAM records pertaining to that project. Similarly, each EMPLOYEE record owns all
the TEAM records pertaining to that employee. There is one TEAM record for each
occurrence of the original TEAM relationship.

(c)   SCHEMA NAME IS ENERGY.

```
RECORD NAME IS PROJECT;
  KEY PROJECT-KEY IS PROJECT-NO
          DUPLICATES ARE NOT ALLOWED.
      PROJECT-NO; TYPE CHARACTER 2.
      PROJECT-NAME; TYPE CHARACTER 8.

RECORD NAME IS EMPLOYEE;
  KEY EMPLOYEE-KEY IS EMPLOYEE-NO
          DUPLICATES ARE NOT ALLOWED.
      EMPLOYEE-NO; TYPE CHARACTER 2.
      EMPLOYEE-NAME; TYPE CHARACTER 5.

RECORD NAME IS TEAM.

SET NAME IS PROJ-TEAM;
  OWNER IS PROJECT;
  ORDER IS DEFAULT.
  MEMBER IS TEAM;
      INSERTION IS AUTOMATIC
      RETENTION IS FIXED;
  SET SELECTION IS THRU PROJ-TEAM IDENTIFIED BY APPLICATION.

SET NAME IS EMP-TEAM;
  OWNER IS EMPLOYEE;
```

```
ORDER IS DEFAULT.
MEMBER IS TEAM;
      INSERTION IS AUTOMATIC
      RETENTION IS FIXED;
SET SELECTION IS THRU EMP-TEAM IDENTIFIED BY APPLICATION.
```

Notice that the TEAM record type contains no user data, but merely serves as a link between the other record types. TEAM *could* have included user data items. For example, (a) where would you store an attribute of the relationship, such as startingDateForEmployeeOnProject, and (b) how could access be provided to EMPLOYEE records in EMPLOYEE-NO order within PROJECT-NO, and to PROJECT records in PROJECT-NO order within EMPLOYEE-NO?

2. (a)

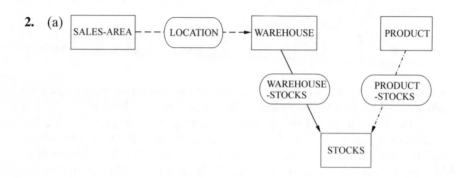

(b)

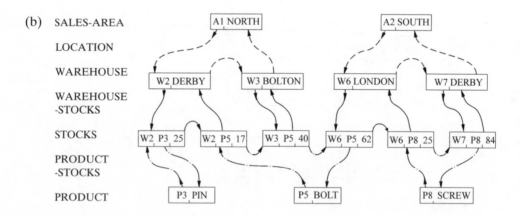

The warehouseNo and productNo values in the STOCKS records could be deleted, as they can be found from the owner records in the WAREHOUSE-STOCKS and PRODUCT-STOCKS sets respectively.

(c) The schema should include record type declarations for SALES-AREA, WAREHOUSE, STOCKS and PRODUCT, and set type declarations for LOCATION, WAREHOUSE-STOCKS and PRODUCT-STOCKS. STOCK-LEVEL should be a data item in STOCKS.

3.   (a)

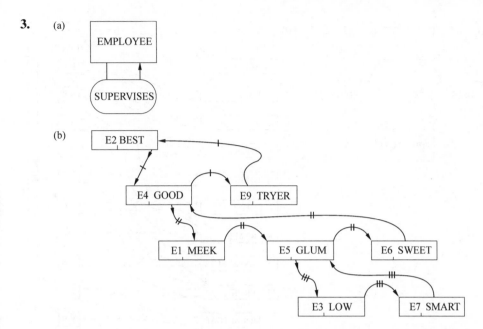

(b)

The single, double and triple bars are used to distinguish between set occurrences. For a non-recursive set type, each record has only one conceptual pointer slot for each set type in which it participates, but for a recursive set type, each record has two conceptual pointer slots, one for its role as an owner, the other for its role as a member. A record at the top or bottom of the hierarchy will use only one of these slots.

(c)   SCHEMA NAME IS PERSONNEL.

```
RECORD NAME IS EMPLOYEE;
   KEY EMP-KEY IS EMPLOYEE-NO
         DUPLICATES ARE NOT ALLOWED.
      EMPLOYEE-NO; TYPE CHARACTER 2.
      EMPLOYEE-NAME; TYPE CHARACTER 25.

SET NAME IS SUPERVISES;
   OWNER IS EMPLOYEE;
   ORDER IS DEFAULT.
   MEMBER IS EMPLOYEE;
      INSERTION IS MANUAL
      RETENTION IS OPTIONAL;
   SET SELECTION IS THRU SUPERVISES IDENTIFIED BY APPLICATION.
```

A MANUAL insertion class is obligatory for a recursive set type. Why?

4.   Part (a) of the solution is derived from the decomposition of the many:many Structure relationship into two 1:many relationships.

In part (b), the USES set connects each PART record to those STRUCTURE records for which that PART is a major part. The USED-ON set connects each PART record to those STRUCTURE records for which that part is a minor part. The fact that there are equal numbers of PART and STRUCTURE records is coincidental.

(a)

(b)

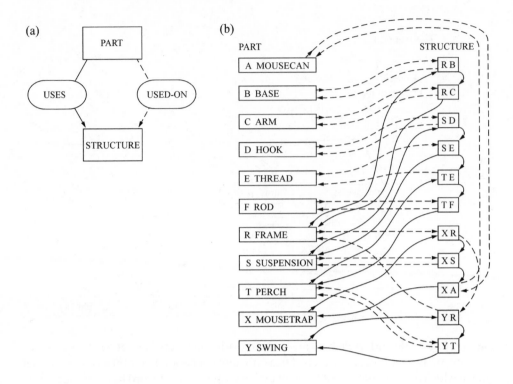

(c) SCHEMA NAME IS ASSEMBLY.

```
RECORD NAME IS PART;
  KEY PART-KEY IS PART-NO
          DUPLICATES ARE NOT ALLOWED.
      PART-NO; TYPE CHARACTER 1.
      PART-DESCRIPTION; TYPE CHARACTER 10.

RECORD NAME IS STRUCTURE;
      MAJOR-PART-NO; TYPE CHARACTER 1.
      MINOR-PART-NO; TYPE CHARACTER 1.

SET NAME IS USES;
  OWNER IS PART;
  ORDER IS SORTED BY DEFINED KEYS.
  MEMBER IS STRUCTURE;
      INSERTION IS AUTOMATIC
      RETENTION IS FIXED;
      KEY IS ASCENDING MINOR-PART-NO
          DUPLICATES ARE NOT ALLOWED
          NULL IS NOT ALLOWED;
  SET SELECTION IS THRU USES OWNER IDENTIFIED BY KEY PART-KEY.

SET NAME IS USED-ON;
  OWNER IS PART;
  ORDER IS SORTED BY DEFINED KEYS.
  MEMBER IS STRUCTURE;
      INSERTION IS MANUAL
      RETENTION IS FIXED;
      KEY IS ASCENDING MAJOR-PART-NO
```

```
      DUPLICATES ARE NOT ALLOWED
      NULL IS NOT ALLOWED;
  SET SELECTION IS THRU USES OWNER IDENTIFIED BY KEY PART-KEY.
```

The solution demonstrates ordering of the STRUCTURE records within sets. If this is not required, the data items could be omitted from STRUCTURE. If direct access to STRUCTURE records is required, the data items should be retained and supplemented with a declaration of one or more record keys. The insertion class cannot be AUTOMATIC for both set types as two PART-NO values, one for the major part and the other for the minor part, would have to be nominated simultaneously. Is this true for other set selection options?

5. The 1:1 relationship could be represented with PATIENT as the set type owner and CONTAINS as the member, or *vice versa*. The choice will affect the membership class constraints which may be imposed. As there is only one member record per set occurrence, there is no point in declaring an ORDER other than DEFAULT for a 1:1 relationship.

6. Include a member sub-entry for each member record type.

7. (a) Advantages are (i) IN-PATIENT records would be members of CONTAINS, so their insertion class could be AUTOMATIC; (ii) attributes of the relationship could be included in IN-PATIENT but omitted from OUT-PATIENT. A disadvantage is that transfer between in-patient and out-patient status would be more complicated.

(b) Declare a singular set with both IN-PATIENT and OUT-PATIENT record types as members, and with PATIENT-NAME as the sort key.

8. The schema should include two set types, each with owner DEPT and member EMPLOYEE, but with different sort keys.

9. With a recursive set type, a record may be an owner in one occurrence of the set, but a member in another occurrence. It will not be clear which of these occurrences should be selected if set selection is "THRU ... APPLICATION" (unless the DML statement can indicate which should be used).

10.

```
MOVE INPUT-PROJ-NO TO PROJECT-NO.
FIND ANY PROJECT USING PROJECT-NO.
[Then loop around the following statements].
FIND NEXT TEAM WITHIN PROJ-TEAM.
FIND OWNER WITHIN EMP-TEAM.
GET EMPLOYEE.
MOVE EMPLOYEE-NAME TO [data item in output record].
[Display output record].
```

A2

Further Codasyl schema facilities

A2.1   Introduction

We now review some further Codasyl facilities for the conceptual schema, and outline the subschema (external schema) and storage schema (internal schema) facilities.

A2.2   Conceptual schema facilities

Figure A2.1 illustrates syntax for the facilities described below. The line numbers quoted in the text refer to this schema.

```
SCHEMA NAME IS PERSONNEL.                                     1
  CALL PROC-1 BEFORE ALTER;                                   2
  CALL PROC-2 AFTER ALTER;                                    3
  CALL PROC-3 BEFORE LOCKS;                                   4
  CALL PROC-4 ON ERROR DURING COPY;                           5
  ACCESS CONTROL LOCK FOR ALTER, LOCKS IS "CIA";              6
  ACCESS CONTROL LOCK FOR DISPLAY IS "MI5" OR PROC-5.         7

RECORD NAME IS DEPT;                                          8
  KEY DEPT-KEY IS DEPT-NO                                     9
      DUPLICATES ARE NOT ALLOWED                             10
  CALL PROC-12 BEFORE, AFTER DELETE;                         11
  CALL PROC-13 BEFORE MODIFY;                                12
  CALL PROC-14 AFTER STORE;                                  13
  ACCESS CONTROL LOCK FOR MODIFY, DELETE IS PROC15.          14
    DEPT-NO; TYPE CHARACTER 3;                               15
        CHECK DEPT-NO IS WITHIN ("AOO" THRU "D99");          16
        CALL PROC-16 BEFORE MODIFY;                          17
        ACCESS CONTROL LOCK FOR MODIFY IS "DOS".             18
    DEPT-NAME; TYPE CHARACTER 20.                            19
    NO-OF-EMPLOYEES; TYPE FIXED 3;                           20
        RESULT OF PROCEDURE PROC-17 ON CHANGE TO             21
        TENANCY OF ALL MEMBERS OF DEPT-EMP.                  22

RECORD NAME IS EMPLOYEE;                                     23
  KEY EMP-KEY IS EMP-NO                                      24
      DUPLICATES ARE NOT ALLOWED                             25
  ACCESS CONTROL LOCK IS "CPM".                              26
    EMP-NO; TYPE CHARACTER 6;                                27
        CHECK EMP-NO IS NOT NULL.                            28
```

```
EMP-NAME; TYPE CHARACTER 25;                              29
    CHECK EMP-NAME IS NOT WITHIN ("MORIARTY").            30
EMP-QUALS; TYPE CHARACTER 5 OCCURS 4 TIMES;              31
    DEFAULT IS "-----".                                  32
TAX-CODE; TYPE CHARACTER 4;                               33
    RESULT OF PROCEDURE PROC-18 ON CHANGE TO             34
    DATA EMP-NAME OF THIS RECORD.                         35
DEPT-NUM;                                                 36
    SOURCE IS DEPT-NO OF OWNER OF DEPT-EMP.              37
SET NAME IS DEPT-EMP;                                     38
  OWNER IS DEPT;                                          39
  ORDER IS DEFAULT;                                       40
  CALL PROC-19 BEFORE FIND;                               41
  ACCESS CONTROL LOCK FOR REMOVE IS "MPM".               42
  MEMBER IS EMPLOYEE;                                     43
     INSERTION IS AUTOMATIC                               44
     RETENTION IS MANDATORY;                              45
  SET SELECTION IS THRU DEPT-EMP OWNER                    46
        IDENTIFIED BY KEY DEPT-KEY;                       47
  CALL PROC-20 BEFORE, AFTER INSERT, REMOVE;             48
  ACCESS CONTROL LOCK FOR INSERT, REMOVE IS "MPM".       49
```

Fig. A2.1   Codasyl conceptual schema

The conceptual schema language specification assumes that certain basic functions will be available in any data manipulation language (DML) which makes use of a schema description; however, the precise definition of a DML is no concern of the conceptual schema language. Consequently, keywords such as DELETE, FIND, GET, INSERT, which are used in this section to describe these basic functions, may differ from the keywords used for the same functions in any particular DML. For instance, the COBOL DML does use FIND and GET, but DELETE becomes ERASE, and INSERT becomes CONNECT or RECONNECT.

ACCESS CONTROL

Access to the database can be controlled by declaring locks at the schema, record, data item, data aggregate (e.g. repeating group), set and member levels. An application program must provide the correct access control key in order to access locked data. A lock may be declared as a literal, a data name, or a procedure name. In the latter case, the procedure determines whether the access control key is valid.

Locks included in the schema entry (lines 1–7) control access to the schema declaration, not the stored data. The operations which may be locked are ALTER (line 6), DISPLAY (line 7) LOCKS (line 6) and COPY. The LOCKS operation must be used in order to view, create or change access control locks. COPY is used to extract information for the purpose of constructing a subschema.

A record type may have locks specified for DELETE, FIND, GET, INSERT (connect into a set occurrence), MODIFY (update), REMOVE (disconnect from a set occurrence) and STORE operations. Line 26 applies to all of these operations. Line 14 applies to the MODIFY and DELETE operations only.

A data item (or data aggregate) may have locks specified for GET, MODIFY (line 18), or STORE operations.

Locks may be specified for a set type in two ways. Firstly, locks may be declared against FIND, INSERT or REMOVE (line 42) operations on occurrences of a set. Secondly, locks may be declared against FIND, INSERT or REMOVE (line 49) operations on occurrences of a member record type.

TYPE

A TYPE clause may be used to describe an arithmetic data item as base BINARY or DECIMAL, with scale FIXED or FLOAT, and with mode REAL or COMPLEX. REAL implies a single value, COMPLEX a pair of values for the real and imaginary parts of the number. Defaults for base, scale and mode are DECIMAL, FIXED and REAL, respectively. A TYPE clause may also be used to describe a string data item as BIT or CHARACTER; the item may be of variable length if a DEPENDING ON . . . clause is used.

CHECK

A CHECK clause may be appended to a data item declaration to specify that a validity test is to be applied whenever a value of the item has been changed or added to the database. If the test fails, the DBMS reports an exception condition. The validation criterion may be an individual value (line 30), a list of values, a value range (line 16), a non-null test (line 28), a procedure call, or some combination of these. It is also possible to declare a CHECK clause for the record as a whole (e.g. between lines 10 and 11), in which case a procedure call is not allowed, but the check may involve more than one of the data items in the record.

RESULT

A RESULT clause specifies that the data item's value is to be supplied by the execution of a named procedure, and states the conditions under which the item's value is to be evaluated. For example, the RESULT clause may state that the data item is to be evaluated whenever any data item in the record is updated, or whenever particular data item(s) are updated (lines 34–35). In this context updating includes the storing of a new record. If the RESULT clause is attached to a data item in an owner record type, evaluation may be triggered by a change in the value of a member record's data item, or by the connection or disconnection (i.e. a 'CHANGE TO TENANCY') of a member record in the set occurrence (lines 21–22). In line 22, ALL actually means ANY.

SOURCE

A SOURCE clause (line 37) specifies that the value of a data item in an owner record should appear to be present also in the member records themselves. This does not necessarily mean that the data item will be physically duplicated in storage, that depends on the storage schema description, but it will appear to be duplicated as far as an application program is concerned. Application programming is therefore simplified because, having accessed the member record, the SOURCE data item is immediately available; there is no need to write further commands to FIND and GET the data item from the owner record.

OCCURS

An OCCURS clause (line 31) is used to describe a *data aggregate*. In our terminology, the term repeating group includes the special case of a repeating item (or *vector*).

Codasyl terminology distinguishes between a vector and other kinds of repeating group. The Codasyl term data aggregate includes both vectors and (Codasyl) repeating groups.

CALL
The ability to CALL procedures has already been mentioned in connection with the ACCESS CONTROL, CHECK and RESULT clauses, but the facility is more general than this. A procedure may be called BEFORE, ON ERROR DURING and/or AFTER:

(a) an ALTER, DISPLAY, COPY or LOCKS operation on the schema (lines 2–5);
(b) a DELETE, FIND, GET, INSERT, MODIFY, REMOVE or STORE operation on a record (lines 11–13);
(c) a GET, MODIFY or STORE operation on a data item or data aggregate (line 17);
(d) a FIND, INSERT, or REMOVE operation on an occurrence of a given set type (line 41);
(e) a FIND, INSERT or REMOVE operation on an occurrence of a given member record type in a set (line 48).

DEFAULT
When an application program stores a record in the database, it will supply values for those data items present in its external schema (subschema) view. Any data item in the conceptual schema record which is not included in the external schema record will be given a default value. The latter may be explicitly specified by a DEFAULT clause (line 32), otherwise the data item is set to null.

Questions

1. In what ways does the effect of an access control lock on member records differ from a lock applied to a set as a whole? (2 min)
2. What value would you expect the DBMS to place in a SOURCE data item if its host record occurrence does not belong to an occurrence of the set quoted in the SOURCE clause? (1 min)
3. What penalty would you associate with the prolific use of access control locks and procedure calls? (1 min)

A2.3 External schema facilities

External schemas (or *subschemas*) are defined using a *subschema data description language* tailored to the style of a particular host language. Figure A2.2 is an example of a COBOL subschema based on the conceptual schema of Fig. A2.1.

The TITLE DIVISION names the subschema and relates it to its parent conceptual schema. A subschema cannot be associated with more than one schema.

```
TITLE DIVISION.
SS  SKILLS WITHIN PERSONNEL.

MAPPING DIVISION.
ALIAS SECTION.
AD  RECORD STAFF IS "EMPLOYEE".
AD  SET AFFILIATION IS "DEPT-EMP".
AD  EMP-CODE IS "EMP-NO".

STRUCTURE DIVISION.

REALM SECTION.
RD  SKILLS-REALM CONTAINS STAFF, DEPT RECORDS.

RECORD SECTION.
01  DEPT.
    02  DEPT-NO PICTURE A99.
    02  DEPT-NAME PICTURE X(20).
01  STAFF.
    02  EMP-QUALS PICTURE X(5) OCCURS 4 TIMES.
    02  EMP-CODE PICTURE X(6).

SET SECTION.
SD  AFFILIATION.
```

Fig. A2.2   COBOL subschema example

The optional MAPPING DIVISION allows *aliases* to be defined, so that names used in the conceptual schema for record types, set types and data items can be altered to suit the needs of the application programs which use the subschema. For example, aliases would be declared to avoid clashes between names used in the conceptual schema and reserved words in COBOL.

The STRUCTURE DIVISION includes a REALM SECTION, a RECORD SECTION and a SET SECTION. A *realm* consists of a collection of specified record types. A subschema may define several, possibly overlapping, realms. An application program must open a realm (using a READY command) in an appropriate way for the type of processing required (e.g. EXCLUSIVE UPDATE). The RECORD and SET sections declare the records, the data items within those records, and the sets, which are to be included in the subschema.

Some other ways in which a subschema may differ from a conceptual schema include the declaration of:

(a)   aliases for individual characters used in defining names in the conceptual schema;
(b)   different data item formats (i.e. data types);
(c)   local validation rules;
(d)   set selection clauses, which may override those in the conceptual schema.

A2.4   Internal schema facilities

A Codasyl internal (or *storage*) schema is defined using a language known as the *data storage description language* (DSDL). The DSDL is designed to be independent of any particular operating system, so an implementor must provide some means for translating the DSDL into a form which the operating system can understand.

The description of the DSDL given here is based on the 1981 Codasyl report on a Draft Specification of a Data Storage Description Language. The following extract from this report defines the terms used in the DSDL:

'A *storage area* is a named subdivision of the storage space allocated to a database. It is a container for storage records and indexes.

A *page* is an individually numbered subdivision of a storage area, each storage area consisting of an integral number of pages of the same capacity. Successive access to storage records is fastest if they are stored within the same page, and successive access to pages with adjacent page numbers is generally faster than access to non-adjacent pages. Typically a page is the unit of transfer between the database and the database management system buffers.

A *storage record* is a variable length addressable container for data and pointers associated with a single conceptual schema record. The contents of a storage record are defined in the storage schema. A storage record is usually stored wholly within one page.

An *index* is a structure which supports access paths to storage records. It consists of a sequence of elements, each of which contains a pointer and, where specified, a key.

A *storage schema* consists of DSDL entries describing storage areas, storage records and indexes which support records and sets described in the conceptual schema.'

(Some minor amendments to the text have been made in the above extract and the one which follows.)

A good idea of the flexibility in tuning database performance which the DSDL offers to the database administrator is given by a further extract from the report:

'Some of the differences between the conceptual schema and storage schema descriptions that may imply data transformations are:

* at the storage schema data item level
(a)   The order of data items within a storage record type may be different from the order implied by the conceptual schema.
(b)   Items may be declared as occupying no space if they are derived from other items.
(c)   Items may be aligned on specified boundaries.
(d)   Items may be separated by fillers.
(e)   The format of a data item may be changed.
(f)   Items may be duplicated.

* at the record level
(a)   A storage record may contain all or part of a conceptual schema record.
(b)   Different occurrences of a conceptual schema record type may be represented by storage records of different types.'

Questions

1.   In a conventional COBOL file, what construct is equivalent to a DSDL page?
(1 min)

2.   Why might data items in a conceptual schema be duplicated in an associated storage schema? (1 min)

3. Why might data items in a conceptual schema be omitted from an associated storage schema?   (2 min)
4. Why might a conceptual schema record be split between several storage records?
                                                                                  (1 min)

A2.4.1   Representation of schema data

Record pointers
Storage records may contain pointers to other storage records. A *direct pointer* indicates the page in which the target record is stored. An *indirect pointer* references an index entry which itself contains a direct pointer to the target record. If the storage location of a record which is the target of several direct pointers is changed, then all the direct pointers will need to be updated. If indirect pointers had been used, only the index entry would need to be altered, but access to the target record would be slower.

Record representation
As indicated in the previous section, the mapping from conceptual to storage records may be quite elaborate. A conceptual schema record may be mapped into one or more storage records, though each storage record is associated with only one conceptual schema record. The same conceptual schema data item may be represented in more than one of the storage records. Different mappings may be requested for different occurrences of the same record type, the mapping actually used being determined by the contents of the conceptual schema record.

Whenever a conceptual schema record is split among several storage records, the latter must be connected by link pointers so that the complete record may be reconstituted when necessary.

Set representation
Figure A2.3 shows the access paths which are declarable in the storage schema in order to represent a conceptual schema set. Starting at any owner or member record it is possible to find the next or prior record, and starting at any member record it is possible to find the owner record. The DSDL permits the declaration of a pointer for each arrow shown in the diagram, namely first and last pointers for set owners, and next, prior and owner pointers for set members. Not every set type will need to use all these pointers. For example, if an owner record is never accessed from a member record there is no merit in including an owner pointer. In general, any or all of the owner, prior and last pointers may be omitted to save storage space.

Figure A2.4 shows a second method of representing a set. The owner record points to a set index, whose entries point to the member records. The index entries may also contain a key to facilitate direct access to members and the ordering of member records.

Questions

1. Compare the suitability of the pointer chain structure (Fig. A2.3) with the set index structure (Fig. A2.4) for (a) sequential access to all the members in a set occurrence, and (b) direct access to a member record in a set occurrence given the record's key. In each case assume that the starting point is the owner record.   (2 min)

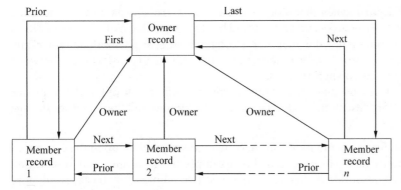

Fig. A2.3   Pointer chain representation of a set

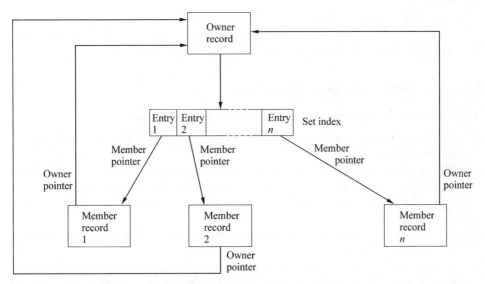

Fig. A2.4   Set index representation of a set

2.   For a given set type, access from a member record to the owner record is required very infrequently. Should owner pointers be declared?   (2 min)

A2.4.2   Record and index placement

Conditions can be stipulated to control the *gross placement* of storage records into storage areas, or parts thereof. The *fine placement* of storage records into pages within a storage area is controlled by the following options:

(1)   CALC specifies random (hashed) placement. A transformation algorithm is used to convert a nominated key in the storage record into a page address. The algorithm may be a named procedure or, by default, a system-supplied procedure.

(2)   CLUSTERED specifies that storage records that are associated with the same conceptual schema set occurrence should be stored near each other, if possible. A cluster may contain just the 'member' storage records, or else both 'member' and 'owner' storage records with a specified number of pages (possibly zero) between the 'member' and 'owner' records.

(3)   SEQUENTIAL specifies that storage records should be stored in the sequence (ascending or descending) determined by a nominated key in the storage record.

Both gross and fine placement options may be made dependent upon the content of the schema records being represented. For example, in an airline seat reservation system, records representing flights due in the next two months may be accessed more frequently than those due at a later date, so different placement options may be appropriate to achieve the best compromise between access time and storage requirements.

An index supporting a non-singular set may be placed near the set owner or, using the CALC placement method, within a nominated storage area. In all other cases an index is placed within a specified page range of a selected storage area.

A2.4.3   DSDL schema structure

A DSDL storage schema may contain the following entry types:

(a)   The *storage schema entry* names the storage schema, and states which conceptual schema it represents.

(b)   The *mapping description entry* defines the mapping of each conceptual schema record into one or more storage schema records. This entry may be omitted if there is a 1:1 correspondence between records in the conceptual schema and the storage schema.

(c)   A *storage area entry* defines the name, initial size, expansion increment, and page size of a storage area.

(d)   A *storage record entry* names a storage record type, defines its contents, and specifies how its occurrences are to be placed in the database (i.e. the gross and fine placement). The contents declared for the storage record may include data items (and their formats), and links to other storage records (where a conceptual schema record is mapped into several storage records).

(e)   A *set entry* declares the pointers which are required to support the sets to which occurrences of a record type may belong. First, last, and index pointers may be specified for owner record types, and next, prior, owner, and index pointers for member record types. It is possible to state, for each set type in which a record participates, whether pointer space is to be allocated permanently (STATIC allocation) or as required (DYNAMIC allocation).

(f)   An *index entry* names an index and describes where it is to be stored, how it is to be accessed, and its role within the database structure (e.g. whether it is a disjoint index to storage records of a given type, regardless of set membership, or whether it is an embedded index as in Fig. A2.4).

A2.4.4   Reorganisation

To facilitate reorganisation, the description of an object in the storage schema may exist in several *versions*, each of which applies to different occurrences of the object in the database. For example, the implementation of a particular set type may be changed from pointer chain to set index. Use of the DSDL version facility allows existing occurrences of the set to be reorganised, not necessarily immediately, but as and when they are accessed.

Question

1.   The Codasyl DDLC JOD distinguishes between *static* and *dynamic* reorganisation. What do you think is meant by these terms?   (1 min)

Assignments

1.   Is it feasible for a DBMS to automatically tune the internal schema to optimise performance? Would languages such as DSDL then be redundant?
2.   Discuss the effect on the structures shown in Fig. A2.3 and A2.4, of splitting schema records into more than one storage record.

Answer pointers

Section A2.2

1.   A lock on member records does not control access to owner records, and different locks may be applied to each member record type should there be multiple member record types in a set type.
2.   Null. Codasyl defines null as a state, not a value, so application programs do not have to avoid using some particular bit pattern.
3.   Slow execution of database operations.

Section A2.4

1.   The blocking factor (BLOCK CONTAINS. . .). But note that the page size for a given storage area is fixed in DSDL, so occurrences of different record types must share the same page size if they are stored within the same storage area.
2.   To improve performance. As the duplication would be under DBMS control, consistency should not be a serious problem.
3.   The storage schema is being developed and tested in stages. Parts of the conceptual schema are not yet in use. The storage schema represents one section of a distributed database.
4.   To improve performance. For example, different subschemas may relate to different (possibly overlapping) parts of a conceptual schema record. Some operations, e.g. accessing the whole conceptual schema record, may become slower if the record is split into several storage records, but access to individual parts may be faster.

Section A2.4.1

1.   The pointer chain structure should offer slightly faster sequential access, as there is no set index to be read, and some saving on storage. The set index structure should offer faster direct access to member records, as the set index can be searched quickly. The DSDL does not define the structure of an index in detail, for example whether it is an (ordered) list or an indexed sequential structure.

2.   If a pointer chain set representation is used, the next pointers would be sufficient to access the owner record from a member record, although if a fast response is needed it might still be necessary to include owner pointers. If a set index representation is used, owner pointers are mandatory, otherwise an owner could not be accessed from its member records.

Section A2.4.4

1.   In *static* reorganisation, application programs are not allowed to access the database until the reorganisation has been completed. In *dynamic* reorganisation, application programs may continue to run while reorganisation proceeds. Dynamic reorganisation may take the form of either *background* or *incremental* reorganisation. In the former a background utility is run; in the latter individual record occurrences are reorganised only when they are accessed. Static, background and incremental reorganisation could all be used on the same database.

A3

Further Codasyl DML facilities

A3.1 Introduction

Several of the Codasyl COBOL DML statements have been discussed, or at least mentioned in passing, in parts A1 and A2. These, and other statements and facilities are reviewed here to give a more complete picture. The treatment is based on the 1981 Codasyl COBOL Journal of Development.

Most of the examples refer to the SKILLS subschema of Fig. A2.2, which contains the realm SKILLS-REALM, and record types DEPT and STAFF connected by set type AFFILIATION.

A3.2 Run units

A *run unit* is an individual execution of an application program (which may itself consist of one or more interacting program modules). If the same application program is run on two separate occasions it exists as two distinct run units; similarly, an application program executed concurrently by two independent users (using duplicate copies of the program, or the same copy written in re-entrant code) would exist as two distinct run units.

A3.3 Subschema invocation

A subschema is invoked via a DB entry in the SUB-SCHEMA SECTION of the DATA DIVISION.

```
DATA DIVISION.
SUB-SCHEMA SECTION.
DB   SKILLS WITHIN PERSONNEL.
```

Only one DB entry may appear in a separately compiled program.

A3.4 Currency

The idea of currency has been implicit in previous discussions of DML statements, but we now take a closer look at the subject. For each run unit there is a currency indicator for:

(a)   the run unit;
(b)   each record type;
(c)   each set type;
(d)   each realm.

Currency indicators are updated by the successful execution of certain DML statements, except that some DML statements (FIND, FETCH, STORE) can optionally specify that one or more of the record type, set type, or realm currency indicators should not be altered by the statement's execution. This facility allows, for example, a run unit to keep its present position among the occurrences of a given record type, while taking a sideways glance at another occurrence of the same record type, and without the use of a keep list (see next section). Prior to the execution of the run unit's first DML statement, all currency indicators are set to null. Each currency indicator can contain a database key value (see next section) to identify a current record; set and realm currency indicators can also specify a position, as explained below.

The *run unit currency indicator* always identifies the last database record for which a DML statement has been successfully executed by the run unit.

Each *record type currency indicator* identifies the current record of that record type, if one exists, otherwise it is null.

Each *set type currency indicator* can be in one of three states:

(a)   It identifies a tenant (i.e. owner or member) record in the set, and also the position of that record within the set.
(b)   It does not identify any record, but does point to a position within the set. This situation will arise when a member record identified by a set type currency indicator is deleted.
(c)   It is null, in which case it identifies neither a record nor a position.

The value of a set type currency indicator is updated by the DBMS following successful completion of a DML statement affecting a tenant record of that set type. The set occurrence, if any, to which a set type currency indicator points, is known as the current set of the set type. (For a singular set, the current set occurrence is always the occurrence of that singular set, regardless of the value of the currency indicator.) The record type, if any, to which the set type currency indicator points, is known as the current record of the set type. Where NEXT or PRIOR ordering of member records is specified in the conceptual schema, the point of insertion for a member record is determined by the contents of the relevant set type currency indicator.

Each *realm currency indicator* can be in one of three states:

(a)   It identifies a record in the realm, and also the position of that record within the realm.
(b)   It does not identify any record, but does point to a position within the realm.
(c)   It is null, in which case it identifies neither a record nor a position.

If the DBMS cannot accomplish all the changes specified by a statement which attempts to alter the database, then no changes are made to the database or to the currency indicators.

A run unit may set any of its currency indicators to null by using the appropriate FREE statement option. For example:

```
FREE CURRENT.
FREE STAFF.
FREE WITHIN AFFILIATION.
FREE WITHIN SKILLS-REALM.
```

The first example refers to the current record of the run unit, and the last three examples refer to the current record of the nominated record type, set type, and realm, respectively.

A3.5 Database keys

During the life of a run unit, each record in the database is identifiable by a unique *database key* assigned by the DBMS. Conceptually, a database key is equivalent to the physical storage address of the record, and may indeed be implemented as such. Database keys may be *used* by a run unit, although their actual values are never directly *visible* to the run unit. For instance, if it is known that a record will be retrieved several times during a run unit's life, processing will be more efficient if the run unit notes the value of the record's database key after the first retrieval, and then uses this value for each subsequent retrieval. However, database key values cannot be passed from one run unit to another; their use is strictly local to a run unit.

The construct provided for handling database keys is the *keep list*. One or more keep lists may be declared in the SUB-SCHEMA SECTION. For example:

```
DB  SKILLS WITHIN PERSONNEL.
LD  LIST1 LIMIT IS 5.
LD  LIST2 LIMIT IS 20.
```

LIST1 is able to hold a maximum of five database keys, and LIST2 a maximum of twenty.

A database key is added to a keep list by using a KEEP statement. For example:

```
KEEP  CURRENT USING LIST1.
KEEP  FIRST WITHIN LIST1 USING LIST2.
KEEP  LAST WITHIN LIST1 USING LIST2.
KEEP  CURRENT STAFF USING LIST1.
KEEP  CURRENT WITHIN AFFILIATION USING LIST2.
KEEP  CURRENT WITHIN SKILLS-REALM USING LIST1.
```

In each case the database key is added to the end of the keep list nominated in the USING phrase. The first example refers to the current record of the run unit, the next two examples transfer database keys between keep lists, and the final three examples refer to the current records of the nominated record type, set type, and realm, respectively.

A run unit makes use of the database keys on a keep list through commands of the form:

```
FIND FIRST WITHIN LIST1.
FIND LAST WITHIN LIST1.
```

The FIND statement makes the record referenced by the database key the current record of the run unit but, as noted previously, a FIND statement does not itself transfer the record.

A database key may be discarded from a keep list by a FREE statement. For example:

```
FREE FIRST WITHIN LIST1.
FREE LAST WITHIN LIST1.
FREE ALL FROM LIST1, LIST2.
```

Questions

1. Suggest why the values of database keys may not be transferred between run units.
    (2 min)
2. Suggest why the value of a database key is never directly visible to a run unit as data.
    (1 min)

A3.6   Further DML functions

A3.6.1   Storing new records

The STORE statement instructs the DBMS to place a new record in the database. For example:

```
STORE STAFF.
```

The record becomes the current record of the run unit, and is made a member of an occurrence of each set type in which it has automatic membership. A RETAINING phrase may be attached to specify that the currency indicators for all realms, and/or all record types, and/or nominated set types, are to be left unaltered. For example:

```
STORE DEPT RETAINING RECORD, AFFILIATION, CURRENCY.
```

will preserve the currency indicators for all the record types and for the AFFILIATION set type, but the currency indicators for the realm(s) to which the record belongs will be updated.

If a currency indicator points to a position, but not a record, and the new record is stored at that position, then the currency indicator will be altered to point to the new record, even if a RETAINING phrase is present.

A3.6.2   Managing set membership

The CONNECT statement makes a record a member of a set. For example:

```
CONNECT STAFF TO AFFILIATION.
```

will insert the CURRENT record of the STAFF record type into the AFFILIATION set occurrence determined by the relevant set selection criterion.

The DISCONNECT statement removes a member record from a set. For example:

```
DISCONNECT STAFF FROM AFFILIATION.
```

The RECONNECT statement moves a member record from one occurrence to another of the same set type, or between one position and another in the same occurrence of the set type. For example:

```
RECONNECT STAFF WITHIN AFFILIATION.
```

The record is disconnected from the set occurrence of which it is a member, and reconnected to the occurrence determined by the relevant set selection criterion.

The record name may be omitted from a CONNECT, DISCONNECT or RECONNECT statement, in which case the current record of the run unit is assumed. A statement may specify a list of set names or, for CONNECT and DISCONNECT only, the keyword ALL.

A3.6.3   Locating and retrieving data

Various formats of the FIND statement have been discussed previously. We merely note here that the RETAINING phrase described for the STORE statement may also be applied to the FIND statement, and that a variation on the FIND statement is available which enables the current record of a given record type, set type or realm to be made the current record of the run unit; for example:

```
FIND CURRENT STAFF.
FIND WITHIN AFFILIATION.
FIND WITHIN SKILLS-REALM.
```

The GET statement places all, or part, of the current record of the run unit in its associated record area. For example:

```
GET.
GET DEPT.
GET DEPT-NAME.
GET DEPT-NO, DEPT-NAME.
```

The first example refers to the whole of the current record of the run unit. Where a record name or data item name is specified, the DBMS will check that it is valid for the current record of the run unit.

The FETCH statement combines the functions of FIND and GET. For example:

```
FETCH NEXT STAFF WITHIN AFFILIATION USING ONLY EMP-QUALS.
FETCH ANY DEPT USING DEPT-NO USING ONLY DEPT-NAME.
```

In the second statement, the first 'USING' identifies a DEPT record; the second 'USING' names the data item(s) required.

A3.6.4   Updating records

The MODIFY statement replaces the contents of one or more data items within a record. For example:

```
MODIFY DEPT-NAME.
```

will replace the contents of DEPT-NAME in the current record of the record type with the contents of DEPT-NAME in the DEPT record area. The MODIFY statement may specify a record name, or a list of data item names associated with the same record. If the keyword MODIFY is used on its own, it references the current record of the run unit.

A3.6.5   Deleting records

The ERASE statement deletes one or more records from the database. The effect of ERASE is complicated by the fact that the record to be erased may own member records, in which case the DBMS needs to know whether it should erase the owner but leave the members, or erase the member records along with the owner, or raise an exception condition to alert the run unit.

The four options for ERASE are:

```
ERASE.
ERASE ALL.
ERASE <record name>.
ERASE ALL <record name>.
```

The first two options refer to the current record of the run unit. The last two options refer to the current record of the nominated record type.

If the ALL phrase is not specified, the record cannot be erased unless all its member records have FIXED or OPTIONAL membership in the set(s) which it owns, in which case member records with FIXED membership are erased and those with OPTIONAL membership are disconnected from the set(s). If the ALL phrase is specified, both the record and its members are erased regardless of the members' retention classes.

A member record owned by the record which is the object of the ERASE statement may itself be an owner record. If so, the above rules apply to the member record as though it were the object record.

A3.6.6   Reordering member records

The ORDER statement is used to change the logical ordering of the member records in a set occurrence. For example:

```
ORDER AFFILIATION LOCALLY ON ASCENDING KEY EMP-CODE.
```

The set occurrence affected by the ORDER statement is the one in which the current record of the set type is a tenant. The optional keyword, LOCALLY, means that the reordering will be local to the run unit and will remain in effect only until the termination of the run unit or the next quiet point (see section A3.6.8), at which time the original ordering will be restored.

A3.6.7   Opening and closing realms

The READY statement makes one, or more, realms available to the run unit. For example:

```
READY SKILLS-REALM USAGE-MODE IS RETRIEVAL.
READY SKILLS-REALM USAGE-MODE IS UPDATE.
```

Both RETRIEVAL and UPDATE may be qualified by the prefix SHARED (the realm may be updated by other run units), PROTECTED (the realm cannot be updated by other run units), or EXCLUSIVE (the realm cannot be accessed in any way by other run units).

The FINISH statement terminates the availability of one, or more, realms. For example:

```
FINISH SKILLS-REALM.
```

A3.6.8   Recovery

To facilitate on-line recovery, the database changes made by a run unit are not accessible to other run units until the run unit which made the changes issues a COMMIT statement. If the run unit detects a situation which invalidates an update, then it can issue a ROLLBACK statement to nullify any changes made since the run unit's last *quiet point*. A quiet point exists at the completion of a COMMIT or ROLLBACK statement, and also at the beginning or end of the run unit. The significance of a quiet point is that no updates will be in progress at that instant. Both COMMIT and ROLLBACK empty all the run unit's keep lists, and set all its currency indicators to null. When the run unit is terminated the DBMS executes an implicit ROLLBACK.

A3.6.9   Exception handling

The COBOL USE statement is extended to include an option for specifying procedures to be executed when a database exception is generated. For example:

```
USE FOR DB-EXCEPTION.
USE FOR DB-EXCEPTION ON "0502400".
USE FOR DB-EXCEPTION ON OTHER.
```

USE statements are placed in the DECLARATIVES portion of the PROCEDURE DIVISION, and each is followed by zero or more paragraphs to specify appropriate exception processing. The first example above would apply to any database exception, the second example applies only to an exception for which the database status indicator is set to 0502400 (a *notfound* exception), and the final example is self-explanatory. The same exception condition must not be the subject of more than one USE statement.

A3.6.10   Database conditions

The COBOL IF statement may be used to test certain database conditions known as the *tenancy, member* and *database key* conditions, respectively.

The tenancy condition determines whether or not the current record of the run unit is a member, or an owner, or either in one or more specified sets. For example:

```
IF MEMBER OF AFFILIATION ... .
IF MEMBER ... .
```

The first example checks whether the current record of the run unit is a member of an AFFILIATION set occurrence. The second example checks all set types in the subschema to see whether the current record of the run unit is a member of at least one of them. Similar tests can be done with OWNER or TENANT in place of MEMBER.

The member condition determines whether there are any member records for one or more specified set types. For example:

```
IF AFFILIATION EMPTY ... .
IF EMPTY ... .
```

The first example checks whether there are any members in the current set occurrence of the AFFILIATION set type. The second example checks all the set occurrences owned, within the subschema, by the current record of the run unit to see whether they are all empty.

The database key condition tests database key values held by currency indicators or stored on keep lists. It can determine whether or not a database key is null, whether or not two specified database key values are identical, or whether or not a specified database key value is identical to any database key value in a specified keep list. Database key values are equal if, and only if, they identify the same database record or are null. A few of the many options are:

```
IF CURRENT STAFF IS NULL ... .
IF CURRENT STAFF IS ALSO CURRENT WITHIN SKILLS-REALM ... .
IF CURRENT DEPT IS ALSO FIRST WITHIN LIST1 ... .
IF CURRENT DEPT IS WITHIN LIST2 ... .
IF FIRST WITHIN LIST1 IS ALSO LAST WITHIN LIST2 ... .
```

A3.7   Concurrent update

The following description, which is taken almost verbatim from the 1981 Codasyl COBOL Journal of Development, explains how concurrent update is controlled via a system of update locks and selection locks. Mention of the FOR UPDATE phrase has been deferred until this point because of its association with update locking.

Record locking
Record locking is provided to maintain integrity while allowing concurrent run units to update a database. Conceptually, every record may have an *update lock* and a *selection lock*.

Update locks
A run unit holds the *update lock* of each record that has been the object of a CONNECT, DISCONNECT, ERASE, FETCH FOR UPDATE, FIND FOR UPDATE, MODIFY, RECONNECT or STORE statement executed by the run unit since its last quiet point. The update locks held by a run unit are released when the run

unit executes a COMMIT statement, a ROLLBACK statement, a STOP RUN statement, or by abnormal termination. The database changes made by a run unit will be available to concurrent run units only after a COMMIT statement is executed by the run unit which holds the locks.

Selection locks
A run unit holds the *selection lock* of each record identified by any of its currency indicators or keep lists. A selection lock held by a run unit is released when the record is no longer identified by any of the run unit's currency indicators or keep lists. Thus, selection locks may be released by the FREE statement or any statement that changes currency indicators. Furthermore, any selection locks held by a run unit are released when its update locks are released.

Effect of record locking
Holding an update lock prevents the record from being the object of a CONNECT, DISCONNECT, ERASE, FETCH, FIND, MODIFY or RECONNECT statement executed by concurrent run units. Holding a selection lock prevents the record from being the object of a CONNECT, DISCONNECT, ERASE, MODIFY or RECONNECT statement executed by concurrent run units. Detection and resolution of any deadlock situations that occur as a result of the locking mechanism is implementor-defined.

Questions

1. A record type may be the owner in the conceptual schema of set types and record types which do not appear in the subschema used by a run unit. Should these non-subschema set types and record types be immune from the effects of an ERASE statement executed by the run unit on an occurrence of the owner record type?

(3 min)

2. Suggest a rationale for the rules which govern the effect of retention class on the outcome of the statement:

`ERASE.`   (3 min)

3. It is not always obvious what effect a DML statement should have on the currency indicators. Propose your own set of rules for the statements CONNECT, DISCONNECT and RECONNECT, and compare your proposal with the rules quoted in the answer pointer.

(15 min)

Assignment

1. Explain why the relational model has superseded the Codasyl model. Consider, among others, the following aspects:

- the representation of relationships;
- the type of data manipulation language;
- changes in business information system requirements;
- developments in hardware performance;
- optimisation of application code.

Answer pointers

Section A3.5

1. Database integrity would be endangered. A run unit might use a database key which had been stored months, or even years, earlier. There would be severe practical difficulties in ensuring that a database key continued to identify the same record indefinitely in the face of database reorganisation and restructuring.

2. A run unit could store a database key for input by another run unit.

Section A3.7

1. No. Otherwise, records with fixed or mandatory retention class could be left without an owner. The non-subschema record types and set types are treated in this context as though they are within the subschema.

2. Fixed retention is used where member records have no right to be in the database unless owned by a particular owner record, so if the owner is deleted the members should go too. Optional retention is used where member records can be detached from their owner, so there is no call to delete the members when the owner is deleted. Mandatory retention is used where member records can be moved between owners in the same set type but each member must belong to one or other of the owners. Were an owner to be deleted, its members ought to be transferred to another of the owners, but the DBMS would not know which to choose (or there might not be another owner), so deletion of the owner is blocked.

3. The rules given in the 1981 Codasyl COBOL Journal of Development are:

CONNECT
The object record becomes the current record of the run unit. The currency indicator for each set type to which the record is connected is modified such that the object record becomes the identified record, and the position of that record in the set becomes the position specified by the currency indicator. No other currency indicators are modified.

DISCONNECT
The object record becomes the current record of the run unit. The currency indicator for each set type from which the record is disconnected is modified only if that record is the current record of that set type. These currency indicators are modified such that no current record is identified. The position specified by these currency indicators is not changed. No other currency indicators are modified.

RECONNECT
The execution of a RECONNECT statement does not change the position specified by any currency indicator. If a set type currency indicator identifies the object record and execution of the RECONNECT statement causes the position of the record to be changed within a set of that set type, or causes the record to be reconnected to a different set of that set type, the currency indicator is modified such that no record is identified. If a set type currency indicator specifies a position, but does not identify a record, and the execution of the RECONNECT statement causes the object record to be inserted at that position, the currency indicator is modified to identify the object record.

Bibliography

Items marked with an asterisk (*) are recommended for the next stage of tutorial reading.

* BENNETT, S., McROBB, S. and FARMER, R. 1999: *Object-oriented systems analysis and design using UML*. McGraw-Hill.

A comprehensive introduction to object-oriented systems analysis and design, making extensive use of the UML (Unified Modelling Language) notation. Substantial bibliography.

* BRITTON, C. and DOAKE, J. 2000: *Object-oriented systems development: a gentle introduction*. McGraw-Hill.

An introduction to the basic ideas that underpin the development of object-oriented systems.

CHEN, P. P.-S. 1976: The entity-relationship model—toward a unified view of data. *ACM Transactions on Database Systems* 1(1), 9–36.

The original paper on the entity-relationship model.

CODASYL COBOL Committee Journal of Development. 1981.

Specifications of the Codasyl COBOL data manipulation language and the subschema data description language.

CODASYL Data Description Language Committee Journal of Development. 1981.

Specifications of the Codasyl conceptual schema DDL and the draft internal schema DSDL.

CODD, E. F. 1970: A relational model of data for large shared data banks. *Communications of the ACM* 13(6), 377–87.

The original paper on the relational model.

* CONNOLLY, T. and BEGG, C. 1998: *Database systems*. 2nd edn. Addison-Wesley.

Subtitled 'A Practical Approach to Design, Implementation and Management', this book covers in a readable style a wide range of database topics, including relational modelling, entity-relationship modelling, SQL, object-orientation, Web databases, data warehousing and data mining. Extensive references and bibliography.

* DATE, C. J. 1999: *An introduction to database systems*. 7th edn. Addison-Wesley.

A thoughtful and lucid account of the fundamentals of database systems with particular reference to the relational model. It includes consideration of the major concepts of SQL, the divergence between SQL and the principles of the relational model, and a critical analysis of object-orientation and its relevance to the relational model. Extensive annotated literature references and bibliography.

DATE, C. J. with DARWEN, H. 1997: *A guide to the SQL standard.* 4th edn. Addison-Wesley.

A critical analysis of the SQL92 standard, with some material on SQL99. Includes a careful analysis of inconsistencies in the standard.

* GRUBER, M. 2000: *Mastering™ SQL.* Sybex.

A comprehensive tutorial on the SQL92 standard. Also includes material on SQL99 and the JDBC/SQLJ interfaces between SQL and the Java programming language.

GULUTZAN, P. and PELZER, T. 1999: *SQL-99 Complete, Really.* Miller Freeman Inc.

A comprehensive tutorial on the SQL-99 standard.

ISO. 1992: *Database language SQL* (ISO/IEC 9075:1992). International Organization for Standardization.

Specification of the SQL92 standard.

ISO. 1996: *Information technology—Database languages—SQL—Technical corrigendum* 2 (ISO/IEC 9075: l992/Cor.2:1996(E)).

Revisions and corrections to the previous reference.

Unified Modeling Language (UML). http://www.omg.com.

The Object Management Group (OMG) downloadable specification of UML.

Index